Frommer's®

P9-DCG-629

GERMANY'S
BEST-LOVED
DRIVING
TOURS

Ⓦ Wiley Publishing, Inc.

Written by Adi Kraus

Revised eighth edition published 2008
Revised seventh edition published 2006
Revised sixth edition published 2004
Revised fifth edition published 2002
Revised second edition published in this format 1998
First published January 1992

Edited, designed and produced by AA Publishing.

Published by AA Publishing

Published in the United States by
Wiley Publishing, Inc.
111 River Street, Hoboken, NJ 07030

Find us online at Frommers.com

Frommer's is a registered trademark of Arthur Frommer.
Used under license.

ISBN 978-0-470-22693-3

Color separation: Daylight Colour Art, Singapore

Printed and bound by G. Canale & C. s.p.a., Torino, Italy

Right: *traditional maypole*

A03367

CONTENTS

ABOUT THIS BOOK

This book is not only a practical guide for the independent traveller, but is also invaluable for those who would like to know more about the country.

It is divided into 5 regions, each containing between 3 and 8 tours, which start and finish in major towns and cities we consider to be the best centres for exploration.

Each tour has details of the most interesting places to visit en route. Panels catering for special interests follow some of the main entries – for those whose interest is in history, wildlife or walking, and those who have children. There are also panels which highlight scenic stretches of road along the route and give details of special events, crafts and customs. The simple route directions are accompanied by an easy-to-use tour map, at the beginning of each tour, along with a chart showing intermediate distances in kilometres and miles. This can help you to decide where to take a break and stop overnight, for example. (All distances quoted are approximate.)

Before setting off it is advisable to check with the information centre at the start of the tour for recommendations on where to break your journey and for additional information on what to see and do, and when best to visit.

Tour information
See pages 167–76 for addresses, telephone numbers and opening times of the attractions mentioned in the tours, including telephone numbers of tourist offices. The opening times of museums and other attractions listed in this book are subject to change. Places may be closed on some public holidays and visitors are advised to check opening times locally beforehand.

Accommodation & Restaurants
See pages 160–66 for a list of recommended hotels and restaurants for each tour.

Business Hours
Banks: open Monday to Friday 8.30–1, 2.30–4 (to 5.30 on Thursdays). Exchange offices of the Deutsche–Verkehrs–Kredit–Bank are located at main railway stations and road and rail frontier crossing points, and are usually open from early morning until late at night.

Post offices: generally open Monday–Friday from 8–6 (to noon on Saturday). *Post restante* mail is issued on presentation of an identity card or passport. Money orders telegraphed from abroad are cashed in euros (€). Post boxes are bright yellow.

Shops: usually open Monday to Friday 9–6, Saturday 8.30–2, but this may vary in certain areas.

Credit Cards
Credit cards can be used in establishments displaying the appropriate signs. Cash can be obtained at banks and some cash dispensers.

Make a note of your credit card numbers and emergency telephone numbers. If they are lost or stolen, advise the company immediately.

Currency
There are 100 cents in 1 euro (€). Notes are available in the following denominations: €5, €10, €20, €50, €100, €200 and €500; coins are available in the following denominations: 1, 2, 5, 10, 20 and 50 cents, €1 and €2.

Customs Regulations
Visitors from non–EU countries can take in 200 cigarettes or 50 cigars or 100 cigarillos or 250g of tobacco, one litre of spirits and two litres of table wine without paying duty.

There are no restrictions for EU visitors where duty has been paid. Guidelines have been set for the amounts that are considered reasonable for personal use: 800 cigarettes or 200 cigars or 400 cigarillos or 1kg of tobacco; 10 litres of spirits or 20 litres of liqueur, 90 litres of table wine and 110 litres of beer. There are no currency restrictions.

Electricity
230 volts on a continental two-pin plug.

Emergency Telephone Numbers
Police and Ambulance 110
Fire 112

Entry Regulations
An identity card or valid passport is required by EU nationals. Nationals of Australia, Canada, New Zealand and the US need a valid passport. Nationals of other countries should check their visa requirements.

Health
No vaccinations are needed to enter Germany. Citizens of other EU countries are entitled to some free medical treatment, on production of an EHIC (European Health Insurance Card). You must obtain this before leaving home. It is wise to get travel insurance as well.

Motoring
For information on motoring in Germany, see pages 158–59.

Public Holidays
1 January: New Year's Day
6 January: Epiphany (Baden-Württemberg and Bavaria)

Painted buildings brighten the streets of Oberammergau, a town best known for the Passion Play it stages every 10 years

Good Friday/Easter Sunday/
Easter Monday
1 May: Labour Day
Ascension Day (in May)
Whit Sunday and Whit Monday
(in May)
18 June: Corpus Christi
(observed only in certain areas)
15 August: Maria Himmelfahrt
(Assumption of the Blessed
Virgin Mary, observed only in
Bavaria and Saarland)
3 October: Day of German
Unity
1 November: All Saints' Day
(observed only in certain areas)
Day of Prayer and Repentance
(in November, exact date
changes annually)
25/26 December: Christmas

Route Directions

Throughout the book the
following abbreviations are used
for German roads:
A – Autobahn
B – Bundesstrasse (federal/
national roads*)
* on tour maps B roads are
indicated by number only.

Telephones

International calls can be made
from public telephone kiosks
showing a black receiver in a
green square. Some take euro
coins, but phone cards are more
generally used.

Cheap rates operate during
the weekend and from Monday
to Friday 8pm–8am.

The international code for
Germany is 49.

Time

Germany is one hour ahead of
Greenwich Mean Time (GMT)
in winter and two hours ahead in
summer.

Tourist Offices

Offices of the German National
Tourist Office can be found at
the following locations:
UK: PO Box 2695, London W1A
3TN. Tel: 020 7317 0908;
e-mail: gntolon@d-z-t.com
USA: 122 East 42nd Street, 52nd
Floor, New York, NY 10168-
0072 Tel: (212) 661-7200, e-mail:
gntonyc@d-z-t.com

Useful Words

The following words and
phrases may be helpful.
English *German*
hello *Guten Tag: Grüss Gott* (in
 the south)
goodbye *Auf Wiedersehen*
do you speak English? *Sprechen
 Sie Englisch?*
yes/no *ja/nein*
please *bitte*
thank you *danke* (can also
 mean 'no thank you')
I don't understand *Ich verstehe
 nicht*
where is/are *Wo ist/sind*
the bank *die Bank*
the nearest toilets *die nächsten
 Toiletten*
open/closed *Geöffnet/
 Geschlossen*
I would like *Ich hätte gern*
single room *Einzelzimmer*
double room *Doppelzimmer*
with bath *mit Bad*
May I see the menu please?
 Die Speisekarte bitte?
How much is *Wieviel kostet*
1 to 10 *eins, zwei, drei, vier, fünf,
 sechs, sieben, acht, neun, zehn*

THE NORTHERN LOWLANDS & THE EAST

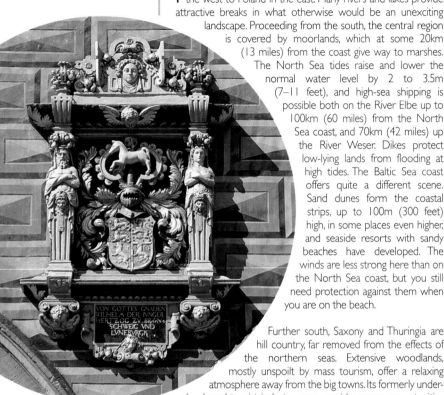

The North German plain covers a wide area from Holland in the west to Poland in the east. Many rivers and lakes provide attractive breaks in what otherwise would be an unexciting landscape. Proceeding from the south, the central region is covered by moorlands, which at some 20km (13 miles) from the coast give way to marshes. The North Sea tides raise and lower the normal water level by 2 to 3.5m (7–11 feet), and high-sea shipping is possible both on the River Elbe up to 100km (60 miles) from the North Sea coast, and 70km (42 miles) up the River Weser. Dikes protect low-lying lands from flooding at high tides. The Baltic Sea coast offers quite a different scene. Sand dunes form the coastal strips, up to 100m (300 feet) high, in some places even higher, and seaside resorts with sandy beaches have developed. The winds are less strong here than on the North Sea coast, but you still need protection against them when you are on the beach.

Further south, Saxony and Thuringia are hill country, far removed from the effects of the northern seas. Extensive woodlands, mostly unspoilt by mass tourism, offer a relaxing atmosphere away from the big towns. Its formerly under-developed tourist industry now provides more opportunities for holidays and relaxation for the hard-pressed urban population.

Celle's elaborate town crest documents its importance in medieval times

The livelihood of the people on the northern shores is provided by the sea, with shipbuilding and a large fishing industry as the main employers. A special dialect, called *Plattdeutsch* (or *Platt*) is spoken here, especially in the ports, and is not easily understood by outsiders, even German-speakers.

Berlin has been established as the capital of the united Germany and its economy is supported by a fair amount of local industry. Extensive building is still under way.

Saxony used to be one of Germany's prime industrial centres, but has witnessed serious neglect in the modernisation of its plant and machinery. It will take nothing short of a major investment programme to improve local industry, but judging by Saxony's previous industrial record, before communist control, it can be expected to steadily improve its economic prospects.

Tour 1

There is 'water, water everywhere' on this tour of Germany's northern tip. From Hamburg, on the Elbe estuary, the route takes a break on the island town of Ratzeburg, in the middle of a lake, before crossing into what used to be East Germany, and Schwerin, the 'Town of the Seven Lakes'. Then it's up to the Baltic Sea coast and the once-powerful ports of the Hanseatic League, afterwards heading northwest from Lübeck to Kiel through a region of lakes called the 'Holsteinische Schweiz' (Switzerland of Holstein). The Elbe and its estuary provide a natural border to the south, and guide the way back to Hamburg.

Tour 2

Starting in Bremen, an historic German port, this tour journeys into an area where the clearest German is spoken, and a strong link between the Hanoverian and English crowns was forged in the 18th century. Industry and commerce are happily balanced here with old traditions and notable reminders of the past. A fascinating detour into the vast tracts of the heathland known as the Lüneburger Heide rounds off this tour. Wildlife and flora flourish in this carefully protected environment, where, in certain defined areas, the car becomes off-limits and horse-drawn carts provide the only transport.

Tour 3

Berlin is still undergoing big changes in consequence of the reunification in 1989–90. The extensive building programme is by no means finished, although the move of the Government offices has been completed. New hotels, restaurants and shopping centres have sprung up in the former eastern sector, and gradually the former division of the city is becoming less noticeable on the ground, even if a psychological divide still remains.

On the human side, the West Berliners still do not quite accept their brothers from the East as equals, as the East is still receiving enormous subsidies from the West – and this situation is likely to continue.

Tour 4

This tour travels from the bustling environs of Leipzig, via Meissen, known for its delicate porcelain, to a resurrected town. The job of restoring Dresden is not finished yet, but the work so far has been little short of miraculous, as was shown in the reopening of the war-devastated Frauenkirche. One of the great highlights here is the priceless Zwinger collections of art treasures and porcelain displayed in a baroque palace. Further on, past the attractive castle of Moritzburg, there are startling natural wonders in the form of bizarre rock formations. The tour ends with a visit to the World War II POW camp, Colditz.

Tour 5

A passing acquaintance with German literature brings this tour alive. The itinerary starts in Weimar, a historic cultural centre that was once home to the painter Lucas Cranach and the poets Goethe and Schiller. Then the route continues on to Jena, cradle of 18th-century German philosophy and 19th-century scientific discovery, to Eisenach, where Martin Luther translated the New Testament between 1521 and 1522. Later still, the beautiful, unspoiled Thuringian Forest provides much-needed relaxation, as they must have done for past generations of great thinkers.

View of the Elbe River from the Bastei (the Bastion) rocks near Bad Schandau

Northern Ports
& Two Seas

Hamburg is not only Germany's second largest city, but also its major port. The Hamburg–America shipping line continues in the tradition of the Hanseatic League, an association of Northern Ports, set up in the Middle Ages to control and secure the northern shipping lanes.

2/3 DAYS • 550KM • 341 MILES

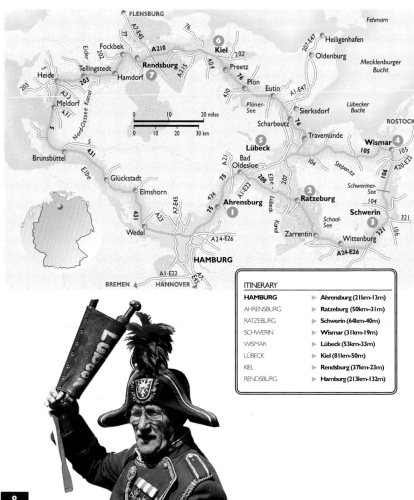

ITINERARY		
HAMBURG	▶	**Ahrensburg** (21km-13m)
AHRENSBURG	▶	**Ratzeburg** (50km–31m)
RATZEBURG	▶	**Schwerin** (64km-40m)
SCHWERIN	▶	**Wismar** (31km-19m)
WISMAR	▶	**Lübeck** (53km-33m)
LÜBECK	▶	**Kiel** (81km-50m)
KIEL	▶	**Rendsburg** (37km-23m)
RENDSBURG	▶	**Hamburg** (213km-132m)

ⓘ Steinstrasse 7, Hamburg

▶ From Hamburg take the
B75 northeast for 21km
(13 miles) to Ahrensburg.

❶ Ahrensburg, Schleswig-
Holstein
Built around 1595, the moated
castle of Ahrensburg lies north
of the town and was reopened
to the public in 1955, after
complete renovation. Today it is
in excellent condition and its
cosy interior has remained
largely unchanged over the
centuries. The façade consists
of three sections with gabled
roofs, flanked by two towers,
all in late-Renaissance style.
Valuable furniture and paintings
adorn the interior.

ⓘ Stadtverwaltung, Rathausplatz 1

▶ Continue on the **B75** to
Bad Oldesloe, then take
the **B208** southeast for a
distance of 50km (31 miles)
to Ratzeburg.

❷ Ratzeburg, Schleswig-
Holstein
Three dams and bridges
connect the charming island
town of Ratzeburg with the
mainland. An observation tower
on the lake embankment offers
particularly attractive views of
the town and its surroundings.

The magnificent Dom
(cathedral) is one of the largest
and oldest Romanesque church
buildings in northern Germany.
Built of brick, it was founded in
1154 by Heinrich der Löwe
(Henry the Lion), and stands on
the northern part of the island.
Ancient paintings can be seen
in the cloister while the high
altar is decorated by an illustra-
tion of the *Crucifixion*. Do not
miss the chapel in the south
transept, furnished with beautiful ornaments finished in old
gold. Near the cathedral, the
Herrenhaus (Gentlemen's
House) was erected for the
dukes of Mecklenburg and now
houses a local museum.

ⓘ Schlosswiese 7

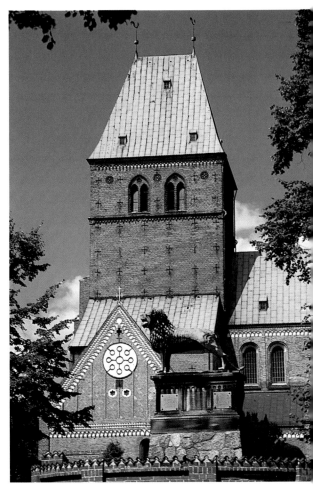

The impressive tall red-brick
Romanesque cathedral in
Ratzeburg

▶ Drive southeast via Zarrentin
and Wittenburg to the **A24**,
then continue east on the
A24 to the Hagenow exit
and turn north to Schwerin,
64km (40 miles).

❸ Schwerin, Mecklenburg-
Vorpommern
Also called the 'Town of the
Seven Lakes', Schwerin was
founded by the Saxon Duke
Heinrich der Löwe (Henry the
Lion) in 1160. After he defeated
the Slavonic tribe of the
Obotriten (Abodrites), Heinrich

expelled their leader, Duke
Niklot, from his castle on the
Schlossinsel (Castle Island),
founded the County of
Schwerin in 1167 and started to
rebuild the castle.

In 1358, Albrecht II bought
Schwerin, and from then on the
castle, with few interruptions,
became the residence of the
dukes of Mecklenburg until the
demise of the German monar-
chy in 1918.

Today's castle is the handi-
work of several architects and
builders, notably Gottfried
Semper and Adolph Demmler.
The latter was heavily
influenced by the French-style
elegance of Château Chambord

in the Loire Valley. The surrounding gardens are planted with many exotic trees, and brilliant green lawns are interspersed with ponds. There is also an orangerie lined with colonnades, which transform the inner courtyard into a romantic setting for evening concerts and recitals.

The interior of the castle is beautifully appointed with inlaid parquet floors, highly polished wood-panelled walls and gilded beams supporting the ceilings. Highlights include the Throne Room, the Ancestor's Gallery, the Smoking Room and the Equerry's Chamber. Overlooking the Burgsee (Castle Lake), one wing houses a history museum exhibiting articles dating back to the Stone Age; and the Renaissance-style Schloss-kapelle (chapel) built between 1560 and 1563 is lavishly decorated.

In the old town, which is situated between two lakes, the Pfaffenteich and the Burgsee, the historic streets and squares have been thoroughly restored,

including the market square and the Rathaus (Town Hall), a part of which dates back to the 14th century. The Court Architect, Demmler, added its neo-Gothic façade in 1835.

The State Museum, a model of late classicism, received Italian Renaissance ornaments to improve its modest façade. The exhibits include many paintings by Flemish, Dutch, German and French masters of the 17th and 19th centuries. The Dom (Cathedral) was built between the 13th and early 15th centuries. Especially noteworthy are the Gothic Altar of the Cross, brass tomb plates and the Gothic font.

ⓘ *Markt 14*

RECOMMENDED WALKS

At Schwerin you can take a pleasant walk along the Schweriner See and the Schlosspark.

The romantic castle at Schwerin, a Loire-style château on a North German lake

▶ *Take the B106 north for 31km (19 miles) to Wismar.*

4 Wismar, Mecklenburg-Vorpommern

The Baltic seaport of Wismar is protected from the open sea by the island of Poel. First mentioned as *Aqua Wissemara*, it was probably founded by the nearby town of Lübeck. In 1259, the ports of Wismar, Lübeck and Rostock on the Baltic Sea formed a pact against pirates, which later developed into the all-powerful Hanseatic League. The Swedish Crown owned the town from 1648 to 1803, and then mortgaged it to Mecklenburg. It was 1903 before Wismar was truly returned to the province of Mecklenburg.

Views over the large market square are dominated by the Wasserkunst, a grandiose Dutch Renaissance-style former pumping station

View over the Baltic coastal town of Lübeck, taken from St Peter's Church

which supplied the town with fresh water. Around the square there are a number of attractive, carefully restored old houses with gabled roofs, plus a historic residence called 'The Old Swede' dating from 1380 – the oldest in Wismar and now a fine restaurant.

SPECIAL TO...

The curiously named Baumhaus (Tree House) in Wismar's old harbour is the point from which ships' movements were monitored. At night, a tree was placed across the harbour to prevent ships entering or leaving.

ⓘ *Markt 11*

▶ *Take the B105 west to Lübeck.*

5 Lübeck, Schleswig-Holstein

Although the Altstadt (Old Town) shows its past, Lübeck is a major port on the Baltic Sea, and also the northern end of the important Elbe–Lübeck Kanal, which carries the Elbe river traffic out into the Baltic.

The town was founded in 1143 by Count Adolf I of Holstein, and became a Free Imperial City in 1226. It was the capital of the Hanseatic League, an association of ports and towns on the Baltic and North Sea coasts founded in the mid-14th century, and later joined by many other German

---

FOR HISTORY BUFFS

The Buddenbrookhaus in Lübeck, at Mengstrasse 4, was owned by the well-known novelist Thomas Mann's family from 1841 to 1891. Built in 1758, it is named after one of Mann's most famous novels, *Buddenbrooks*, which describes the decline of a wealthy Lübeck family. He was awarded the Nobel Prize for Literature in 1929.

Detail of the architecture in the Altstadt (Old Town) of Lübeck

cities further south. The object of the association was primarily to safeguard and control shipping in the region, but it was also a powerful trading entity, and guarded its neutrality with great care.

From the 16th century, Lübeck declined in importance with the gradual dissolution of the Hanseatic alliance. By the 19th century, the town had to endure French rule which, together with competition from other ports, seriously affected the fortunes of the city. However, the opening of the Elbe–Lübeck Kanal prompted a rush of industrialisation, and the fall of the nearby East German frontier attracted better fortunes. Lübeck does a good trade in red wine, even producing its own Rotspon label. Hanseatic merchants first brought back marzipan from the Orient and, with a couple of improvements, it has become one of Lübeck's gourmet specialities.

The outline of the city is basically oval-shaped and surrounded by water. The entrance from the west is the mighty Holstentor, the old city gate with its twin towers, which were completed in 1477, and recognised as the emblem of the town. Traffic passes by on either side, and above the entry portal is a Latin inscription meaning 'Unity inside, peace outside'.

Beyond the Holsten gate, there is a fine vista of red brick-built churches and slim spires, and it is a short walk to the imposing Rathaus (Town Hall) which stands in the market square and is one of the most grandiose in Germany. Building commenced when Emperor Friedrich II granted Lübeck the status of a Free Imperial City in 1226. A close inspection reveals several styles, the oldest part being the Gothic south façade, followed by the Renaissance-style Neues Gemach annexe. A

tour of the interior includes the wine cellars, which together with the Admiral's Room and the Brautgemach (Bridal Suite) should not be missed.

A stroll through the city is highly recommended. Stop off to see 13th-century St Marienkirche (St Mary's Church), the prototype for many of the typical brick-built churches scattered around the Baltic area. It has a memorial chapel whose bell crashed down during the air bombardments of 1942. There are several other fine churches in the Old Town, and the Dom (Cathedral) houses Bernt Notke's superb 1477 *Triumphkreuz* (Triumphal Cross). One of Lübeck's finest restaurants occupies the Schabbelhaus on Mengstrasse,

an old merchant's house painstakingly restored to its original design after having been completely destroyed during World War II.

FOR CHILDREN

Not far north of Lübeck, Hansa-Park at Sierksdorf is easily reached by taking the A1 and turning right at the Eutin exit for Sierksdorf. This excellent fun park offers a great variety of exciting entertainment from shows like 'Butterflies' and the 'Water Circus' to dolphin and sea-lion performances. There is also the Pirates bay and a 'Mexican Beach' for a taste of the exotic, and many funfair rides for the whole family in the pleasant gardens.

BACK TO NATURE

At Heiligenhafen (from Lübeck take the A1 – Oldenburg/B207), there is the Graswerder nature reserve and bird sanctuary, offering daily tours between April and September, to see large colonies of breeding birds, including several species of terns and black-headed gulls.

Keep a lookout for white storks. These large white and black birds have big red bills. They feed in the marshes and fields and sometimes build their nests on rooftops.

SPECIAL TO...

The Sommerspiele festivities at Eutin, between Lübeck and Kiel, offer annual open-air theatre performances in the Schlossgarten (castle garden) every July and August. Composer Karl Maria von Weber's opera *Der Freischütz* always features on the programme here, in honour of his position as the town's most famous son.

ℹ️ *Holstentorplatz 1*

RECOMMENDED WALKS

About 1.5km (1 mile) north of Lübeck is the Brodtener Steilufer, a 4km (2½-mile) long cliff, with fine views over the sea, and a golf course.

▶ *From Lübeck follow the **B75** north via Travemünde to Scharbeutz and continue on the **B76**, via Eutin, to Kiel, 81km (50 miles).*

6 Kiel, Schleswig-Holstein
Kiel is the main ferry port for traffic to Scandinavia and a favourite destination for cruise ships. The North Sea–Baltic or Kiel Canal from Brunsbüttel ends here, near the point where the Elbe reaches the North Sea. The busiest canal in the world, it is 97km (60 miles) long and ships take between seven and nine hours to pass from one end to the other.

The yachting world knows Kiel for its annual June regattas (Kieler Woche), and the Hindenburg Ufer (quay) is a good spot from which to view all the port activities.

ℹ️ *Andreas Gayk Strasse 31*

▶ *Take the **A210** west for 37km (23 miles) to Rendsburg.*

7 Rendsburg, Schleswig-Holstein
Rendsburg lies between the River Elbe and the important Kiel Canal. Its Altstadt (Old Town) is situated on an island in the Eider. The Altes Rathaus (Old Town Hall) is a timber-framed building dating back to 1566. Near by is the 13th-century Marienkirche (St Mary's), its interior decorated with valuable 14th-century wall paintings and a splendid 1649 baroque altar.

But it is Rendsburg's technical achievements which are of greatest interest, such as the railway bridge spanning the Kiel Canal at a height of 42m (137 feet), avoiding any obstruction to the funnels of passing ships. A suspended transporter ferry runs underneath the railway lines for passengers and cars. The 1,280m (4,200-foot) long Kanaltunnel passes 20m (66 feet) beneath the canal and carries road traffic with an escalator tunnel (the longest in Europe) running parallel for pedestrians.

ℹ️ *Altstädter Markt*

▶ *Take the **B203** to Heide, then the **B5** to Brunsbüttel and continue on the **B431** to Hamburg, 213km (132 miles).*

SCENIC ROUTES

Between Lübeck and Kiel, the route passes through the picturesque Holsteinische Schweiz (Swiss Holstein) region. Take the main road from Lübeck to Travemünde, and then the B76 via Eutin to enjoy the delights of this popular lakeland holiday destination.

A detour from Wismar to Rostock and its seaport of Warnemünde should be rewarding. The route runs close to the shores of the Baltic Sea. Look out for the Gothic Rathaus in Rostock.

The desolate, windswept shoreline of the Baltic coast

The Royal
Connection

2/3 DAYS • 484KM • 300 MILES

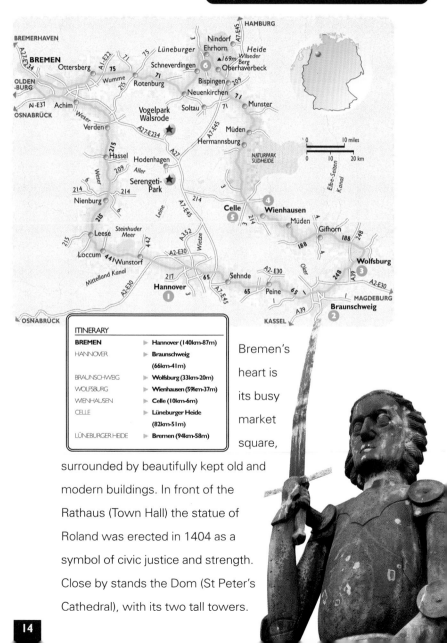

Bremen's heart is its busy market square, surrounded by beautifully kept old and modern buildings. In front of the Rathaus (Town Hall) the statue of Roland was erected in 1404 as a symbol of civic justice and strength. Close by stands the Dom (St Peter's Cathedral), with its two tall towers.

Carved detail on Bremen's Rathaus (town hall)

important industrial and trading centre on the busy east–west Mittelland Kanal.

Despite industrialisation, the city's legacy of green open spaces interspersed with lakes lends credence to its claim to be the Grossstadt im Grünen (the Green Capital).

Written records first mention a market-place called *vicus Hanovere* in 1150. Heinrich der Löwe (Henry the Lion) gave it city status, and a treaty in 1495 brought Hannover under the rule of the Calenberg family, whereupon Duke Georg von Calenberg moved his residence here. Hannover flourished under Kurfürst (Elector) Ernst August. In 1658 the Duke married Princess Palatine Sophia, a granddaughter of James I of England. Their son, George Ludwig, later succeeded to the English throne as George I, forming a union between the Hanoverian and the English crowns which lasted up until the Victorian era.

During the 19th century, the city enjoyed a further golden age of economic and cultural

growth. Fashionable architect/builder George Ludwig Laves founded the Opera House, and created plans for the future outline of the city.

To explore the most interesting sights of the city, start on the quayside by the River Leine at the Beginenturm, a sturdy round stone tower which stands on the spot of the original settlement. Next, the 14th-century Marktkirche (Market Church) is a Gothic brick-built structure which succeeded a Romanesque church first mentioned in 1238. On the market square, the late Gothic Altes Rathaus (Old Town Hall) dates from the first half of the 15th century, and has been beautifully restored.

Kramerstrasse leads off the square, and its historic timber-framed houses are some of the few remaining examples of Old Hannover, most of which was destroyed by bombing during World War II. Not far from the Friedrichswall, the early 20th-century Neues Rathaus building is unmistakably Prussian. Erected during the Wilhelmine

i *Am Bahnhofsplatz, Bremen*

▶ *From Bremen head southeast to Verden, via Achim, turn south on to the B215 to Leese and continue south on the B441 to Hannover, 140km (87 miles).*

❶ **Hannover,** Niedersachsen Hannover (Hanover in English) is the capital of the province of Niedersachsen (Lower Saxony). Its strategic position and transport links have made it an

The Herrenhäuser gardens in Hannover, combining centuries of European garden designs

Katharinenkirche – St Katharine's Church – at the Hagenmarkt in Braunschweig

era, this grandiose neo-Gothic edifice sports an enormous dome, rather out of proportion with the rest of the building. A lift provides access to the top.

The Herrenhäuser Gärten, in the grounds of Herrenhäuser Castle, are regarded among the finest gardens in Europe. Laid out in 1714, they consist of four quite different and separate sections. The oldest section, the Grosser Garten (Grand Garden), is French-influenced, with flower borders and allegorical statues positioned in the corners; while the Berggarten (Mountain Garden) is of specialist interest on account of the variety and rarity of its species. Do not miss the greenhouses which contain a wealth of orchids, cacti and other tropical flowers; and there is a mausoleum dedicated to the House of Hannover in the northern part of the garden which contains the sarcophagus of King George I of England.

Hannover can offer a choice of interesting museums including the excellent Kestner Museum which exhibits 5,000 years of Egyptian, Greek and Roman antiquities, plus European decorative art –

ceramics and art nouveau silverware. The Niedersächsische Landesmuseum (Museum of Lower Saxony) has a historical department dealing with the evolution of man in the area, among other exhibitions, and the Sprengel Museum of 20th-century art is situated across from the Maschsee Park.

[i] *Ernst-August-Platz 8*

▶ *Take the **B65** east for 66km (41 miles) to Braunschweig (Brunswick).*

2 Braunschweig,
Niedersachsen
Braunschweig is a town very much associated with its mighty prince, Heinrich der Löwe, Duke of Saxony and Bavaria, who made it his residential seat. Heinrich himself erected the fine bronze statue of a lion which still stands in the town's central square, the Burgplatz. He also built the Burg Dankwarderode (fortress) in 1175, much altered from 1887 onwards, and then greatly restored after World War II. The bomb damage to the town was so extensive that only a few buildings and corners of Old Brunswick remained to be repaired.

Another building which owes its origins to Heinrich's initiative is the Romanesque-Gothic Dom (St Blasius' Cathedral), built between 1173 and 1195. In the central nave lies the tomb of Heinrich and his wife, Mathilda of England.

Built in 1591, the Renaissance-style Gewandhaus on the Altstadtmarkt (Old Town Marketplace) boasts a superbly ornate east façade and gable. The house belonged to the tailors' and cloth-dealers' guild. Apart from trading purposes, it was used as a banqueting hall, and was later transformed into a restaurant.

The Altstadt Rathaus (Old Town Hall) dates back to the 13th century and overlooks the 1408 Marienbrunnen (Mary's Fountain), erected in the middle of the square and cast from molten lead. Consecrated in 1031, the well-restored Magnikirch (St Magnus' Church) was one of the original buildings to grace Brunesguik, which later evolved into Braunschweig. The interior is an interesting mixture, with modern stained-glass windows and a 15th-century font. Behind the church a small number of 16th-century timber-framed buildings remain intact.

The Herzog-Anton-Ulrich Museum is well worth a visit. It houses a collection largely devoted to 17th-century Flemish and Dutch masters with paintings by Rembrandt, Rubens, van Dyck, Ruysdael, Vermeer and others.

i Vor der Burg I

▶ Take the **B248** for 33km (20 miles) to Wolfsburg.

FOR HISTORY BUFFS

South of the old part of Braunschweig lies the Bürgerpark (Citizens' Park) and the adjoining Schloss Richmond. This charming castle was built between 1768 and 1769 in late baroque style for the Duchess Augusta.

---

3 Wolfsburg,
Niedersachsen
Wolfsburg's great claim to fame is the massive Volkswagenwerk (Volkswagen plant), home of the VW Beetle. Austrian engineer Ferdinand Porsche was the originator of the company's most famous model, which was years ahead of its time. The distinctive outline concealed a revolutionary engine, which was air-cooled and very simple to maintain. The whole engine block at the rear of the car could be taken out and exchanged in a matter of minutes without any special tools.

Volkswagen's factories were built from scratch on empty fields employing state-of-the-art manufacturing and production designs. Subsidised housing was provided for the workers, and from a few small villages Wolfsburg has now grown into a town of 130,000 inhabitants. A visit to the factory is strongly recommended to see the highly automated manufacture and production processes.

Another object of civic pride is mighty Schloss Wolfsburg. Built during the Renaissance period, it was restored in the 1970s and serves as a cultural centre and conference venue.

i Willy-Brandt-Platz 3

▶ Head west from Wolfsburg on the **B188**. About 10km (6 miles) beyond Gifhorn turn north for Ettenbüttel and continue via Müden and Langlingen to Wienhausen.

SCENIC ROUTES

The stretch of road between Wolfsburg and Gifhorn (B188) is one of the loveliest sections of the Deutsche Ferienstrasse (German Holiday Road). One of Europe's finest natural preserves, the Lüneburger Heide offers a wealth of magnificent views and plenty of native wildlife.
Away from the highways, on the route from Bispingen to Ehrhorn, it is hard to believe that the great industrial cities of the north are less than an hour's drive in all directions.

---

4 Wienhausen,
Niedersachsen
A well-kept secret, Wienhausen's medieval treasures attract art experts from far and wide. Its Kloster (Convent) and the Nonnenkirche (Nuns' Church) contain some of the most valuable works of art in Europe. Originally founded by the Cistercians in the 13th century and consecrated by the Bishop of Hildesheim, the convent was adopted by a Protestant order after the Reformation. Superb collections of tapestries, frescoes and glass paintings, sculpture and furniture all illustrate tremendous wealth during the 13th to 15th centuries.

The Nonnenkirche was built around 1300. Its choir section and Allerheiligen Kapelle (All Saints' Chapel) still retain their original wall paintings, but the medieval tapestries are so valuable that they are only shown to the public once a year – for 11 days from the Friday after Whitsuntide – to prevent damage. The famous winged altarpiece with its beautifully carved figures presents the life of the Virgin.

▶ Continue west to join the **B214**, then follow the road north to Celle, about 10km (6 miles).

5 Celle, Niedersachsen
The Dukes of Brunswick and Lüneburg resided here from 1292 to 1866, and the town grew under their patronage. Celle was first documented around 990 by Otto III, who knew the town as Kellu, meaning 'a settlement on a river'. Later this was changed to Zelle, and then Latinised to Celle. Heinrich der Löwe was active here, too, granting the settlers privileges for storing goods on the developing long-distance trade route via the town.

The Schloss was founded in the Gothic period, but rebuilding and alterations changed its shape considerably and only in

Decoration runs riot on the
Hoppener Haus in Celle

the 20th century, after the
Prussian takeover, did it emerge
in its present form. The reception and banqueting halls are of
interest, and the unique
baroque-style theatre, which is
supposed to be the oldest small
theatre in Germany, once had
its own company.

The Altes Rathaus (Old
Town Hall), with its
Renaissance gable, stands
among a fine collection of richly
decorated houses, which exude
a comfortably patrician air of
days gone by. Take a stroll down
attractive Kalandgasse, passing
the old Latin Schoolhouse. At
the southern end of the narrow
lane is the Stechbahn, where
jousting tournaments were
staged. Back on the market
place, the Stadtkirche (Parish
Church) contains the epitaphs
and tombstone of the last Duke
of Celle, and a burial vault of

the Danish Queen, Caroline
Mathilde, who died in Celle
Castle in 1775.

[i] *Markt 14–16*

▶ *From Celle drive north to
Hermannsburg and continue
via Münster and Bispingen to
Oberhaverbeck. No cars are
allowed from Oberhaverbeck
to Wilseder Berg and back,
82km (51 miles).*

BACK TO NATURE

From Celle, take the B214
west for 28km (17 miles) to
join the A7 north. Take the A27
to Walsrode Süd exit and
north through town. Vogelpark
Walsrode is an amazing bird
sanctuary. Its feathered
inhabitants have been gathered
from around the globe, but
seem quite at home in the
delightful gardens.

RECOMMENDED
WALKS

For a taste of the wide open
spaces, nothing beats the trail
from Oberhaverbeck to the
Wilseder Berg, across the
heart of the wild Lüneburger
Heide heathland. Spectacular
views extend all the way to
Hamburg on a clear day, and
the heather is alive with the
buzz of honey bees during the
late summer.

From Bispingen, drive north
on the A7 to the Garlsdorf
exit and turn left to the
Lüneburger Heide Animal Park.
There are idyllic walks through
the woods here, passing enclosures inhabited by deer, boar,
wolves and bears. Paths are
well marked, and routes are
divided into short walks which
take about 30 minutes, medium
trails of about 45 minutes,
and longer walks of around
an hour.

6 Lüneburger Heide, Niedersachsen

Covering some 7,200sq km (2,800 square miles), Lüneburger Heide (Heath) stretches from Hamburg in the north to Hannover in the south, and from Bremen in the west, east to the Lüneburg–Braunschweig road and beyond. It is the largest expanse of pure heathland in Europe, with its highest point at Wilseder Berg – a small mountain at just 169m (554 feet) above sea level. Residents of the surrounding towns find a welcome respite from the crowds on the heath, which is best visited in August and September, when the heather is in blossom. At other times, especially in winter, it is a melancholy landscape, scattered with ancient *Hühnengraber*

(megalithic tombs) which bear witness to the brief tenure of prehistoric man. Later, the infertile soil prevented any further agricultural encroachments, and now nature reserves maintain the delicate status quo of this unique ecosystem. At the heart of the area, the village of Wilseder has a museum dedicated to the heath, and on a clear day there is a spectacular view from the top of the Wilseder Berg. Weather permitting, binoculars can pick out the church spires of Hamburg 40km (25 miles) to the north.

ℹ *Rathaus (Town Hall), Borsteler Strasse 6, Bispingen*

▶ *From Oberhaverbeck drive north to Ehrhorn and continue west, crossing the*

> #### FOR CHILDREN
>
> Just west of the A7, Heide-Park, Soltau combines the interest of an animal park with the excitement of trips by monorail, narrow-gauge train rides, boating excursions on 'rough water' or on rafts and plenty of other attractions – a real funfair in natural surroundings.

B3. Take the next road south to Schneverdingen, continue south, then turn northwest just before Neuenkirchen for the B71 and the B75 to Bremen, 94km (58 miles).

Historic houses along Lüneburg's Ilmenau River in the Old Port

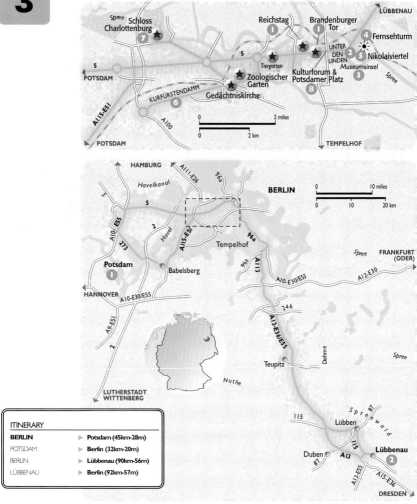

New Berlin –
Capital of Germany

2/3 DAYS • 259KM • 161 MILES No city was more in the news during 1989–90, and Berlin's emergence from 40 years of division is one of the historic landmarks of our age. The city is the seat of the German Government and has regained its former political and cultural importance.

i *Berlin Hauptbahnhof, Europlatz, Berlin*

❶ Brandenburger Tor & Reichstag

The Brandenburg Gate was erected at the end of the 18th century and has since become the emblem of Berlin. It is crowned by a *Quadriga*, a bronze statue of an ancient chariot drawn by four horses. Napoleon took a liking to it and packed it off to Paris, but after Waterloo, Marshal Blücher took it back to Berlin. Destroyed in World War II, it was recast after the original mould was found.

The nearby Reichstag (Parliament) building was restored by the British architect Sir Norman Foster, who added a glass cupola to bring daylight into the building. Visitors can take a lift right to the top for fine views of the city. The Kanzleramt (offices) was inaugurated in May 2001 and portrays a striking example of modern architecture in Berlin.

Schloss Charlottenburg, one of Berlin's finest buildings, is dedicated to Queen Sophie Charlotte

▷ *Continue from the Kanzleramt southeastwards past the Brandenburg Gate to Unter den Linden.*

❷ Unter den Linden

From the Brandenburger Tor across Pariser Platz, Berlin's famous boulevard is lined with magnificent buildings that date from the 18th and 19th centuries. These include the Old Palace of Wilhelm I, the Humbold University, the German State Opera and the Neue Wache (new guardhouse). Now dedicated to the victims of war and tyranny. It contains the tomb of the unknown soldier and an unknown victim of a concentration camp. Its most moving feature is the *Mother and her Dead Son* sculpture by Käthe Kollwitz, set in bare and sombre surroundings. Unter den Linden ends at the Zeughaus (arsenal), which now houses the German Historical Museum.

▷ *Continue in an easterly direction and cross the Schlossbrücke over the Spree-canal to reach the Museumsinsel.*

The war-damaged tower of the Kaiser Wilhelm memorial church (Gedächtniskirche)

❸ Museumsinsel

Berlin is endowed with an abundance of museums and many are centered on a man-made island between the Spree river and its canal. An ambitious renovation programme has not

yet been completed. The Alte Nationalgalerie, the Altes Museum and the Bodemuseum have reopened. The Egyptian Museum, housed in the Altes Museum is the proud owner of a unique bust of Queen Nefertiti, which is estimated to have been cast around 1350 BC. The beautiful lines created by the sculptor gave the bust its deserved worldwide reputation.

The Pergamon museum, parts of which are still being restored, is perhaps the most interesting and should not be missed. A complete ancient altar, dedicated to Zeus and Athene, was transported from Pergamon in West Turkey and erected in one grand hall in the museum. Other priceless objects include a Roman market gate from Milet, a layout of the Babylonian Processional Way and the façade of the Throne Room of King Nebuchadnezzar II, to name only a few of these magnificent monuments.

▷ *The tour continues past the Berliner Dom on Karl-Liebknecht Strasse towards the easily visible Fernsehturm.*

4 Fernsehturm

A modern landmark in former East Berlin, the Fernsehturm (television tower) looms 365m (1,196 feet) above the city. The rotating Tele-Café, at a height of 207m (678 feet), affords views extending up to 40km (25 miles) across the surrounding countryside.

The *Quadriga*, with the victory goddess, on top of the Brandenburg Gate

▷ *South of the Fernsehturm Rathausstrasse leads in a southwesterly direction past the Rotes Rathaus (Red Town Hall). The road continues to the Nikolaiviertel.*

5 Nikolaiviertel

The Nikolai quarter was the oldest in Berlin, but had to be completely rebuilt after World War II. In the centre stands the St Nikolai church, and other remaining landmarks are the Ephraim-Palais and the Knoblach-Haus, named after the family that owned it for 170 years. This is now open to visitors to show former upper bourgeois life.

The East German government had tried to re-create the original medieval, bohemian atmosphere of the Nikolai quarter, but the destruction was too severe for the attempt to be called successful. However, its many restaurants and pubs can provide a very welcome and relaxed evening for a tired museum visitor.

6 Kurfürstendamm

Berlin is made up of a conglomeration of little 'villages', or districts. The Kurfürstendamm was the centre of prosperous West Berlin before the unification of the city. Locally it is

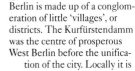

RECOMMENDED WALKS

To get the best out of the centre in one fell swoop, start at the Brandenburg Gate and follow the length of Unter den Linden, then continue to Alexanderplatz, with its World Time Clock. There is plenty to see and some of the city's best-preserved historic buildings can be seen en route.

known as the 'KuDamm', and many prestigious hotels and restaurants are there. At the top end stand the remains of the Kaiser Wilhelm I Gedächtniskirche, built in memory of Wilhem I between 1891 and 1895. After World War II it was left in its badly damaged state, as a reminder of the horrors of war.

New hotels have opened in the former central and eastern sections of the city, and the western way of life is emerging in former eastern areas.

▶ *The nearest U-Bahn stations for Schloss Charlottenburg are Sophie-Charlotte Platz (U2) and Richard-Wagner Platz (U7).*

7 Schloss Charlottenburg

The castle was founded in 1695 and built for Queen Sophie Charlotte, the wife of Emperor Friedrich I. The apartments have been carefully restored and the rococo-style Golden Galerie (gallery) is where Friedrich's notable collection of French 18th-century paintings is exhibited. The Porcelain Room displays pieces that mostly come from China, while the Antikenmuseum features displays of arms, bronze ware and utensils from ancient Greece, Etruria and Crete. The Schatzkammer (Treasury) holds a glittering display of gold and silver artefacts from the Mediterranean area and Roman finds in Germany.

SPECIAL TO...

At the point where Friedrich-strasse crosses Kochstrasse, the Allied border control post 'Checkpoint Charlie' is one of the most evocative symbols of the Cold War years. The museum here is a reminder of the human tragedies initiated by the Wall.

▶ *Take U2, S1 or S2 to Station Potsdamer Platz.*

8 Kulturforum & Potsdamer Platz

Two very different centres were established around the south-eastern corner of the Tiergarten. The Kulturforum, planned and built in the 1950s and 60s was thought to be a West Berlin answer to Berlin's cultural heritage, which lay mostly in the Eastern sectors. The Neue Gemäldegalerie (New Picture Gallery) is itself an impressive

Statues of the gods surround visitors in the Rotunda in the Altes Museum

building when viewed from the inside. It houses famous classical paintings from the 13th to the 18th centuries. The nearby Neue Nationalgalerie (New National Gallery) displays works by 19th- and 20th-century artists. The importance of music is acknowledged in the Berlin Philharmonie, the ultramodern home of the Berlin Philharmonic Orchestra.

Quite different are the new designs for Potsdamer Platz, an area near Hitler's former power bases, including his chancellery and the bunker where he died. All this is now buried, by history as well as by the buildings of New Berlin. Famous names such as Daimler-Benz (now Daimler-Chrysler), Sony and other industrial giants have erected their modern and prestigious buildings here, creating the image of a new century.

The attractive Schloss Cecilienhof in Potsdam, a 1916 Tudor-style mansion house

EXCURSION 1

▶ *From Berlin Centre drive west on the **A5** to the ring road, **A10/E55**. Head south for exit Potsdam-Babelsberg and drive west to Potsdam.*

Potsdam, Brandenburg
Potsdam, a satellite town of Berlin, is a favourite destination with Berliners wanting a relaxing excursion. Capital of the province of Brandenburg, the town is set amid pleasant woodland, interspersed with lakes formed by the River Havel.

A settlement was mentioned here as early as AD 993, but Potsdam's golden hour did not arrive until 1660, when Friedrich Wilhelm, Elector of Brandenburg, chose the town as the residential seat for the ruling Hohenzollern dynasty. He also encouraged the immigration of French Huguenots (Protestant exiles from the reign of Louis XIV), who invested their considerable wealth and craftsmanship in the development of the town. Friedrich der Grosse (Frederick the Great) was a keen admirer of all things French. He commissioned a mini-Versailles and the result was the delightful Schloss Sanssouci, the focal point of the town, with grounds that cover a substantial area of Potsdam. This intimate rococo building has only 12 rooms, and was a great success with the King. He paid considerable attention to other parts of the estate, and the architect Knobelsdorff was instructed to build an orangery, later named the Neue Kammern (New Chambers), used to accommodate the King's guests, including the French writer-philosopher Voltaire and the musician Carl Emanuel Bach. Then followed the Neptune Grotto, Chinese Tea House, Drachenhaus (Dragon's House) and the Belvedere. The Neues Palais, erected between 1763 and 1769, has a richly appointed interior that boasts the impressive Marmorsaal (Marble Hall) and the Schlosstheater, a private showcase for the ruler's personal entertainment.

Other sights include the present Orangerie, added in the middle of the 19th century and modelled on Italian Renaissance palaces; and the

---

SPECIAL TO...

At the Alexanderplatz, locally called the 'Alex', and a popular meeting point for Berliners, stands the Urania World Clock. It is a solidly built circular presentation of the globe, showing the time in all parts of the world. It is displayed in a 24-hour system. The Alex was named in honour of Tzar Alexander I of Russia.

FOR HISTORY BUFFS

Only 66km (41 miles) south of Potsdam lies Lutherstadt Wittenberg. The Schlosskirche set the scene for religious upheaval when Martin Luther posted his 95 theses against the indulgence of the church hierarchy on the church gate on 31 October, 1517. It caused an uproar among the ruling clergy and resulted in a war that lasted for 30 years. The Lutherhalle and palace church are also worth a visit.

Raffaelsaal, which displays 47 copies of paintings by Raphael.

Potsdam's Schloss Cecilienhof is a copy of an English Tudor-style mansion house. This is where Churchill, Truman and Stalin decided the fate of post-war Germany and signed the Potsdam Treaty on 2 August, 1945. The actual conference room and offices of the three leaders can be

visited; the rest of the castle functions as a hotel.

ⓘ *Brandenburger Strasse 3*

▶ *From Potsdam drive through Babelsberg to join the A115/E51 and turn north-east back to Berlin Centre, 32km (20 miles).*

EXCURSION 2

▶ *From Berlin Centre take the A96a/A113/A13-E36/E55 southeast to the exit for Lübbenau and continue east to Lübbenau.*

Lübbenau, Brandenburg
The Spreewald, southeast of Berlin, makes an interesting excursion for its special landscape and inhabitants. The people of the Spreewald are mostly of Slavonic descent, refugees from Poland, who have retained their own traditions and language. Called Sorbs, they have adapted their lifestyle to the special requirements of

RECOMMENDED WALKS

If you don't take to a boat or a punt in Lübbenau, take a walk alongside the many waterways where you can enjoy watching those who pass by.

this wet lowland region, interrupted by sandy islands, which divide the Spree into numerous small rivers and lakes. Houses are built on the islands and transport is mainly by flat-bottomed barges or punts. Lübbenau is the starting point for boat trips into the heart of the Spreewald.

ⓘ *Ehm-Welk Strasse 15*

▶ *From Lübbenau take the B115 north via Lübben to the A13/E36 and continue north to Berlin.*

The 18th-century Chinesiches Teehaus (Chinese Teahouse) in the gardens of Schloss Sanssouci

The Upper Elbe,
Rocks & Castles

Leipzig is famous for its literary and musical associations. Friedrich von Schiller, one of Germany's greatest poet– dramatists, studied at Leipzig University, and Johann Sebastian Bach lived and worked here, as did Mendelssohn, Schumann and Richard Wagner. The focus of civic life here is the mid-16th-century Altes Rathaus (Old Town Hall). Behind it lies the Naschmarkt square, its northern end adorned with the 17th-century Alte Handelsbörse (Old Trading Exchange).

1/2 DAYS • 322KM • 200 MILES

ITINERARY		
LEIPZIG	➤	**Meissen (80km-50m)**
MEISSEN	➤	**Dresden (24km-15m)**
DRESDEN	➤	**Moritzburg (14km-9m)**
MORITZBURG	➤	**Königstein (52km-32m)**
KÖNIGSTEIN	➤	**Bad Schandau (5km-3m)**
BAD SCHANDAU	➤	**Colditz (106km-66m)**
COLDITZ	➤	**Leipzig (41km-25m)**

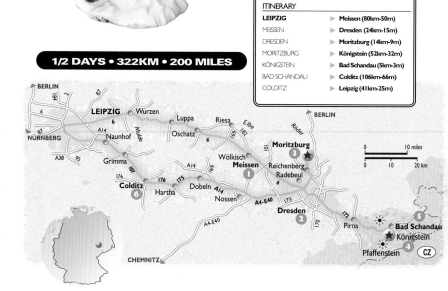

i *Richard Wagner Strasse 1, Leipzig*

▶ *From Leipzig take the B6 east to Meissen.*

❶ Meissen, Sachsen

The 1,000-year-old town of Meissen lies on the River Elbe, a short distance northwest of Dresden. Meissen is, of course, known the world over for its beautiful porcelain – identified by the distinctive trademark featuring two crossed swords.

The town's history begins with Heinrich I, who founded Misni Castle in AD 929. Forty years later it became the seat of a bishop, an important step in those days for a growing town. Around AD 1000, Meissen was granted *Marktrecht*, a decree permitting the settlement to hold its own markets; and in 1150 it was first officially documented as a Stadt (town). Further development was

Battlement walls and entrance gateway to the Cathedral and former Bishop's Castle in Meissen

hampered by the wars of the Middle Ages, but in 1719 Friedrich August der Starke (The Strong) founded the Königliche Porzellanmanufaktur (Royal Porcelain Works) in the Albrechtsburg (castle). It was transferred to the valley of the Triebisch River during the last century.

The best views of the Albrechtsburg are from the opposite bank of the Elbe. Founded in AD 929, the castle is a good example of late Gothic architecture, and was intended to be the seat of Dukes Ernst and Albrecht who ruled over Saxony and Thuringia. The adjoining Dom (cathedral) was started in 1260. Its early Gothic origins have almost disappeared under many extensions and annexes, such as two western towers which were partly destroyed by lightning in 1547, and rebuilt between 1903 and 1908. St Afra's Church and the former Fürstenschule (Duke's School) are interesting.

South of the Nikolaikirche (St Nicholas's), the head office

of the Staatliche Porzellan-Manufaktur, owned by the State of Saxony, is open to visitors, who can inspect a selection of porcelain objects, and there are demonstrations of the various processes involved in porcelain manufacture.

On a more relaxing note, Meissen is the centre of a wine-growing district. There are plenty of traditional old wine cellars in the town where thirsty travellers are welcome to sample the product.

i Markt 3

SPECIAL TO...

Keep an eye out for the local wines. Elbewein comes from the vineyards along the banks of the Elbe. The Weinstube Vincenz Richter is a famous timber-framed wine cellar dating from the 16th century. Look out for its gory collection of antique weaponry and instruments of torture.

Above: the Zwinger Palace, in classical baroque style, Dresden's most famous sight

▶ *From Meissen continue on the* **B6** *for a further 24km (15 miles) to Dresden.*

2 **Dresden,** Sachsen
On a bend of the Elbe, Dresden is now a thriving centre of half-a-million inhabitants, a far cry from the smoking ruins of a city almost totally destroyed by massive British and American bombing in February 1945.

Historically, the driving force behind the city's development was the Saxon ruler Friedrich August der Starke (The Strong) and his son, August II. The latter initiated the golden age of Dresden baroque architecture by bringing in Matthäus Daniel Pöppelmann as chief designer, and Balthasar Permoser, the sculptor, to build the Zwinger Palace. Originally planned as an orangery, the building grew and grew between 1709 and 1732.

Later it was decided to house a gallery there, and Gottfried Semper was commissioned to design a wing that would close the river end of the garden which had previously remained open. The central view from the gardens to the Wall Pavilion or the Glockenspiel Pavillon

Left: statues on the façade of the
Zwinger Palace

Although the Zwinger complex
was totally destroyed during
the devastating bombing raids
of 1945, the structure was carefully rebuilt and completed in
1964, a symbol of Germany's
determination to maintain her
cultural heritage.

Bordering the Zwinger,
Theaterplatz (Theatre Square)
makes sightseeing easy, as
nearly all Dresden's buildings
are there. The Semperoper
(Opera House), built to plans
by Gottfried Semper, was one
of the most beautiful theatres
in Europe, erected between
1871 and 1878. Reduced to a
ruin in 1945, it was rebuilt
between 1977 and 1985, keep-
ing as close as possible to the
original designs. On 13
February, 1985, exactly 40
years after its destruction, it
reopened with the Weber opera
Der Freischütz. Opposite the
Opera House stands the
Hofkirche (cathedral),
designed by Italian architect
Chiaveri and founded in 1738.
Chiaveri never finished the
baroque-style building, which
was subsequently consecrated
in 1751 and completed in 1755.
Bombing destroyed the interior
and parts of the walls, but the
tower remained upright and
was restored after the war.
Notable features of the interior
are Permoser's pulpit, carved in
1722; the altar painting, the
Ascension of Christ; and the
magnificent Silbermannorgel
(organ). The catacombs contain
the tombs of the kings and
princes of Saxony, and August
the Strong's heart in an urn.

The magnificent
Frauenkirche (Church of Our
Lady), destroyed by wartime
bombing, has been carefully
restored and reopened. This
masterpiece of baroque architecture was consecrated in
1736, and its bell-shaped dome
was a highlight of Dresden's
skyline and a symbol of the
city. The city gate, the
Georgentor, has been restored
and can be seen on the
Schlossplatz (Castle Square),
next to the Hofkirche.

(Carillon) on the opposite side,
amply demonstrates Semper's
genius. The unusual carillon
itself, consisting of 40 bells, is
all made of Meissen porcelain
and was added at the beginning of the century.

The Wall Pavilion displays
the joint coat of arms of Saxony
and Poland, reflecting August
the Strong's additional role as
King of Poland. Art lovers are
in for an enormous treat in the
palace's Picture Gallery – the
emphasis is on Old Masters.

The *porzellansammlung*
(porcelain collection) is equally
magnificent – the Zwinger
Collection is said to be the
second largest in the world,
featuring early Chinese ceramics and porcelain and a unique
display of Meissen products.

ℹ *Prager Strasse 2a*

▶ *From Dresden head northwest to Moritzburg, 14km
(9 miles).*

FOR HISTORY BUFFS

In Dresden, do not miss the
impressive golden equestrian
statue of Friedrich August II,
Der Starke (The Strong),
Elector of Saxony and King of
Poland. Erected in 1736, it was
designed by the French Court
sculptor Vinache, cast in
copper and gilded by
Wiedeman.
In the centre of the town, near
the Augustusstrasse, the
Fürstenzug (Train of Princes)
decorates the wall of the
Langer Gang (Long Gangway).
Some 24,000 porcelain tiles
from the Meissen
factory were used to create
images of the rulers of the
House of Wettin, including a
few eminent artists and scientists. It was erected between
1870 and 1876 using a sgraffito
technique.

FOR CHILDREN

A visit to the Zoologischer
Garten (zoo) in Tiergarten-
strasse is always recom-
mended. Its penguin house is
particularly appealing. Or try
the Karl May Museum at
Radebeul, just northwest of
Dresden, which houses
fascinating collections of relics
from the North Americans. It
is a memorial to Karl May, who
wrote many novels about the
'Wild West' of North America.

8 Moritzburg, Sachsen
Surrounded by a nature reserve,
Schloss Moritzburg, built by the
Duke of Moritzburg in the 16th
century, was once a hunting
lodge. It escaped war damage,
and its well-preserved interior
houses a museum of baroque

furniture and exhibits on the history of hunting. The *Hengstdepot* (stud farm) was founded in 1828 to rear race and cart horses. Now mainly race horses are bred and during the summer, horse shows are staged for buyers and visitors, attracting some 50,000 people to the Parade of the Stallions.

ℹ️ *Schlossallee 3b*

SCENIC ROUTES

The drive from Dresden to Bad Schandau via Königstein runs parallel to the course of the Elbe and offers very attractive scenery.

▶ *Return to Dresden, then take the B172 to Königstein, 52km (32 miles).*

4 Königstein, Sachsen
The massive and impregnable Festung Königstein squats on a rocky hill above the Elbe. Although there was mention of a fortress here as early as 1241, the present buildings were erected between 1589 and 1631 by the Elector Christian I. From the 17th century, the castle cellars were used to store huge barrels of wine, some holding 250,000 litres (55,000 gallons).

Königstein was also used as a secure prison. Christian I locked up his chancellor Krell here; Böttger, the European discoverer of porcelain, spent some time incarcerated at the castle; then it was the turn of the 1849 revolutionaries. During World War II, several important Allied prisoners pitted their wits against the castle's security, and the French General Giraud made a daring escape during 1942.

There are fine views from the castle over the Elbe Valley, which is also called Sächsiche Schweiz (Saxon Switzerland).

The main entrance gate to Colditz Castle

RECOMMENDED WALKS

Cross the Elbe, then continue on foot to the Lilienstein mountain on a bend in the river. There are beautiful views from the 414m (1,360-foot) plateau, and the ruins of a medieval fortress. Or head south to the 427m (1,400-foot) Pfaffenstein, with its interesting rock formations, particularly one called Barbarine.

ℹ️ *Schreiberberg 2*

▶ *Continue on the B172 to Bad Schandau.*

5 Bad Schandau, Sachsen
A favourite base for many possible excursions in the area, Bad Schandau also boasts a sanatorium offering the popular Kneipp cure. This is based on physiotherapy with the objective of developing resistance to common ailments. Hydrotherapy is also part of the cure.

The favourite local beauty

Jagged sandstone cliffs tower above the River Elbe

spot is the Bastei, a high stone bridge linking a chain of sandstone peaks above the Elbe. From the bridge, there are fine views over the rocky landscape, ideal terrain for climbing. Walkers can explore some 1,200km (745 miles) of footpaths around the area. Popular hiking destinations further afield include the Lichtenhainer Waterfall, the Kuhstall and the Obere Schleuse. For relaxed sightseeing, try a boat trip on one of the pleasure steamers.

[i] *Markt 12*

▶ *Take the **B172** back to Dresden, then the **A4/E40** to Abzweigung Nossen and turn right for the **A14** to Döbeln. Turn south for the **B175** and*

*right after Hartha on the **B176** to Colditz, a distance of 41km (25 miles).*

6 Colditz, Sachsen
On the return to Leipzig, a short detour leads to Colditz, a small town in the shadow of its castle. Popularised by many films and books, Colditz Castle is best known for the daring escapes by its Allied prisoners of war. A tour reveals one of the escape tunnels. Most of those sent to Colditz were considered particularly troublesome, but stories of the castle's impregnability only spurred them on to plot ever more daring escape plans. Statistics record that of 460 prisoners who tried to escape, 300 were caught at the outset, 130 got out but were captured in Germany, while just 30 actually scored the elusive 'home run' and reached their final destination. Reminders of

---

BACK TO NATURE

For something a little out of the ordinary, check out the strangely shaped Schrammstein rocks south of Bad Schandau. The Bastei is another bizarre rock formation to the north of the town. The rock formations in this area are unique to Europe and were created by the Elbe river which eroded the sandstone mountains.

---

the period can be found in the nearby Escape Museum. Since the war, the castle, once the seat of the Dukes of Saxony, has been used as a hospital.

[i] *Markt 1*

▶ *From Colditz take the **B107** to Grimma. Head northwest back to Leipzig via Naunhof.*

Towns &
Forests of Thuringia

Weimar was appointed as European City of Culture for 1999, and its Altstadt (Old Town) is listed as a historic monument. The baroque-style Deutsches Nationaltheater (German National Theatre) maintains Weimar's traditional status as an important centre of German literature, art and music. Goethe, Schiller, Herder, Cranach, Bach, Liszt and Weber head the list of the former residents.

2 DAYS • 346KM • 215 MILES

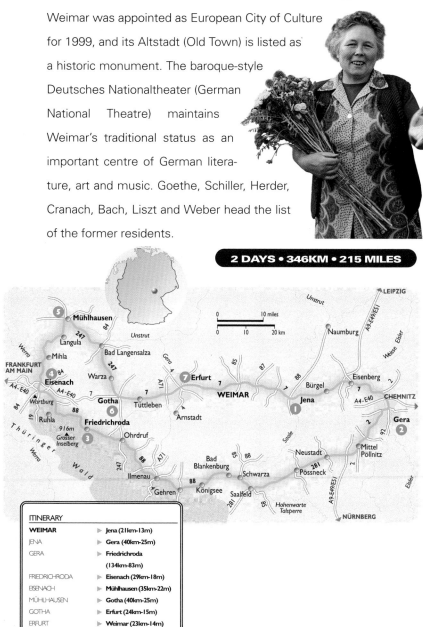

ITINERARY	
WEIMAR	▶ **Jena (21km-13m)**
JENA	▶ **Gera (40km-25m)**
GERA	▶ **Friedrichroda (134km-83m)**
FRIEDRICHRODA	▶ **Eisenach (29km-18m)**
EISENACH	▶ **Mühlhausen (35km-22m)**
MÜHLHAUSEN	▶ **Gotha (40km-25m)**
GOTHA	▶ **Erfurt (24km-15m)**
ERFURT	▶ **Weimar (23km-14m)**

i *Markt 10, Weimar*

▶ *From Weimar the **B7** runs east for 21km (13 miles) to Jena.*

1 Jena, Thüringen

Jena used to belong to the Duchy of Saxony and Weimar. In the Middle Ages it flourished as a manufacturer of agricultural products and wine, while later it became famous for more intellectual pursuits. Once accused of being a 'hoarder of knowledge', Jena was the centre of the German philosophy movement, and had its own university. Schiller was invited to lecture here in history and philosophy, and Goethe was one of the university's patrons.

The scientific reputation of Jena rests on the achievement of three men: Carl Zeiss, a mechanic; Ernst Abbe, a physicist; and Otto Schott, a glass manufacturer. Together they laid the foundations for the development and manufacture of optical and other precision instruments using glass. Zeiss installed his mechanical workshop at Jena in 1846. He was joined by Abbe, who was experimenting with microscopes, and Schott, the chemical and glass engineer who provided the raw materials.

The Zeiss Planetarium, opened in 1926, is one of the oldest of its kind in Germany. it is a listed building, and was renovated between 1983 and 1985 when it was equipped with the latest state-of-the-art advances in technology.

Jena suffered badly during World War II, and the Marktplatz (Market Square) is the only reminder of the past. It is flanked by a neat, comparatively small Gothic-style Rathaus (Town Hall) with two parallel roofs and a clock tower in between.

The statue of the Elector Johann Friedrich der Grossmütige (The Generous) stands in the square, an imposing figure with a huge sword in his right hand. He was the

founder of Jena's university. To the south of the city centre, the Optisches (Optical) Museum is a fascinating experience. Some 12,000 valuable mechanical and optical instruments are exhibited here, and there is a model of the type of camera used in space explorations.

i *Johannisstrasse 23*

▶ *Continue east on the **B7**, via Eisenberg, to Gera.*

2 Gera, Thüringen

Gera's name derives from the Old German *Geraha*, meaning a large body of water. Nearly 1,000 years old, the town was

Duchess Anna Amalia's Wittums-palais at Weimar, now a museum for German literature

SPECIAL TO...

From Jena the B88 leads 33km (20 miles) northeast to Naumburg. The Dom of St Peter and St Paul is one of the most valuable historical monuments in Europe. The crypt is the oldest part, dating from 1170, but the main part of the building was started some time before 1213, and frequently altered until its completion in the 19th century. It houses many treasured works of art.

chosen as the seat of the von Weida family at the beginning of the 13th century.

The lovely market square is edged by the Renaissance Rathaus (Town Hall) and a

collection of colourful and well-restored burghers' houses. At the centre of the square is the 17th-century Simonsbrunnen (fountain). Also of note is the 17th-century pharmacy, topped with an ornate circular Renaissance oriel.

i *Heinrichstrasse 35*

▶ *Take the **B2** south to Mittelpöllnitz, turn right on to the **B281** to Saalfeld, then turn north to Schwarza. Turn left for the **B88** for Friedrichroda, via Ilmenau, 134km (83 miles).*

8 **Friedrichroda,** Thüringen
The road runs through the lovely green hiking countryside of the Thüringer Wald (Forest of Thuringia) and into the resort of Friedrichroda. The town developed around the nearby

SCENIC ROUTES

One of the loveliest sections of the route between Gera and Friedrichroda is the stretch between Saalfeld and Bad Blankenburg, before the road actually reaches and runs parallel to the Thüringer Wald. Once you reach the Thüringer Wald, there is a rewarding detour into the forest from Ilmenau.

Kloster (abbey) built by Landgrave Ludwig. The abbey was destroyed in the 16th century, and a castle built on its site. The gardens are very attractive with century-old trees and a little Japanese-style garden with artificial cliffs built into the scenery. The monks also created fishponds, which

are still used for trout and carp farming.

Friedrichroda prides itself on being one of the oldest tourist resorts and celebrated 160 years of tourism in 1997. The Thüringerwaldbahn (Thuringian Forest Railway) provides a handy connection to the Marienglashöhle, one of the most attractive and longest crystal caves in Europe, which houses the fabulous Marienglasgrotte, a grotto noted for its translucent gypsum crystals of amazing length. Another recommended excursion is a trek up the Grosser Inselberg, a 916m (3,000-foot) mini-mountain which can best be reached from the nearby villages of Ruhla, Brotterode or Tarbarz. The final ascent has to be started from the Kleiner Inselberg and the Grenzwiese near Rennsteig, which is the terminus for cars and coaches. There are superb views from the mountaintop.

i *Marktstrasse 13*

▶ *Continue northwest on the **B88** to Eisenach, 29km (18 miles).*

The richly decorated entrance door to Gera's Renaissance Rathaus (Town Hall)

4 **Eisenach**, Thüringen
Sometimes known as the
Wartburgstadt Eisenach, the
town of Eisenach lies at the
northwestern end of the
Thüringer Wald, below the
Wartburg Mountain, and its
imposing Wartburg Castle. One
of the most interesting German
fortress complexes, the
Wartburg is believed to have

*In the Thüringer Wald, the well-
tended villages generally have red
roofs and grey slate house façades*

been founded in 1067. As the
local lords prospered, the castle
grew in importance, from a
fortress into a seat of government and ducal residence.

The Reformist Martin
Luther lived here between 1521
and 1522, under the protection
of the Kurfürst (Elector), after
he had been outlawed by the
reactionary bishops at the Diet
of Worms. Within a mere ten
weeks he had translated the
New Testament from the original Greek into German and, by
doing so, laid the cornerstone
for the development of the
German language. The present
fortress was constructed
between the 11th and 16th
centuries and then renovated in
the 19th century. The interior of
the Wartburg Castle is
enchanting, with
timber-

framed structures bordering its
two courtyards. The castle
museum, the Neue Kemenaten,
displays several exquisite works
of art, including paintings by
Lucas Cranach the Elder, sculptures by the famous woodcarver,
Tilman Riemenschneider, a
carved trunk designed by
Albrecht Dürer, and late-Gothic
tapestries.

The market square is the
heart of the Altstadt (Old
Town). At the northern end, the
baroque-style Stadtschloss
(Town Castle) houses the
Thüringer Museum and its
collection of local faïence,
porcelain and glass. The
Rathaus (Town Hall) has a
markedly leaning tower.

The Parish Church of St
George boasts a richly decorated interior with tombstones
erected for the Counts of
Thuringia. Luther preached
here and Johann Sebastian Bach
was christened in the church.
The Lutherhaus near by, and
the Bachhaus on Frauenplan,
can be visited.

i *Markt 9*

▶ *Continue north for 35km
(22 miles) to Mühlhausen.*

Old Wartburg model in
Eisenach's car museum

Medieval houses in the handsome market town of Gotha

5 **Mühlhausen,** Thüringen
A visit to Mühlhausen is like stepping back into the Middle Ages. This small town of timber-framed houses, narrow streets and numerous churches is still surrounded by its ancient city walls. Historically, it is renowned as the crucible of the German Peasants' Revolt of 1524 to 1525, and is sometimes called Thomas Müntzer Stadt after the leader of the revolt. Müntzer's crusade set out to free the peasants from the system of hefty payments demanded by the feudal landlords.

The Parish Church of Divi Blasii stands on the square between the Untermarkt and Johann Sebastian Bachplatz (Bach Square). Near by, the Annenkapelle dates back to the 13th century, and a little further on there are several beautiful medieval houses. Parts of the old city walls, interspersed with towers, are still standing, and the largest tower, Rabenturm, houses a museum.

[i] *Ratsstrasse 20*

▶ *From Mühlhausen take the* ***B247*** *southeast to Gotha, a distance of 40km (25 miles).*

6 **Gotha,** Thüringen
Dominating the view of Gotha is Schloss Friedenstein, an early baroque building. It stands on the site of the former Grimmenstein fortress, which was conquered in the 16th century and later razed to the ground. The 365-room castle complex includes the Schlosskirche (church), which contains the tombs of the rulers of Gotha; and the Schloss-museum, which has a fine art collection. The castle's Ekhof Theatre is named after Conrad Ekhof, who established a resident theatre company here. Leave enough time for a visit to the extensive castle gardens, where there is plenty of scope for restful walks.

Overlooking the town centre from the castle, there is a good view of the red-painted Rathaus, built between 1567 and 1577. The market square in front of the town hall is lined with burghers' houses. On the right, coming from the castle, stands the house of artist Lucas Cranach the Elder (1472–1553).

[i] *Hauptmarkt 2*

▶ *From Gotha take the* ***B7*** *east for 24km (15 miles) to Erfurt.*

7 **Erfurt,** Thüringen
Erfurt's main claim to fame is its position as a centre for horticultural activities. Its permanent Internationale Gartenbauaustellung (International Horticultural Exhibition) attracts many thousands of visitors.

SPECIAL TO...

The town of Gotha prides itself on a long-established reputation in the map business. Maps and atlases have been designed and printed here since the 18th century, and the Museum Kartographisches (Cartographic Museum) was opened in 1985 to celebrate 200 years of map craft.

A town with a population of some 200,000 inhabitants, it has undergone an extensive restoration programme and, fortunately, the Altstadt (Old Town) remained largely intact after World War II.

The medieval churches on the Domberg – the Dom (cathedral) and the Severikirche next to it – are impressive ecclesiastical buildings and should not be missed. The cathedral was founded in the 8th century, and then completed in 1154 as a Romanesque basilica. The middle of its three towers contains the Maria Gloriosa, one of the largest church bells in the world, and christened the Gloriosa on account of its beautiful sound.

The 600-year-old Krämerbrücke (Krämer Bridge), which spans the River Gera, used to connect the old east–west trading route. Lined with 33 timber-framed and gabled houses, it is one of the town's top sights. Close by, the old Furt, a shallow part of the river used as a crossing before the bridge was built, has been uncovered.

One of the oldest streets in the town is the Anger, a fascinating place for a stroll. Now completely restored, many of its houses hosted a number of important visitors in the past: No 11, Zum Schwarzen Löwen

(The Black Lion), was visited by Queen Marie-Elenore of Sweden in 1632, and Tsar Alexander of Russia was entertained at No 6 in 1808.

i *Benediktsplatz 1*

▶ *Take the **B7** heading east for 23km (14 miles) back to Weimar.*

Painted shutters in Erfurt's Altstadt, an area full of unconsidered architectural trifles

THE GERMAN MIDLANDS

South of the North German plain the map changes and from west to east a hilly and mountainous landscape emerges, cloaked with beautiful forests, lakes and rivers. One scenic route follows another, and as the mountains, with few exceptions, do not reach heights above 1,000m (3,280 feet), there are the advantages of easier walks. The difficulties encountered crossing from one valley to another in higher mountain ranges do not occur here. Heading into the countryside from the towns and cities of the Ruhr, the visitor is pleasantly surprised by the change in scenery and by the many little villages which present quite a different image of Germany, a Germany for holidays and relaxation.

The gentle rolling countryside of the Sauerland region

The Harz region is called 'The Heart of Germany', and since unification it is definitely more in the middle of the country than before, when it formed the border with the eastern provinces. The Harz Mountains were exploited for their valuable ore deposits from as early as the 10th century, with the trees above the mines providing the necessary fuel for the refining operations. Forestry and the creation of hydroelectric power are two major industries to be found here, along with tourism.

Numerous forests, interrupted by the tributaries of the Weser, make this a very pleasant area to explore. Nature parks compete with medieval towns for attention, and it is little wonder that the Deutsche Märchenstrasse (German Fairy Tale Road) runs right along the Weser and its riverside towns. The towns themselves often seem to have been plucked straight from the pages of a fairy tale.

Further down, in the unspoilt northern regions of the province of Hessen, there is no geographical border, but visitors arriving from the north are greeted by three large nature parks to the west and east of Kassel, with the Reinhards Wald (forest) bordering the northern approach to Kassel itself. Historic towns full of fine buildings and surrounded by forests provide a balanced landscape between the city and nature. The Sauerland region consists of tree-covered hills, rivers and the massive dams which supply the mighty industries of the Ruhr Valley to the west with water and power. Far from interfering with the natural balance of the surroundings, the dams have actually enhanced the beauty of the scenery and the new lakes have created valuable recreational facilities, a bonus for watersports enthusiasts.

Statue of the *Rattenfänger* (Pied Piper) of Hameln

Tour 6

One of the best areas for recreational pursuits and holiday-making in Germany, the Harz region enjoys a great location – not too far from the capital Berlin, and within easy reach of the Ruhr, Bremen and Hannover. Although this is a mountainous region, it is not too strenuous for gentle strolls or hikes, and visitors to the area will find the many lakes and rivers provide a wealth of beautiful scenery to just sit and enjoy. There is plenty of history, too, and a great number of superb medieval buildings, many of which are classified as national treasures.

Tour 7

Weserbergland lies between the arms of the River Weser. The river and its main tributaries, the Fulda and the Werra, seem to have inspired many German legends and fairy-tales, some of which have achieved international fame. The Deutsche Märchenstrasse (German Fairy Tale Road) links up many of the myths and stories of the past with their original settings. Weserbergland is at the centre of this giant fairy-tale, with the town of Hameln, or Hamelin, its most famous location.

Tour 8

Forests and rivers provide the main backdrop to this scenic tour, and historic towns furnished with beautiful old buildings offer additional interest. It would seem that all the major holiday routes lead here, too. In the town of Alsfeld, the Deutsche Märchenstrasse crosses the Deutsche Ferien-strasse (German Holiday Road); and Kassel is the starting point of the Deutsche Historische Strasse (German Historical Road), while the town of Marburg lies on the Lahn-Ferienstrasse (Holiday Road). It just goes to prove that this is a marvellous area to explore and follow up a wide variety of interests, from general sightseeing to boat trips on the Eder Dam near Waldeck and hiking in the plentiful natural parks covering the north of the region.

Tour 9

Bordering the Ruhr Valley, Germany's industrial heartland, the Sauerland is the vital power behind the might of German industry. Its numerous lakes and rivers supply water and hydroelectric power, but on the human side the landscape provides an excellent recreation area. A wide variety of watersports can be enjoyed here, and there are some great lakeside walks and camping grounds. Out of the 15 artificial lakes, only six do not permit sports and bathing.

A richly decorated door in the lovely old town of Goslar

Harz Mountains
& Forests

Goslar's monumental Kaiserpfalz (Emperor's Residence) is an imposing sight and one of the largest non-ecclesiastical structures of the 11th century. The market square, with its 15th-century Rathaus, was built by wealthy burghers. The former Ratsherrnzimmer (council meeting chamber), open only for viewing, is beautifully restored, its walls and ceiling decorated with images of the Holy Roman Emperors and scenes from the life of Christ.

2 DAYS • 176KM • 109 MILES

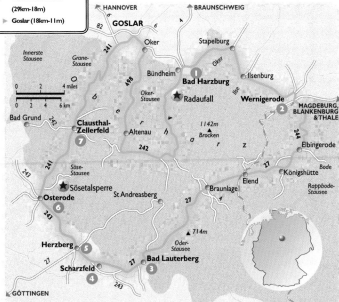

i *Markt 7, Goslar*

▶ *From Goslar take a short drive east to Oker, turn south on to the B498, then turn sharp east past Altenau for the B242. Turn north on to the B4 for Bad Harzburg, 48km (30 miles).*

❶ **Bad Harzburg,**
Niedersachsen

Away from the big towns, skimming the northern end of the Harz Mountain range, Bad Harzburg is a spa town with all the facilities for a relaxing and healthy stay. A natural spring delivers water at a constant 32°C (89°F) to the Hallenbad (covered pool), and there is an open-air annexe where the water temperature drops to a mere 29°C (84°F).

BACK TO NATURE

The Wild Deer Park at Bündheim, near Bad Harzburg, contains moufflon and red deer, among other animals.

FOR CHILDREN

South of Bad Harzburg a stream cascades down on to rocks to the Radaufall (waterfall). This forms the background for a Kinderparadies (Children's Paradise) which offers all kinds of entertainment and features rides on a miniature railway. The Märchenwald, near the cable-car station at Bad Harzburg, exhibits scenes from well-known fairy-tales in little wooden chalets. There are some 100 handcarved figures on display arranged on rotating stages.

The only historical remains here are the ruins of the Harzburg, an 11th-century fortress first founded by Heinrich IV, later destroyed by the Saxons, then rebuilt under Emperor Friedrich Barbarossa,

Traditional decorations on the façade of one of Goslar's old half-timbered houses

only to be demolished again in the middle of the 17th century. A cable-car ride makes short work of the 500m (1,640-foot) climb up the Burgberg. The commanding view from the top explains the positioning of the fortress, and there are several gentle strolls around the area which make this a pleasant excursion.

i *Nordhäuser Strasse 4*

▶ *Head east for 20km (13 miles) to Wernigerode.*

SPECIAL TO...

The Harzquerbahn is a real old-time steam train which runs on narrow-gauge tracks from Wernigerode to Nordhausen, a distance of 60km (37 miles). The line was first opened on 27 March, 1899, and it was hoped it would eventually run as far as Hamburg in the north and Vienna in the south.

2 **Wernigerode,** Sachsen-Anhalt

Located in what was formerly East Germany, Wernigerode is a beautifully preserved town with a medieval centre that is listed as a monument. The focus is the Marktplatz (Market Place) with its unique Rathaus (Town Hall), which looks as if it has been lifted straight from the pages of a fairy-tale. This little jewel of medieval architecture has a raised ground-floor entrance that is reached by two staircases, flanked by a pair of oriel spires, and all its façades are painted and decorated. First documented in 1277 as a Spelhus, from the word for a playhouse or theatre (Spielhaus), this was not only a place for entertainment, it also served as a law court administered by the ruling Counts. After a fire in 1543 its function changed to that of a town hall,

and weddings still take place there today.

Other interesting buildings include the Waaghaus, whose scales date back to the 16th century, which adjoins the rear of the Rathaus; and there are a number of beautiful timbered houses all around the town centre bearing witness to an era of great and stylish architecture. On Breite Strasse, the Krummelhaus, at No 72, was built in 1674 and decorated with carved ornaments which completely conceal the timber-framed façade. The smallest house in town is found on Kochstrasse, just 4.2m (13½ feet) up to the eaves and less than 3m (10 feet) wide. Then there is the Schiefe Haus (Leaning House), formerly a mill, which started to lean when the water from the stream beneath attacked the foundations.

The town of Wernigerode is famous for its richly coloured half-timbered houses

A few remnants of the old town fortifications can still be seen, including the moat and one of the city gates, the Westerntor. A tour of Schloss Adalbert gives several insights into the changing demand for creature comforts through the ages.

About 7km (4 miles) from Wernigerode, towards the mountains, is the Steinerne

---

BACK TO NATURE

The Wernigerode Wildlife Park in the Christianental is a good place to spot all sorts of indigenous animals, from moufflon, red and roe deer, to birds of prey.

Renne with a waterfall and Ottofelsen (Otto's Rock). The rock can be climbed with the aid of fixed steel ladders and offers beautiful views from the top.

ⓘ *Marktplatz 10*

▶ *Take the **B244** south to Elbingerode and continue on the **B27** via Braunlage to Bad Lauterberg, 40km (25 miles).*

FOR HISTORY BUFFS

When walking around Wernigerode, do not miss the house at No 95 Breite Strasse. Built in 1678, it is called Krell'sche Schmiede (Smithy), and above the door a horse's head juts out and horseshoes denote the nature of the occupant's trade. There has been a smithy here since the house was built.

❽ Bad Lauterberg,
Niedersachsen

It is worth considering a stop in Braunlage, before going on to Bad Lauterberg. Braunlage is one of the most developed resorts in the Harz mountains. It is officially classified as a climatic health resort and offers a great variety of entertainment for all tastes. The sports-minded can take their pick of tennis, bowling, swimming, water gymnastics and skiing in winter, to name a few. The body-conscious can visit the beauty studio or undergo a course of the Scarsdale diet, while children can enjoy their favourite activities, and competitions are arranged for them in the Maritim Kinder Club (Maritime Children's Club). You can take a trip by cable-car to the top of the 971m (3,185-foot) Wurmberg (Worm Mountain) for fine views and to see the excavations of an ancient place of worship dating back to about 100 BC. The Grosse Wurmbergstrasse (Great Wurmberg Road) can also be

taken from Braunlage and leads along hairpin bends up to the mountain.

Bad Lauterberg is an officially classified health resort. There is no shortage of things to do here as the spa town is at the centre of an extensive network of nature walks, and its other great attraction is the Oder-Stausee, an artificial lake which offers a wide range of water-sports facilities. Canoeing, rowing and sailing are all available on the 310m (1,016-foot) long stretch of water. On a more relaxed note, a chair-lift operates rides up to the Hausberg, with views over Bad Lauterberg from the Burg-Restaurant.

ⓘ *Ritscherstrasse 4*

SCENIC ROUTES

The Harz Mountain region offers an abundance of scenic routes. The drive between Braunlage and Bad Lauterberg is particularly lovely. It is always useful to map out a circular drive, and there is a good circuit from Bad Lauterberg to St Andreasberg and back via Herzberg. From Osterode you can take the scenic Deutsche Ferienstrasse (German Holiday Road) to Clausthal-Zellerfeld.

▶ *From Bad Lauterberg take the **B27/B243** west to Scharzfeld.*

❹ Scharzfeld,
Niedersachsen

The Steinkirche (Stone Church) in Scharzfeld is really a cave once used by prehistoric people as living quarters and then by early Germanic tribes for religious ceremonies. Later made into a church, the cave was used as a place of worship into the 16th century. Its former church bell is now housed in the local village church.

Another intersting cave near by is the 400m (1,310-foot) long Einhornhöhle (Unicorn Cave),

The Romkerhaller waterfall in the Okertal valley, near Goslar

noted for the skeleton of a prehistoric animal that was found here.

▶ *Continue on the **B27/B243** for 4km (2 miles) to Herzberg.*

❺ Herzberg, Niedersachsen
Herzberg's claim to fame is its timber-framed schloss (castle), formerly a hunting lodge, then seat of the local rulers. Built in 1510, it was the birthplace of Ernst August of Hannover, who later founded what was to become the English-Hanoverian royal dynasty.

ⓘ *Marktplatz 32*

▶ *Continue on the **B243** for 11km (7 miles) to Osterode.*

❻ Osterode, Niedersachsen
The River Söse flows out of the Harz Mountains past the picturesque medieval town of Osterode. The main square, Kornmarkt (Grain Market), is edged with a collection of splendid historic buildings,

The timber Marktkirche in Clausthal-Zellerfeld

including the Renaissance-style Englischer Hof dating from 1610. Near by is the renovated 16th-century Church of St Agidii; behind that the old Rathaus, built in 1552, stands together with the richly ornamented Ratswaage building, which once housed the official weights and measures office erected one year later. The Heimatmuseum is located in the historical Ritterhaus (Knight's Hall), while the baroque Kornmagazin (Grain Warehouse) was built between 1719 and 1722. Since 1987 it has been used as the town council chambers. The nearby Sösetalsperre (Söse Dam) makes an interesting excursion. Drinking water from the dam is piped as far as Bremen, 200km (124 miles) away. There is a very pleasant footpath that runs around the lake, with traffic restricted to the northern shore.

i *Schachtrup-Villa, Dörgestrasse 40*

Take the ***B241*** *north to Clausthal-Zellerfeld.*

7 Clausthal-Zellerfeld, Niedersachsen

There are two towns rolled into one here, and each boasts its own particular highlight: the Oberharzer Bergwerkmuseum at Zellerfeld, and the Protestant Marktkirche zum Heiligen Geist (Market Church of the Holy Ghost) in Clausthal.

After a serious fire in 1672, Zellerfeld was rebuilt using a grid system. The Oberharzer Museum provides a historical overview of mining activities in the Harz region up until the 1930s. Most appropriately, there is a technical university located here with a noted traditional mining faculty.

Clausthal's Marktkirche has several unusual features. The building is totally constructed from timber, while inside, daylight is filtered through windows set at an angle, so creating an unusual perspective and a unique atmosphere. The altar dates back to 1641.

Side trips from Clausthal-Zellerfeld include the Alte Silberminen (old silver mines) which lie 8km (5 miles) to the north and date back to 1551. Also, a trip to nearby Bad Grund presents the opportunity to visit the Iberger Tropfsteinhöhle (Iberger Caves). Discovered and explored in 1874, the main cave is 150m (490 feet) long, and is made up of a number of smaller caves, with the stalagmites and stalactites mainly found in the upper sections.

i *Bergstrasse 31*

Continue north on the ***B241*** *back to Goslar.*

RECOMMENDED WALKS

The Harz region has more than 8,000km (5,000 miles) of hiking trails. The distinctly picturesque local term for them is Wanderwege, literally 'Wander Ways'.
Drive from Wernigerode via Blankenburg to Thale. From Thale climb up to the Rosstrappe, which can also be reached by chair-lift. It is also possible to walk to the opposite side of the Bode Valley and scale the Hexentanzplatz (Dancing Place of the Witches) for another splendid view.

East & West
of the Weser

Situated on the River Leine, Göttingen is mainly celebrated for its university, founded in 1734 by elector George II, also King of Great Britain, which produced a clutch of Nobel Prize winners. The Markt (market) and the Altes Rathaus (Old Town Hall) form the town centre.

1/2 DAYS • 308KM • 192 MILES

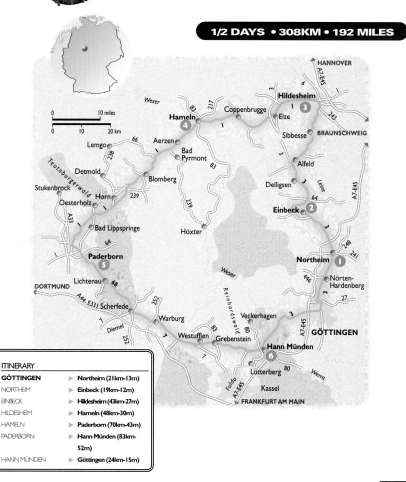

The 'Goose Girl' fountain stands before the Rathaus on the market square in Göttingen

the remainder make idyllic footpaths for walks and part of the moat has been transformed into little ponds.

A special feature of Einbeck is the wooden houses around the market-place. Two of the most outstanding are situated close to a fountain dedicated to the town's famous prankster, Till Eulenspiegel. According to legend, he was a brewery worker, and the composer Richard Strauss set his exploits to music in the symphonic poem, *Till Eulenspiegel*.

The Brodhaus, built in 1552, and the Rats-Apotheke (Town Pharmacy) opposite, are two beautifully preserved and impressive buildings, with interesting high gables and dormer-like ventilation openings in the roofs. The space under the roof was used by brewers for the storage and drying of raw materials, such as hops, barley and malt. Across the square stands the Rathaus, which has become a distinctive emblem with its three asymetrically set oriel windows. Next door is the Ratswaage, the official weights and measures building. Its façade is a picture of Renaissance prosperity, with the doors, window frames and cornices all decorated with mouldings and friezes, and colourfully painted. Tidexerstrasse and Marktstrasse are graced with a further harmonious collection of old houses, their individuality a potent expression of the style and pride of their architect/builders.

[i] *Marktstrasse 13*

▷ *Continue on the **B3** to Alfeld, then turn northeast via Sibbesse to Hildesheim, 43km (27 miles).*

3 Hildesheim,
Niedersachsen
Hildesheim's origins can be traced back by popular legend

[i] *Altes Rathaus (Old Town Hall), Markt 9, Göttingen*

▷ *From Göttingen take the **B3** north to Northeim.*

1 Northeim, Niedersachsen
Northeim is a small medieval-looking town some 700 years old. The past is revealed by remnants of the old city wall and a collection of timber-framed houses. Northeim's distinctive emblem is St Sixti's Church, a late Gothic edifice built between 1467 and 1498. Notable features of the interior are the winged altarpiece and a bronze font in the Christening Chapel. The church organ, and the late Gothic paintings featured in the windows illustrating scenes from Christ's Passion are impressive.

[i] *Am Münster 6*

▷ *Continue on the **B3** north for 19km (12 miles) to Einbeck.*

2 Einbeck, Niedersachsen
'Einbeck invites you back to the Middle Ages,' state the tourist brochures boldly. And it is not far from the truth. The importance of Einbeck stretches back a good few hundred years, and all on account of its beer-brewing activities. The town's famous ale, Ainpockisch Pier as it was called, travelled a long way, even as far as Munich, and the Dukes of Bavaria were already purchasing large quantities of Einbeck beer as far back as 1533. It later became the more familiar Bockbier. The beer was brewed at home by the citizens of Einbeck, and it is thought that there were as many as 700 of these small breweries in the town at the time.

An aerial view of the town clearly shows the circular ring of the old town fortifications; there is also a good view from the top of the Stadtwald, a wooded hill near by. A few towers, walls and ramparts are still standing, while

The Pied Piper plays his pipe and lures the children out of Hameln, never to be seen again

to 815. Ludwig der Fromme (Louis the Pious), so the story goes, was looking for a good site to found a bishopric in the area. One day, at the height of summer, snow fell unexpectedly where roses normally bloomed. The bishop took this as a sign and built his cathedral here. As long as the roses continue to blossom it is said that Hildesheim will flourish too. The rose tree was badly burned during World War II, but miraculously it started to flower again in the winter of 1945. Believing this to be a good omen for the town's future, Hildesheim adopted the thousand-year-old rose bush which surrounds the walls of the cathedral, as its official emblem.

Tragedy struck the town in the final stages of World War II when Allied bombing destroyed 70 per cent of Hildesheim's early Romanesque architecture and wiped out one of Germany's most important centres of Romanesque art.

Southwest of the Altstadt (Old Town) centre the Dom (cathedral) stands on the site of the 9th-century original

Mummy mask in Hildesheim's Roemer-Pelizaeus Museum, which has a world-famous collection of Egyptian antiquities

basilica. The present building is a reconstruction of the 11th-century basilica and was consecrated in 1960. West of the cathedral, the Roemer-Pelizaeus Museum contains the second-most important collection of Egyptian artefacts in Germany, second only to the Bode Museum in Berlin.

Magnificent St Michaelis Kirche (St Michael's Church) is recognised as the best example of the Gottesburg (God's Castle) Ottonian-Romanesque style; it was, and is again, one of the most magnificent Romanesque basilicas in Germany.

The nearby castle of Marienburg, at Pattensen, gives the impression of a medieval fortress, but in fact it was only built by King George of Hanover in the 19th century. The castle houses an interesting museum.

[i] Rathausstrasse 18-20

▶ Take the **B1** west for 48km (30 miles) to Hameln.

4 **Hameln,** Niedersachsen
Hameln, or Hamelin, is the well-known Rattenfängerstadt

SCENIC ROUTES

You can take the scenic Wesertalstrasse (B83) south from Hameln to Höxter for 55km (43 miles), then reverse direction by taking the B239 northwest, through the forests to Rischenau, then back through Bad Pyrmont to the town of Hameln. Alternatively you can head north on the B83 along the Weser. At Veckershagen bear left and drive through the forest of Reinhardswald. From the slopes of the Staufenberg the road carries on to Sababurg, the ruin of a 14th-century hunting lodge built for the Landgraves of Hessen.

(Rat Catcher's Town) of story-book fame. The legendary Pied Piper is said to have come to the town in 1284 and promised to rid it of a plague of rats. Playing his flute, he led the rats into the river where they drowned, but when he went to collect his reward, the city burghers refused to pay. In retaliation, he took up his flute again and enticed the town's children to follow him. Neither he nor the children were ever seen again.

The original settlement of Hamala was founded by peasants and fishermen. In later years, monks from Fulda founded an abbey near the River Weser, which was later called St Bonifatius (St Boniface). On the market square stands the early Gothic Church of St Nicolai, rebuilt between 1957 and 1958. This was originally the rivermen's church and the top of the tower is decorated with a model of a golden vessel, a reminder of its heritage.

On Osterstrasse, east of the market, stands the Renaissance-style Hochzeitshaus (Marriage House), a former reception hall, built between 1610 and 1617. The Rattenfängerhaus (Rat-Catcher's House) is another imposing Renaissance structure with an ornate front gable and splendid decorations. Around the corner, a plaque commemorates the Pied Piper's tale.

☐ *Deisterallee 1*

▶ *Continue southwest on the B1 for 70km (43 miles) to Paderborn.*

SPECIAL TO...

A unique feature of Hameln is the Rattenfängerspiele (Pied Piper plays) which are performed on the terrace in front of the Marriage House during the summer. They are scheduled for midday on Sundays from mid-May to mid-September.

BACK TO NATURE

From Hameln take the B1 southwest to Horn. West of Horn is a strange rock formation called the Externsteine. These bizarre outcrops have been placed under a preservation order. The tallest is 37m (121 feet) high, and one of the rocks is carved with a relief of Christ being taken down from the Cross, the work of an unknown artist around 1130.

---

5 **Paderborn,** Nordrhein-Westfalen

Trading routes between Flanders and Saxony created an early settlement on the site of the present town of Paderborn. Karl der Grosse (Charlemagne) held his first Imperial Diet (Meeting of Rulers) here in AD 777, after he had conquered Saxony, and in the same year Paderborn achieved the status of a city.

In the centre of the Altstadt, the mighty Dom (Cathedral) stands almost as long as its tower is high, nearly 100m (328 feet). Built over two centuries, from AD 1000, the church tower is a massive closed construction of Romanesque design. It dominates the view of the cathedral square and the houses around it. Beneath the floor of the cathedral the foundations of Charlemagne's original basilica were discovered in 1979–80.

Around the cathedral area there are 200 little springs, known as the Paderquellen. These form the River Pader, which, at a mere 4km (2½ miles) long, is one of the shortest rivers in Germany. The Rathaus is located southwest of the cathedral. A late-Renaissance structure with three gables, it was rebuilt after destruction in World War II.

Just 4km (2½ miles) north of town, Schloss Neuhaus is a moated castle which has stood here in its present form since the 16th century. It consists of four wings with a massive tower

on each corner, and was once the residence of the Prince-Bishops. Now the castle houses a school, an exhibition hall for the town's gallery and a concert hall.

☐ *Marienplatz 2a*

▶ *Drive southeast on the B68/B7, via Warburg, to Westuffeln, then turn left to Grebenstein and continue east to Hann Münden.*

FOR CHILDREN

Take the B68 north to Stukenbrock for Safaripark Stukenbrock. The safari park can be visited either by car or bus. Visitors travel through a large monkey reservation, then on to see the lions, tigers, elephants, giraffes and antelopes. Other attractions include a Westernstadt (Western town), a wonderful Hollywood-style theatre and funfair rides.

FOR HISTORY BUFFS

From Paderborn drive north on the B1 for approximately 15km (9 miles), then turn left for Oesterholz and Berlebeck and left again at Hermannsdenkmal. This enormous monument celebrates 1st-century Germanic tribe leader Arminius (Hermann) who is seen here brandishing a 7m (23-foot) sword. Hermann's cunning defeated vastly superior Roman forces when he lured them into the forest and beat them in a three-day battle in AD 89. The raising of the monument coincided with the birth of the German nationalist movement in the mid-19th century and carries the inscription: 'German unity is my strength, and my strength is Germany's power'.

6 Hann Münden,
Niedersachsen

The historic town of Hann Münden enjoys a pleasant position in a valley surrounded by woods, close to the confluence of the rivers Werra and Fulda. Excavations have revealed that a large settlement existed here in Charlemagne's time, but the foundation of the town is credited to Heinrich der Löwe (Henry the Lion).

The Rathaus stands on Marktplatz (Market Square), surrounded by old timber-framed buildings. Its imposing Weser-Renaissance façade was designed by Georg Crossman

Scrollwork, pyramids and statues adorn the entrance gate to Hann Münden's Rathaus

and erected between 1603 and 1613, with ornamented gables, a sumptuous portal and oriel windows. St Blasius's Church, opposite, was built between the 13th and 16th centuries. Features inside include a bronze font, a sandstone pulpit and the tomb of Wilhelm von Braunschweig (William of Brunswick), who died in 1503.

The former Welfenschloss (Castle of the Welfs, an old dynasty) was founded in 1070. It is a picturesque building in Renaissance style and now houses the town's cultural centre and local history museum. Near by is the stone-built Werra bridge.

i *Rathaus (Town Hall),
Lotzestrasse 2*

▷ *From Hann Münden continue on the B3 northeast to Göttingen.*

RECOMMENDED WALKS

There are about 90 suggested circular walks from the car parks in and around Hann Münden. East of Lutterberg, on the B496 south of Hann Münden, the Rinderstall is a popular destination for a stroll. The Kloster Bursfelde (abbey), which dates back to the 12th century, can be reached by driving due north along the eastern bank of the Weser, and there are a number of lovely walks around here.

Nature Parks
& Fairy Tales

On the River Fulda, sheltered by the foothills of the Habichtswald, Kassel has an ideal location for a town. The Altstadt (Old Town) no longer exists, wiped out during World War II. The Wilhelmshöhe Schlosspark is Kassel's real treasure. Commissioned by Landgrave Karl in 1701, it focuses on a giant statue of Hercules, a copy of the Farnese Hercules in Naples, which stands on a stone pyramid, which in turn rests on the Oktogon pavilion.

ITINERARY

KASSEL	▶ **Wilhelmsthal (12km-7m)**
WILHELMSTHAL	▶ **Waldeck (55km-34m)**
WALDECK	▶ **Frankenberg (46km-29m)**
FRANKENBERG	▶ **Marburg/Lahn (39km-24m)**
MARBURG/LAHN	▶ **Alsfeld (46km-29m)**
ALSFELD	▶ **Bad Hersfeld (40km-25m)**
BAD HERSFELD	▶ **Kassel (73km-45m)**

2 DAYS • 311KM • 193 MILES

ℹ Rathaus, Obere Königsstrasse 8

▷ From Kassel take the **B7** northwest and take a left turn after 9km (5½ miles) to Wilhelmsthal.

❶ Wilhelmsthal, Hessen

A detour to Schloss Wilhelmsthal is suggested en route to Waldeck. The castle in its present rococo form was designed by the French architect François Cuvilliés, who built it on the site of an earlier construction dating from the 17th century. The interior is decorated with superb panelling and a whole gallery of beautiful female figures added by the German painter Tischbein the Elder, acting on the instructions of his princely masters.

SPECIAL TO...

From Kassel head north to nearby Immenhausen, and then a further 6km (4 miles) east is Glashütte Süssmuth, whch survived until 1996 as a factory producing hand-blown glass. The former factory now houses the Glasmuseum Immenhausen.

▷ Drive about 5km (3 miles) south to the **B251**, turn right and continue on the **B251** to Sachsenhausen. Take the **B485** east for 5km (3 miles), then turn west for Waldeck.

SCENIC ROUTES

En route from Schloss Wilhelmsthal to Waldeck, a very attractive stretch of road leads through the Habichtswald Nature Park, particularly the section from the village of Ippinghausen to Sachsenhausen. The route from Bad Wildungen to Frankenberg, which passes through the Kellerwald forest, is a very scenic part of the tour.

---

❷ Waldeck, Hessen

Surrounded by woods and an enormous artificial lake, Waldeck is a small town. The Eder Dam, which was completed in 1914, is almost 50m (164 feet) high, between 3 and 5m (10 and 16 feet) thick and 400m (1,310 feet) long. Castle Waldeck, which occupies a commanding position on top of a hill near the town, is said to be a thousand years old, and used to be the seat of the Waldeck princes. Abandoned in the 17th century, it has been restored and is now partly used as a hotel. There is a panoramic view from a terrace overlooking

One of the apartments in the Wilhelmshöhe Palace in Kassel, housing the State Art Collection

the lake, and the interior decorations carefully preserve the romantic atmosphere of the castle. You can still see the dungeon with three prison cells, one on top of the other, in the Hexenturm (Witches' Tower), and there is a museum consisting of two portrait galleries commemorating the glories of the Waldeck dynasty.

A regular boat service plies the lake in summer and there is plenty of opportunity to try out

The inner courtyard of Burg Waldeck, one of Germany's largest feudal castles

Marburg an der Lahn, viewed from the Lahn River

all sorts of watersports. A cabin lift provides an easy connection between the town, the lakes and the castle.

[i] *Altes Rathaus (Old Town Hall), Sachsenhäuser Strasse 10*

FOR CHILDREN

South of Waldeck, near the 400m (1,310-foot) long dam, there is a deer park and power station at Hemfurth, with a cable-car leading to the reservoir.

▶ *Continue on the **B485** to Bad Wildungen, then take the **B253** west to Frankenberg.*

3 **Frankenberg,** Hessen
No fewer than ten little turrets can be counted on Frankenberg's timber-framed Rathaus. A solid tower forms each of the four corners and the space between is filled up by

---

RECOMMENDED WALKS

Take the B252 north from Frankenberg to Korbach and turn left into the Naturpark Diemelsee. Beautiful walking trails explore the forest and the area around the Diemel Talsperre Dam.

---

small oriel turrets, creating a very attractive and unusual outline. The building dates from 1421, but after a fire in 1509 the structure was modified. Its position between the Ober and Unter (Upper and Lower) market squares links the two. A stroll in the upper half of the town reveals an interesting group of 16th-century wooden houses with the timber often protected by a layer of slate. A little higher up is the

---

BACK TO NATURE

Just outside the town of Frankenberg, the Stadtforst Finsterbachtal forest offers a chance to explore a wild deer park inhabited by a wide variety of indigenous wildlife. Look for red squirrels and birds, such as middle-spotted woodpeckers and nutcrackers.

Liebfrauenkirche (Church of Our Lady), built in the 13th and 14th centuries to a design copied from the Elisabeth-kirche in Marburg. A notable feature of the interior is the Marienkapelle (Chapel of Our Lady) which was erected at the height of the Gothic period.

[i] *Obermarkt 7–13*

▶ *From Frankenberg take the **B252** south to Marburg/Lahn, 39km (24 miles).*

The Elisabethkirche is the main attraction in the Altstadt (Old Town), partly for its pre-eminence as the first German Gothic ecclesiastical building, but also because of its connection with Elisabeth of Hungary, daughter of the King of Hungary. The intended bride of the Landgrave Ludwig of Thuringia, she had to leave home in Hungary at the early age of four and was brought up at nearby Wartburg Castle. As a young girl her concern for the sick and poor became well known, then when her husband, the Landgrave, died of the plague in 1227, she withdrew to work in a hospital for the incurables below Marburg Castle, where she died from exhaustion at the age of 24. Canonised in 1235, her body was later placed in the church which bears her name.

St Elisabeth's was constructed between 1235 and 1283. Inside, through the main gate, lies the tomb of Field Marshall von Hindenburg, the last German President, upon whom was thrust the unenviable task of leading Germany after its defeat in World War I, and then dealing with the rise of Adolf Hitler and his National Socialist Party. Hindenburg died in 1934.

The most interesting object in the church is the golden shrine of St Elisabeth, which was built by a craftsman from the Rhineland around 1250; it contained the saint's relics until 1539. Reminders of St Elisabeth are to be found in various parts of the church: a 15th-century wooden statue in the nave; a 13th-century painted window and frescoes in the chancel; and a statue of her personifying Charity.

The Marktplatz (Market Square) and its upper section, known as the Obermarkt, are still surrounded by some beautiful timber-framed houses, especially Nos 14, 21 and 23. The fountain of St George is a popular meeting place for students, while the Gothic Rathaus,

4 Marburg/Lahn, Hessen
On the River Lahn, Marburg was first documented in 1130 as a Thuringian 'marcpurg'. It became part of the province of Hessen in 1248, and in 1527, after the Reformation, it became the seat of the first Protestant university.

FOR HISTORY BUFFS

Some 15km (9 miles) east of Frankenberg stands a former Cistercian abbey, at Haina. During the 16th century it was converted into a mental hospital by Landgrave Phillip der Grossmütige (the Generous), when he underwent conversion to Protestantism. The inside of the church consists of a large Gothic hall with columns in a design peculiar to the Cistercian order. The cloister shows a mixture of Romanesque and Gothic.

---

erected in 1524, forms one end of the square.

Schloss Marburg was built for the former Landgraves of Hesse, and it stands on a hill high above the town with pleasant views from its various terraces. Of special note inside are the large Gothic Rittersaal (Knights' Hall), the Landgrave's study and a small chapel. The Museum für Kulturgeschichte (History of Culture) in the Wilhelmsbau wing exhibits precious objects from St Elisabeth's, fragments of stained glass, 15th-century tapestries and a collection of medieval shields.

The Alte Universität (Old University) was built in 1870 on a rocky site above the Lahn, using the foundations of a former convent. The Aula (Great Hall) is decorated with paintings depicting the history of Marburg; and the Karzer (punishment cell for students) is on view complete with graffiti scrawled by former inmates.

[i] *Pilgrimstein 26*

▶ *Drive east to Kirchhain and take the **B62** southeast to Alsfeld, 46km (25 miles).*

5 Alsfeld, Hessen
First mentioned in 1069, when it belonged to the Landgrave of Thuringia, Alsfeld became part of Hesse in 1247 and was later made a member of the Council of Rhenish towns. In the 14th century it was the occasional residence of Landgrave Hermann of Hessen, who promoted the local guilds; and during the Reformation, Martin Luther stayed here during his appearance before the bishops at the Diet of Worms in 1521.

'European Model Town' in the heritage year of 1975, Alsfeld is very picturesque. The romantic Altstadt has retained its medieval charm right up to the present day, and focuses on the Marktplatz (market square). In prime position is the Rathaus. The two upper storeys are half-timbered and topped by a steeply pitched gabled roof fronted by two oriel windows. Across a narrow road from the Rathaus stands the Weinhaus (Wine House). The Stumpfhaus, named for former Lord Mayor Jost Stumpf, was built in 1609 and is the most elaborately decorated timber-framed house in the town. Further along there are two fine houses: at No 3, the Neurath-Haus is a fine baroque-style half-timbered building; and stone-built No 5, the Minnigerode-Haus, still boasts its original highly unusual wooden staircase built around a tree trunk.

Behind the Rathaus stands the Walpurgiskirche. Built between the 13th and 15th centuries, the church features late Gothic wall paintings and impressive tombs inside. In Untere Fuldergasse there are some funny-looking, crooked half-timbered houses; and further up, one of Alsfeld's few remaining medieval fortifications, a defensive tower called the Leonhardsturm.

ℹ️ *Markt 12*

▶ *From Alsfeld continue on the B62 to Bad Hersfeld.*

6 Bad Hersfeld, Hessen
The origins of Bad Hersfeld can be traced to AD 769, when Archbishop Lullus founded a Benedictine abbey here. After modifications in the 11th and 12th centuries, it was destroyed by French soldiers in 1761. A free-standing bell tower dating from about 1120, houses the 900-year-old convent bells, some of the earliest in Germany.

Picturesque old burghers' houses surround Bad Hersfeld's wide market square, and the Gothic parish church on the eastern side, with its mighty tower, dates back to the 14th century. Opposite the church, the Rathaus was originally built in the 14th century and later enlarged with a Renaissance façade in 1612. The German language expert and lexicographer Konrad Duden (1821–1911) lived here and was responsible for creating the 'bible' of German spelling, since called the 'Duden', the German equivalent of the Oxford English Dictionary.

Bad Hersfeld is also one of the country's most popular spa towns, with its mineral-rich spring water, which is recommended for the treatment of liver complaints.

ℹ️ *Markt 1*

▶ *Take the B27 north to Bebra and go to Kassel on the B83.*

FOR CHILDREN

Do not miss the statue of Little Red Riding Hood near the Rathaus in Alsfeld. The fairy-tale favourite is said to have been based on a former resident of the town.

The town square of Alsfeld with its twin-towered Rathaus

SPECIAL TO...

The ruins of the 1,200-year-old Stiftskirche in Bad Hersfeld provide a spectacular background for the annual Festival of drama, music and opera staged here in June, July and August.

Dams, Lakes
& Woods

2 DAYS • 339KM • 211 MILES

At the centre of the town of Hagen stands the Rathaus (Town Hall), with an image of the sun on its tower. A representation of the solar system is distributed around the town, and bronze plates on the pavements show the orbits of the planets. Hagen has associations with the Jugendstil (art nouveau) movement which flourished from the 1890s.

[i] *Rathausstrasse 13, Hagen*

▶ *From Hagen take the **B7** east for 17km (11 miles) to Iserlohn.*

❶ Iserlohn, Nordrhein-Westfalen

Remnants of the old town fortifications can still be seen in Iserlohn, and another relic of the past is the Oberste Stadtkirche (Upper Town Church), late Gothic with a Romanesque tower. It has a valuable carved altar from Flanders, dating from around 1400. The Bauernkirche (peasants' church) of St Pankratius was originally a Romanesque basilica but was later altered in the Gothic style and became a Protestant church.

The Dechenhöhle (Dechen Cave) at Letmathe, 4km (2½ miles) west of Iserlohn, was discovered by accident when the railway was being built in 1868. Two men lost their tools in a gap in the rocks and while searching for them discovered the caves. Subsequent excavations at the site have revealed animal bones from the last Ice Age. As the temperature inside never reaches more than 10°C (50°F), even in summer, remember to wrap up warmly. Several easily negotiated paths have been laid out which lead to 15 separate chambers. The Wolfsschlucht (Wolves' Ravine) and the Kaiserhalle (Emperor's Hall) are the most impressive.

[i] *Theodor Heuss Ring 24*

▶ *Drive northeast towards Menden, turn right on to the **B515** and continue to Beckum. Turn left and take the **B229** northeast to Arnsberg, 45km (28 miles).*

❷ Arnsberg, Nordrhein-Westfalen

Surrounded by Naturparks (nature reserves), the town of Arnsberg lies just between the Arnsberger Wald in the north, and the smaller Arnsberg Stadtwald in the south, which

Interior of the 300-million-year-old Dechenhöhle (Dechen Cave) near Iserlohn

---

BACK TO NATURE

Adjoining Iserlohn to the east is Hemer, and a further 1km (½ mile) southwest of the town is the Heinrichshöhle (cave), which claims to be the wildest and most romantic part of the Sauerland. Close by, the Felsenmeer (Sea of Rocks) was formed millions of years ago by corals under the ocean. The boulders were created by the collapse of several adjoining caves, and these towers of rocks were given names like Teufelskanzel (Devil's Pulpit) and Paradies (Paradise).

BACK TO NATURE

Visit the wild deer park at Völlinghausen: take the B229 north from Arnsberg to the Möhnesee, and turn right along the south bank to the park, at the eastern end of the lake. The park is home to the indigenous red deer and the Sika.

---

extends to the Naturpark Homert. The Ruhr flows through the middle with Arnsberg on a hill, caught in a loop of the river. Its historic importance as former district capital is demonstrated by the picturesque Altstadt (Old Town) and its attractive timber-framed houses, fortified towers and the Hirschberger Tor, a rococo gate, of 1753.

There is a fine Altes Rathaus (Old Town Hall), complete with bell tower, and a magnificent view across the town and beyond from the ruins of the old Renaissance castle. An example of early Gothic style architecture St Laurentiuskirche is the only remaining building of an abbey founded by the Premonstratensian order in 1173, and later disbanded in 1803. The continuous process of building over the centuries has created a mixture of styles, including a surprising early

baroque high altar finished in marble and alabaster, tombs of local rulers ranging from the 14th to 17th centuries, and a late 18th-century pulpit. The Sauerland Museum exhibits hunting weapons from the 16th to the 19th centuries and finds from the Balver Caves.

Southwest of Arnsberg lies the Sorpesee (Lake Sorpe), a man-made reservoir with a dam supposed to be the longest in Europe. Built between 1928 and 1935, the dam is 700m (2,295 feet) long and 60m (197 feet) high. It created a lake some 8km (5 miles) long, which, apart from supplying electricity, has become a paradise for watersports enthusiasts. Hikers will enjoy walks in the surrounding forests or a stroll round the lake. A motorboat service is also available in summer. Near the southern tip of the lake, in an area called Seidfeld, there is a glider centre. Camping is very popular on the western side of the lake and there is a good choice of sites available.

Due north of Arnsberg, the famous Möhnesee is only a short trip through the Arnsberger Wald. Surrounded by a clutch of 15 little villages, the 10sq km (4-square-mile) man-made lake is named for the River Möhne which feeds it. The Möhnesee's fame is derived from the much-publicised story and film, *The Dambusters*, made about the World War II RAF bomber raid which destroyed the dam with specially designed bombs and a unique technique which allowed the released bombs to bounce along the water to their target.

There are three crossings over the lake for motor vehicles, opening up a variety of different routes. Only the road along the southwest shore leading to the dam is closed to traffic. There are plenty of opportunities for windsurfing, sailing and rowing as well as boat trips by lake steamer during the summer season.

[i] *Neumarkt 6*

> **RECOMMENDED WALKS**
>
> South of the Möhnesee the Arnsberger Wald offers 70 so-called *Wanderparkplätze*, car-parks which are also suggested departure points for hikes through the forest.

▶ *From Arnsberg drive about 8km (5 miles) to Oeventrop, turn left and head northeast to Hirschberg and west to Bilsteinhöhle (Bilstein Cave), about 4km (2½ miles) southwest of Warstein.*

3 Bilsteinhöhle, Nordrhein-Westfalen
A popular tourist attraction, the Bilsteinhöhle (Bilstein Cave) was discovered in 1887. You can visit a 400m (1,310-foot) stretch of the dry upper section of the cave. Close by are the Kulturhöhlen (Caves of Culture), which were once occupied by prehistoric people.

Finds from the caves are displayed in the local museum at Warstein, which also contains information on local history.

[i] *Dieplohstrasse 1, Warstein*

▶ *Return to Hirschberg, then continue south to Meschede.*

4 Meschede, Nordrhein-Westfalen
Meschede lies at the confluence of the Henne and the Ruhr, near the moated 17th-century Schloss Laer which lies about 1.5km (1 mile) west of town. Meschede's parish church is an old historic building dating from the mid-17th century while, in complete contrast, Königsmünster Abbey, in the north of town, is a modern foundation and the monks run a large Gymnasium, a selective secondary school, similar to the old English grammar school system.

[i] *Von-Stephan-Strasse*

> **SPECIAL TO...**
>
> A striking architectural contrast to the mighty Möhne Dam is provided by the nearby Druggelter Kapelle (chapel). Built around 1220, it is said to be the most important Romanesque building in the area. It is a small 12-sided rotunda with sumptuous decorations and sculptures on the capitals.

▶ *Take the **B55** south for about 10km (6 miles) to Herhagen, turn northeast to Remblinghausen, southeast to Westernbödefeld and north to Ramsbeck, 33km (20 miles).*

5 Ramsbeck, Nordrhein-Westfalen
The Erzbergbaumuseum (Mining Museum) in Ramsbeck is well worth a visit for its interesting coverage of centuries of mining techniques in the

Sauerland. There is an original mine shaft where the extraction of lead- and zinc-rich ore is demonstrated, and a fun ride on one of the narrow mining railways is part of the enjoyment.

▶ *Continue north, via Bestwig, and follow the **B7** east to Brilon.*

6 **Brilon,** Nordrhein-Westfalen

In the middle of a high, wide plain, the settlement of Brilon was first documented as early as AD 973. Around 1400, it became the capital of the Herzogtum Westfalen (Duchy of Westfalia), and was also a member of the Hanseatic League.

The historic central Marktplatz (Market Square) is dominated by the Romanesque-style Propisteikirche, consecrated in 1276, whose mighty tower overshadows the Rathaus, an interesting medieval structure dating from the 13th century with a baroque façade. Another feature of the square is the Petrusbrunnen fountain, a fine 16th-century monument.

ⓘ *Derkere Strasse 10a*

▶ *Take the **B7** west, then turn south at Altenburen on to the **B480** to Winterberg. Continue southwest, then south on the **B480** to Balde. Take the **B62** to Sassmanns-hausen and then turn sharp right on the 'Lahn Ferienstrasse' (Lahn Holiday Road) to Siegen, 96km (60 miles).*

7 **Siegen,** Nordrhein-Westfalen

Siegen lies in a region south of the Sauerland, called the Siegerland. The town's Oberes Schloss (Upper Castle) is a successor to the original fortress of the 13th century. It houses the Siegerland Museum which, among other things, celebrates 2,000 years of the production and use of iron in industry. Another department deals with a quite different subject, the painter Peter Paul Rubens, who was born here in 1577 after his parents were exiled from Holland. The museum exhibits several original Rubens paintings and also portraits of former rulers. There is a good view over the town and surroundings from the castle's terrace.

The Unteres Schloss (Lower Castle) is found in the Altstadt (Old Town). Built between 1698 and 1714 in baroque style for Duke Friedrich Wilhelm of Nassau, it was the home of the Protestant branch of the Nassau-Siegen dynasty. The tombs of various counts and dukes are seen below the main building, and the Dicker Turm (Fat Tower) is also worth a visit. West of the Unteres Schloss, Martinskirche (St Martin's church) is a 10th-century Ottonic basilica with a Romanesque font and Gothic features added in the 16th century. East on the market square stands the Nikolaikirche (St Nikolas's church). It houses

the tombs of the Counts of Nassau.

ⓘ *Rathaus (Town Hall), Markt 2*

▶ *From Siegen take the **A45** northwest to the exit for Freudenberg and continue southwest to the town.*

8 **Freudenberg,** Nordrhein-Westfalen

The timber-framed houses in Freudenberg present an amazing sight as you arrive in the old town centre. Built for miners after a devastating fire

in 1666, they are all of roughly the same size and design and give visitors the impression of having just driven into a fairy-tale picture book. The Alter Flecken (Old Spot), as the town centre is called, has preserved its heritage intact over the centuries and the houses are all listed buildings.

A short 8km (5-mile) detour west of Freudenberg, Schloss Krottorf is a moated castle dating back to the 12th century, and offers a deer park in its grounds.

i *Krottorfer Strasse 25*

▶ *Take the **A45** for 80km (50 miles) back to Hagen.*

Freudenberg's black-and-white houses line the hillside

RECOMMENDED WALKS

From Siegen drive north on the B62, and follow the road east for Netphen and Brauersdorf. There are pleasant lakeside walks around the Obernau Stausee and up the slopes of the Sanktkopf.

SCENIC ROUTES

The tour has many scenic stretches of road. Some of the best are from Eisborn, south of Menden, past the Reckenhöhle (cave) to Beckum and Arnsberg; between Arnsberg and Warstein; and Sassmannshausen to Siegen, on the Lahn Ferienstrasse.

BAVARIA

Bavaria forms the southeastern part of Germany, and is the largest and one of the most important states. The north is called Franken and consists mainly of hilly countryside bordered by the ranges of the Thüringer and the Böhmerwald mountains. Further south are the fertile plains of Bavaria and its three main rivers: the Danube, the Isar and the Inn. Towards the Alps, a series of lakes stretches from west to east, before suddenly being confronted by those mighty mountains, with heights of nearly 3,000m (9,840 feet). This district is called Oberbayern, and a turn to the west leads to the Allgäu, well-known for its dairy products. Continuing west towards the Bodensee (Lake Constance), the tour enters Bavarian Swabia, with its distinctive Swabian dialect.

Neuschwanstein Castle, near Füssen, built by Ludwig II

The state is economically strong and has a vigorous industrial capacity as well as a firm agricultural base. Tourism plays an important part, principally in the Oberbayern area. Bavaria was an independent kingdom until the end of World War I; ask a Bavarian about his or her nationality, and the reply will be 'I am a Bavarian' first, with 'and a German' added later.

This is definitely beer country, with the great breweries centred around Munich, although the hops come from the fertile plains of Niederbayern, northeast of the Bavarian capital. Bavarians generally need little prompting to hold a festival. Most are focused around the religious calendar, with Christmas playing the leading role. The traditional fir tree is to be found everywhere and the Christmas celebrations can be very emotional, especially in the Alpine regions. What can be more romantic than Christmas Eve in one of these Alpine villages, with (most years) plenty of snow about and the candlelit Christmas trees to be seen in the charming Bavarian houses? If you wish, why not attend midnight Mass in one of the local village churches.

Tour 10

Franken (Franconia) forms the northern part of Bavaria, and the towns have a strong historical background. They include the home of Queen Victoria's consort Albert and a residence of the Holy Roman Emperor. Opera lovers will know it as the home of the Bayreuth Festival. There is one big difference to the south of Bavaria: it is wine, not beer, which is the favoured drink, and these wines rate among Germany's best.

Tour 11

This tour covers a wide area, starting with some interesting small towns and then proceeding to the famous forests which form the eastern frontier of Bavaria. At the heart of the tour is Nürnberg.

Tour 12

Rivers, forests and beautiful scenery are there to be enjoyed on this tour. Passau is the starting point, and from there it is straight into the forests. A much-treasured jewel of a town set on the Danube, Regensburg is a highlight of the tour.

Tour 13

The tour starts along a large lake with two famous islands dominated by the fairy-tale splendour of one of Bavaria's best-known castles. It then turns south to the Alps, where breathtaking scenery can be enjoyed not only from the mountaintops, but also from the valleys below.

Tour 14

This tour concentrates on a series of Bavarian Alpine lakes which lie at the foot of the mountains. Beautiful scenery can be admired on the drive between the lakes, as the road leads up and down some magnificent mountain passes.

Tour 15

This tour starts by a lake at Starnberg, the favourite weekend destination of visitors from

Picturesque Mittenwald in the Bavarian Alps

the nearby capital of Bavaria. This is followed by resorts famous for their sports and religious affiliations. A charming mountain retreat fit for a king provides an unforgettable experience.

Tour 16

The Danube appears several times along this route, but it has quite a different appearance here to the river it becomes after it leaves Bavaria. The tour enters Bavarian Swabia, where smaller towns attract the interest.

Tour 17

This tour begins and ends on an island in the Bodensee (Lake Constance), but driving on and off it presents no problems. The scenery becomes gradually more dramatic as the route proceeds. Later on, fantasy becomes reality, with a magical castle unmatched by frequent reproductions.

Franconia &
its Historic Towns

Würzburg's prosperity dates from 741, when St Burchard became the first bishop. In the 17th and 18th centuries the Prince-Bishops used their wealth to commission outstanding works of art. The Würzburg Residenz is a major example of south German baroque architecture. The grand staircase by Balthasar Neumann, the magnificent fresco by Tiepolo and the impressive Kaisersaal (Imperial Hall) are masterpieces by 18th-century architects and craftsmen.

2 DAYS • 341KM • 212 MILES

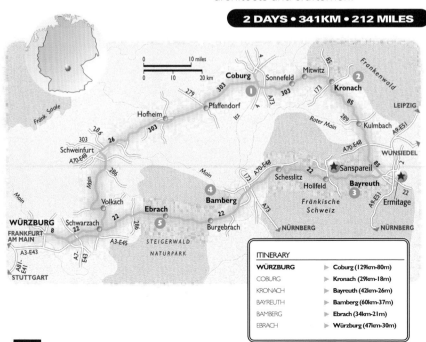

ITINERARY		
WÜRZBURG	▶	**Coburg (129km-80m)**
COBURG	▶	**Kronach (29km-18m)**
KRONACH	▶	**Bayreuth (42km-26m)**
BAYREUTH	▶	**Bamberg (60km-37m)**
BAMBERG	▶	**Ebrach (34km-21m)**
EBRACH	▶	**Würzburg (47km-30m)**

⊞ Congress-Centrum, Würzburg

▶ *From Würzburg take the B22 west to Schwarzach, then north to Volkach, turn left and drive along the west bank of the Main River to Schweinfurt, then on the B303 to Coburg, 129km (80 miles).*

❶ Coburg, Bayern

Coburg lies on the River Itz, and its fortress (Veste Coburg) is a major local landmark. The town is more than 900 years old, and from the 16th century the ruling dynasty of Saxe-Coburg had connections with many of the royal families of Europe. Queen Victoria's beloved Albert was a prince of Saxe-Coburg. His childhood home, the Schloss Ehrenburg, is open to the public.

The Festungstrasse leads up to the fortress, which is known as the 'Fränkische Krone' (Crown of Franconia) because of its layout, well protected by a double ring of walls and numerous watch towers. The original structure dates back to the 12th century, although the present castle is mostly 16th-century. The castle is famous as the place where the Protestant reformer Martin Luther sought refuge. His room, the Lutherstube, can still be seen. In the central wing, a museum displays an art collection acquired over 900 years. It also has the largest weapons collection in Germany, with a chamber devoted to armaments used in the Thirty Years' War (1618–48). The Herzoginbau (Duchess's Building) has a carriage museum, art exhibitions and a display of armour.

The Ehrenburg, Prince Albert's childhood home, has a wonderful collection of French tapestries. Stroll through an arcade up to the Hofgarten, the palace gardens which lead to the Veste (from the German word *festung*, meaning fortress).

The Marktplatz (market square) is typically Bavarian – a feast of Renaissance and baroque buildings, immaculately kept in characteristic German order. Also of interest is a nature museum, which has a collection of over 2,000 birds and exhibits of the natural world. The Rathaus (Town Hall), started in 1500, has a figure called the Bratwurstmännle. He carries a staff supposed to indicate the correct length of the Bratwurst, the celebrated local sausage. The many gables and spires of the town hall give it a most attractive appearance.

⊞ Herrngasse 4

Veste Coburg, one of the country's most splendid strongholds

▶ *Take the **B303** to Kronach.*

❷ **Kronach,** Bayern

In the old town stands the Schloss Rosenberg (Rosenberg Fortress), one of the largest and best-preserved fortresses of the Middle Ages. Although building began in 1128, the last touches were not put to the structure until the 18th century. The numerous wars of the 15th, 16th and 17th centuries meant that the castle was turned into a formidable defence bulwark. Since 1867 it has been used for peaceful purposes and houses both the municipal Franken-wald Museum and the Franconian Gallery.

Kronach's most famous son was the 16th-century painter Lucas Cranach the Elder; three of his paintings are on display here. His house, a timber-framed building, can be seen in the old part of the town.

i *Marktplatz 5*

▶ *From Kronach take the **B85** south to Bayreuth.*

❸ **Bayreuth,** Bayern

Bayreuth received its town charter in 1231 and was later destroyed by the Hussites, the followers of Jan Hus, during their revolt against the clerical privileges in neighbouring Bohemia and Moravia. Hus was excommunicated in 1410 and asked to explain his views at the Council of Constance (1414–18). It suited both the clergy and the emperor to eliminate him, and he was subsequently burned at the stake.

Bayreuth recovered fairly quickly and became the seat of the Margraves of Brandenburg-Kulmbach in 1604. The town blossomed under the rule of Margrave Friedrich and his wife Wilhelmine, the favourite sister of Frederick the Great, King of Prussia. They ruled from 1753 to 1763 and created a building boom, but the fine baroque buildings later decayed, presumably through lack of funds. The town became part of Bavaria in 1810.

In 1847 Richard Wagner had his Villa Wahnfried built, and it now houses the Richard Wagner Museum. The villa is an uninspiring cube-shaped building in neo-classical style. Wagner and his wife Cosima, daughter of the composer Franz Liszt, are buried in the grounds. The Richard Wagner Festspielhaus (Festival Theatre) was built between 1872 and 1876 on the hill northeast of the town, now called Festspielhügel (Festival Hill). King Ludwig II, the 'Mad King' of Bavaria and an admirer of Wagner, supported his work, and the Festspielhaus opened with performances of the four operas of the *Ring Cycle*. Composers Tchaikovsky and Grieg were among the audience, but even a full house could not meet the costs of mounting these lavish operas. Today, the composer's family still carries on the tradition and annual festivals continue to be a highlight of the international music calendar. The Festival Theatre and the ornate Opera House are open to visitors when no performances or rehearsals are in progress.

The Altes Schloss (Old Castle) in Maximilianstrasse is easily recognisable, with its octagonal tower, which has a spiral ramp inside for horses to be ridden up to the top. The castle was burnt out in 1945 but has since been rebuilt. In Ludwigstrasse stands the Neues Schloss (New Castle), commissioned by the princess Wilhelmine in 1753. The interiors were decorated to her taste, with motifs of nature. Birds, insects, palms and Chinese dragons can be seen: the latter were fashionable features of 18th-century interior decoration. The Neues Schloss also contains the municipal museum and a Bavarian state paintings collection.

i *Luitpoldplatz 9*

▶ *From Bayreuth take the **B22/B505** west to Bamberg.*

❹ **Bamberg,** Bayern

The path of the River Regnitz created an island here, which became the centre of this historical town dating from the 10th century. Most of the buildings were erected under the rule of the Holy Roman Emperor Heinrich II, the Saint (1002–24), who upgraded the town to an imperial residence.

The Altes Rathaus enjoys a commanding position on an artificial island on the left arm of the river, and is connected to the other parts of the city by bridges on either side. The building itself is an attractive Gothic structure which dates from 1467, and the long façades facing the river are decorated with fine frescoes. The present Dom, or Kaiserdom (Cathedral), dates from the 13th century and contains many typically

BACK TO NATURE

Leave Bayreuth, heading north on the A9, turn right and follow through the Steinach Valley and the Fichtelgebirge (Fichtel Mountains) to Wunsiedel. Watch the skies for birds of prey soaring overhead. These may include black kites, red kites, honey buzzards and sparrowhawks. The Felsenlabyrinth Luisenburg is a fascinating agglomeration of granite rocks. Marked paths guide the visitor through caves, grottoes and ravines.

beautiful German sculptures, including the enigmatic Bamberger Reiter (Bamberg Horseman). The tomb of Heinrich II is the work of the great Renaissance sculptor Tilman Riemenschneider, a native Bavarian. Not only an eminent sculptor, Riemenschneider became Mayor of Würzburg, but fell into disgrace when he took the side of the oppressed peasants during a rebellion. Imprisoned and tortured, he died in 1531.

Next to the cathedral stands the Alte Hofhaltung (Old Residence), a half-timbered Renaissance structure, once the residence of the former imperial and episcopal rulers. Also of note is the Reiches Tor, the richly decorated entrance portal to the old residence, which offers a fine view into the old courtyard. The Alte Hofhaltung now houses the museum of history, which exhibits documents and maps relating to Bamberg's history.

Look out for the Neue Residenz, built between 1693 and 1703 to express the opulent wealth and power of

Baroque sculptures reflect the golden age of 18th-century Bayreuth under Princess Wilhelmine

the Prince-Electors. The church of St Michael dates from the 11th century, although the site is even older, and the lovely baroque façade was added in the late 17th century.

Bamberg is well-known for its Rauchbier, a beer made from smoked malt using an old recipe.

ℹ️ *Geyerswörthstrasse 3*

▶ *From Bamberg take the B22 west for 34km (21 miles) to Ebrach.*

5 **Ebrach**, Bayern
Ebrach's former Cistercian Abbey, once considered to be one of the finest examples of the order's building style,

is now part of the Steigerwald Naturpark, which lies east of Würzburg and has one of the largest concentrations of beech trees in central Europe. The massive church building is decorated with rich stuccoes, and its organ pipes are arranged around the large round window, the diameter of which is over 7m (23 feet) and composed of 259 pieces of glass. The Kaisersaal (Emperor's Hall) boasts some beautiful frescoes.

ℹ️ *Rathausplatz 2*

▶ *From Ebrach continue west on the B22/A3 for 47km (30 miles) to Würzburg.*

Entrance to the Altes Rathaus (Old Town Hall) in Bamberg

SCENIC ROUTES

A very attractive drive is along the Wiesenttal en route from Bayreuth to Bamberg. The route is actually through a nature park and the area is called Fränkische Schweiz (Franconian Switzerland) which emphasises its scenic and Alpine beauty.

A small detour of 6km (3½ miles) from Hollfeld takes you to the Sanspareil Park, a romantic rock garden with natural caves.

Around Nürnberg
& Regensburg

Nürnberg (Nuremberg), on the banks of the River Pegnitz, suffered from heavy wartime bombing raids, but restored buildings blend well with new ones, and the layout of the town has been preserved.

2/3 DAYS • 458KM • 288 MILES

ITINERARY		
NÜRNBERG	▶	Altdorf (28km-17m)
ALTDORF	▶	Amberg (54km-34m)
AMBERG	▶	Weiden (20km-13m)
WEIDEN	▶	Vohenstrauss (20km-13m)
VOHENSTRAUSS	▶	Kallmünz (129km-80m)
KALLMÜNZ	▶	Kipfenberg (77km-49m)
KIPFENBERG	▶	Eichstätt (22km-14m)
EICHSTÄTT	▶	Weissenburg (27km-17m)
WEISSENBURG	▶	Ellingen (2km-1½m)
ELLINGEN	▶	Abenberg (40km-25m)
ABENBERG	▶	Roth (12km-7½m)
ROTH	▶	Nürnberg (27km-17m)

ⓘ *Königstrasse 93, Nürnberg*

▶ *Leave Nürnberg by the **B4**
southeast, turning right to
Feucht then east to Altdorf.*

❶ Altdorf, Bayern

Altdorf is a historic town with
15th-century gates, city walls
and burghers' houses. The old
university buildings date back
to the 16th century, and many
famous scientists and inventors
have passed through the gates.
The university was dissolved in
1809. The Protestant Church of
St Lorenz was the university
church, and more than 1,100
theology students received their
degrees before the altar.

If you have time, take the
A3 southeast from Altdorf to
Velburg. From there a short and
very enjoyable walk past a
special rock formation called
the Schwammerl (Mushroom)
leads to the König Otto
Tropfsteinhöhle (King Otto
Cave). The cave, with its stalagmites and stalactites, was
discovered in 1895 and is 280m
(918 feet) long. It consists of

Amberg's best-known spectacle –
reflections of the arches forming
the Stadtbrille (City Spectacles)

seven fascinating grottoes and
can be visited daily from April
to October.

ⓘ *Oberer Markt 2*

▶ *From Altdorf take the **A3**
southeast, turn left at exit
Neumarkt and take the
B299 northeast to Amberg.*

FOR HISTORY BUFFS

From Altdorf, a short trip
southeast via Gnadenberg and
Oberölsbach leads to Berg and
the ruin of the oldest
Birgittenkloster (Abbey of St
Bridget) in southern Germany.
It was donated in 1426 by
Pfalzgraf (Count Palatinate)
Johann I and erected to house
both monks and nuns. Its
church was finished in 1483,
but a fire in 1635 destroyed
both the church and the convent. Today's parish church was
erected out of the remains of
the former convent. Easily
recognisable among the ruins
are the remnants of the three
encircling walls, which were a
special feature to which all
Birgittenklöster had to adhere.

---

❷ Amberg, Bayern

'Fortunate Amberg' has almost
totally preserved its medieval
appearance. The town has an
imposing circle of city walls
with four gates, numerous
towers and other fortifications.
One part of the former line of
defence crosses the River Vils
in the form of two arches above
the water, whose reflection
in the water led to the nickname 'Stadtbrille' (the city's
spectacles).

Two Gothic parish
churches, St Martin and
St Georg, dominate the city
centre. Of special note inside
the former is the painting by
C Crayer of the *Coronation of
Holy Mary*, an imitation of the
style of Rubens. This work,
completed in 1658, was
removed from its original place
over the altar and is now above
the sacristy. The tomb of
Ruprecht Pipan, The Pfalzgraf
(Count Palatinate), who died in
1397, stands behind the high
altar. The religious denomina-
tion of the church was changed
from Protestant to Catholic
when the Jesuits acquired the
buildings during the Counter-
Reformation. The adjoining
library hall of the former Jesuit

college is well worth seeing. The Rathaus (Town Hall), on the market square, is a very attractive building, also in Gothic style, with a Renaissance annexe. It features a tall, narrow gable and has various council chambers inside. The small hall has outstanding wood panelling.

Other buildings worth seeing in Amberg are the former residence of the Pfalzgrafen (Counts Palatinate), now used by the local government; the former Kurfürstliche Zeughaus (Electors' Arsenal), dating back to the 15th century; and the Ratstrinkstube (Councillors' Drinking Chamber).

ⓘ *Hallplatz 2*

▶ *From Amberg take the B229/14 north to Gebenbach, continue on the B14 east to Wernberg and from there north on the A93 to Weiden, 51km (32 miles).*

SPECIAL TO...

The 'Glass Road' runs along the Bavarian Forest and links up individual workshops and glass factories, which produce remarkable objects made of glass.

---

8 Weiden, Bayern

Weiden lies on a major crossroads between Regensburg and Leipzig, and between Nürnberg and Prague. The

---

FOR CHILDREN

The Model Railway Club of Weiden has opened a museum at the station building. The trains are in operation on certain days, usually Sundays and public holidays. Check first with a local tourist information centre.

Relaxing in Weiden's town square

town is associated with the composer Max Reger, who came here as a child and received his musical education here. The original Gothic parish church of St Michael, with its onion-shaped spire, was reconstructed in baroque style in the 18th century. Of note inside are the high altar (1791) and the chancel, built in 1787. The Rathaus (town hall), with its 16th- and 17th-century burghers' houses was built between 1539 and 1545 in Renaissance style.

Weiden is an excellent centre for exploring the nearby forests, especially the Böhmer Wald, where some areas are still almost completely unspoilt.

ⓘ *Dr Pfleger Strasse 17*

▶ *From Weiden take the B22 southeast to Bernrieth/ Wittschau, where it crosses* the **B14**. *Continue on the* **B14** *northeast and turn left after about 8km (5 miles) for Vohenstrauss.*

4 Vohenstrauss, Bayern
Situated on the former military road between Nürnberg and Prague, this town's main attraction is Castle Friedrichsburg. Six massive round towers encircle the building, with a very high gabled roof and a wall surrounding the castle yard. The building is unique in its design: a beautiful Renaissance structure erected between 1586 and 1593.

Short detours to the ruin of the fortress Leuchtenberg, 7km (4 miles) southwest, and to the Fahrenberg mountain, 8km (5 miles) northeast, offer fine views to the Fichtel mountain range and the Bohemian forest.

[i] *Marktplatz 9*

RECOMMENDED WALKS

There are very pleasant walks by the Kainzmühl and Reisach Stausees, artificial lakes near Trausnitz, a short drive south from Vohenstrauss. A marvellous view can be obtained from the top of the mountain near Tannesberg.

Colourful mural on a building in the little town of Kipfenberg

▷ *From Vohenstrauss turn south to the* **B14** *and continue northeast to Waidhaus. Turn sharp right south to Rötz and from there head west to Schwarzenfeld. Continue south to Schwandorf and Burglengenfeld via the* **A93** *and* **B15**. *From there drive southwest to Kallmünz.*

BACK TO NATURE

The route from Vohenstrauss to Kallmünz passes through Neunburg vorm Wald, which is 12km (8 miles) past Rötz. A seam of the mineral quartz protrudes in certain places in this area, and one spot where this occurs is Pfahl, near Neunberg – a great attraction for geologists.

---

5 Kallmünz, Bayern
At the meeting of the Vils and Naab rivers lies Kallmünz, a picturesque medieval town. A good view can be had from the River Naab to the rococo-style parish church of St Michael, with the ruins of the former fortress of Kallmünz in the background, delightful for painters and photographers.

The excellent strategic position of the fortress suggests earlier settlements here, and some archaeological findings confirm this. A 10m (33-foot) wall around the fortress was probably erected in the 10th century to protect the inhabitants against attacks from the north. The walls from the fortress went right down to the river, presumably to provide additional protection for the village below. The bridge over the River Naab is noteworthy for its massive pillars and arches, dating back to 1550.

[i] *Marktplatz 1*

▷ *From Kallmünz drive 9km (5½ miles) west to the* **A3** *entry to Beratzhausen, continue northwest and leave the* **A3** *at exit Parsberg in a southwest direction for*

Beilngries. Continue along the Altmühl river to Kinding and turn south to Kipfenberg, a total of 77km (49 miles).

6 Kipfenberg, Bayern
Kipfenberg is a romantic little town surrounded by woods, with its proud Burg standing on a hill. The present fortress was built in the 13th and 14th centuries, but fell into decay and was restored between 1914 and 1925. Remains of the Limes, the wall protecting the Roman Empire against invaders from the north, are near by.

ℹ️ *Marktplatz 2*

▶ *From Kipfenberg continue along the Altmühl Valley southwest to Eichstätt.*

7 Eichstätt, Bayern
Eichstätt is dominated by the imposing Willibaldsburg (St Willibald's Castle), which dates from the 14th century and was fortified and extended in later centuries into a fine castle.
　The town centre is basically baroque in style, and the former bishop's palace has an impressive interior with a double staircase. Some remains are left of the 8th-century cathedral. The 'new' one was built over four centuries and is therefore

The fountain and clock tower in Eichstätt's Residenzplatz

an intriguing mixture of Romanesque, Gothic and baroque styles. The gardens of the summer residence of the

BACK TO NATURE

Eichstätt stands at the heart of the Naturpark Altmühltal, Germany's largest nature park. This landscape of wooded hills, rugged crags and rolling river valleys is speckled with castles and fortresses.

71

Prince-Bishops are arranged in the English manner. There are three pavilions at the southern end – one features a fountain and ornate stuccoes.

☐ *Domplatz 8*

▶ *From Eichstätt take the **B13** northwest for 27km (17 miles) to Weissenburg.*

8 **Weissenburg,** Bayern
The old city walls have survived and the Ellinger Tor and the Spitaltor (gates) remain as formidable entrances to the town. The thermal springs were enjoyed by the Romans, and the layout of their baths was rediscovered in 1977.

The Protestant parish church of St Andreas stands behind the Ellinger Tor and was built in several stages, work finally being completed in 1520.

Sebaldusaltar and the Mariaaltar. The Rathaus (Town Hall) in the market square was built between 1470 and 1476 and is easily recognisable by its richly decorated gable.

☐ *Martin Luther Platz 3*

▶ *From Weissenburg continue for a short drive north on the **B13** to Ellingen.*

9 **Ellingen,** Bayern
The castle at Ellingen is a huge baroque creation, built for the Teutonic Order of Knights. Work began in 1708, and it is one of the most important castles among many created for this order. Napoleon banned the order in 1809, and the building now serves as a museum. The baroque Schlosskirche (castle church) is ornately adorned with stucco and frescoes.

☐ *Weissenburger Strasse 1*

▶ *From Ellingen continue on the **B13** northwest to Gunzenhausen, turn right for the **B466** and 3km (2 miles) after Wassermungenau turn right again for Abenberg.*

10 **Abenberg,** Bayern
Abenberg is a beautiful old town with a walled fortress. The fortress is first mentioned in 1071, but the present building dates from 1250. The 30m (96-foot) square tower offers fine views. Of interest, too, are the gate, in early Gothic style, the circular wall and the moat.

Countess Stilla, who was canonised in 1927, founded a small church in 1132, later turned into a convent. After a fire in 1675, the church was rebuilt in a mixture of Renaissance and baroque styles. There are 68 nuns buried here, the graves being arranged in a design adopted from the catacombs in Rome. The grave-stone of Countess Stilla shows the lady in a long pleated robe,

The statue of Albrecht Dürer in Nürnberg

with a small replica of the church on her arm.

Abenberg was a traditional centre for the manufacture of lace tassels, and has a museum dedicated to the craft.

☐ *Stillaplatz 1*

▶ *From Abenberg head east to Roth.*

11 **Roth,** Bayern
Roth is pleasantly situated on the River Regnitz, among green parkland. George the Pious had the Schloss Ratibor (castle) built from 1535 to 1537, although the towers were not completed until 50 years later. A visit to the Prunksaal, a lavishly appointed banqueting hall and part of the Heimatmuseum (local museum), is recommended. The main building has six gables and surrounds a court. The Riffel-macherhaus on the market square, with its superb carved façade, belongs to one of the areas finest timber-framed houses.

A more unusual museum shows the processes of manufacturing leonic wire and its uses in woven metal products and in the textile industry.

☐ *Schloss Ratibor, Hauptstrasse 1*

▶ *From Roth take the **B2a** north to the **A6**, then north-east to the **B8** to Nürnberg.*

SCENIC ROUTES

The stretch between Weiden and Leuchtenberg en route to Vohenstrauss leads through the nature park called Oberpfälzer Wald. Take a look at the Burgruine Leuchtenberg (castle ruins) from where there are fine views over the forests. One of the most enjoyable routes is the drive between Waidhaus and Rötz. Lakes and small rivers, ruins here and there, and an abundance of forests, will make this drive quite memorable.

The Danube &
the Bavarian Forest

The border town of Passau lies where three rivers – the Donau (Danube), the Inn and the smaller Ilz – join together to form just one: the mighty Danube. An important bishopric since AD 739, Passau has a wealth of beautiful baroque buildings.

2/3 DAYS • 456KM • 283 MILES

ITINERARY	
PASSAU	▶ **Regen (60km-37m)**
REGEN	▶ **Cham (59km-37m)**
CHAM	▶ **Regensburg (53km-33m)**
REGENSBURG	▶ **Donaustauf (12km-7m)**
DONAUSTAUF	▶ **Kelheim (20km-13m)**
KELHEIM	▶ **Essing (8km-5m)**
ESSING	▶ **Riedenburg (8km-5m)**
RIEDENBURG	▶ **Ingolstadt (36km-22m)**
INGOLSTADT	▶ **Landshut (74km-46m)**
LANDSHUT	▶ **Passau (126km-78m)**

ⓘ *Rathausplatz 3, Passau*

▶ *From Passau take the B85 north to Regen.*

SCENIC ROUTES

Soon after leaving Passau the road passes through some charming small villages lined with forests on the Bayerische Ostmarkstrasse.
A detour from Bodenmais en route from Regen to Cham is strongly recommended. It leads to the Risloch waterfalls and the remote Abersee (lake) and into the beauty of the unspoilt Böhmer Wald (Bohemian Forest).

❶ **Regen,** Bayern
Although Regen means rain – and the visitor may feel this is an ominous sign – the name actually comes from the Regen River, flowing through the town. The ruins of the fortress Weissenstein, 3km (2 miles) south, date back to the 11th century, and the keep affords wide views over the Bayerischer Wald (Bavarian Forest). Regen is a good centre to stop and plan side trips into the Bavarian Forest, especially to Arbersee, near the Czech border.

RECOMMENDED WALKS

Parts of the Bohemian Forest are still left to their natural devices and are largely untouched by human hand. Fallen trees form intriguing natural 'sculptures' and some areas are totally covered in moss.
The areas around the Arber and Falkenstein mountains are designated as maintained 'wild' forests. To get there, drive from Regen towards Bayerisch Eisenstein on the B11 or branch off from Bodenmais en route to Cham. Beautiful walks into remote unspoilt nature can be enjoyed here.

ⓘ *Schulgasse 2*

▶ *From Regen drive north via Bodenmais and Kötzting for 59km (37 miles) to Cham.*

❷ **Cham,** Bayern
Having left Regen, a stop is suggested en route at Bodenmais in the Bavarian Nature Park. In the Silberberg (Silver Mountain) there is an old mine, dating back to the 12th century, which is open during the summer.

Passau, on the Danube, has a legacy of glorious buildings from its past as a Free Imperial City

SPECIAL TO...

In Regen, the Pichelsteinerfest takes place around the last Saturday in July and lasts for five days. A special dish of meat, potatoes and vegetables is served, cooked in one pot. The festivities continue in the evenings with a romantic atmosphere provided by gondolas with candlelit lanterns on the River Regen.

In Cham the market square is dominated by the 13th-century parish church of St Jakob. Many alterations and extensions over the centuries have meant that the church is now an attractive mixture of Gothic, baroque and rococo styles. The Rathaus (Town Hall), with its many gables and oriels, was originally built in the 15th century but has been added to many times since.

ⓘ *Propsteistrasse 46*

▶ *From Cham take the B85/B16 southwest to Regensburg.*

❸ Regensburg, Bayern
Regensburg, set on the Danube, must be one of Germany's loveliest cities. The great German poet and philosopher Goethe said that so beautiful a location was bound to attract a city, and Regensburg lives up to its setting. The Roman fort was built here in AD 179 by the Emperor Marcus

---

BACK TO NATURE

Wildlife can be observed in almost any part of the Bavarian Forest. Explore forest tracks on foot looking for orchids such as lady's slipper and dark red helleborine growing in clearings. Mezereon – with red berries in autumn – and butcher's broom are also frequently found here.

FOR CHILDREN

The Churpfalzpark at Loifling has a special section for children with a fairy-tale garden and playing fields.

Aurelius. Later, the Bavarian Dukes made Regensburg their capital, and in the Middle Ages it became a European centre for politics, science and economics. Many Imperial Diets (assemblies) met here, dealing with issues which involved the entire Holy Roman Empire. Napoleon was wounded here in 1809, an event recalled by a plaque; but otherwise Regensburg remained unscathed by centuries of war.

Entering the old town from the north, drivers cross the Danube over the Steinerne

Brücke (Stone Bridge). If traffic allows, stop for a memorable first glimpse of the town before crossing the bridge, which is said to be the oldest in Germany. It dates from 1135 and is a masterpiece of medieval engineering. The old town is entered through the southern bridge gate, which was erected in the 14th century. Not far away on the left is the former North Gate of the Castra Regina, the Roman fort. On the site of a former Romanesque basilica stands the Dom (cathedral). Building began in the 13th century, but its 105m (344-foot) spires were only finished 600 years later. The beautiful stained-glass windows date back to the 14th century. Other

Stone carvings adorn the main portal of St Peter's Cathedral in Regensburg

The undulating hills of the attractive Bavarian landscape, tamed here but largely wilderness

features of note are the 14th- to 16th-century cloisters, the Romanesque All Saints' Chapel and the Annunciation group of 1280. The cathedral also boasts one of the finest boys' choirs in the land – the Regensburger Domspatzen.

The Altes Rathaus (Old Town Hall) dates from the 13th century, although parts of the building were added much later, up to and including the 18th century. In the large Reichssaal (Imperial Hall) many Diets were held. Later this became a permanent institution and could be called a forerunner of the first German parliament. Also on view are the dungeons where prisoners were 'interviewed'.

Schloss Thurn and Taxis belongs to the old dynastic family of Thurn and Taxis, who became powerful by holding the first German mail delivery monopoly until 1867. The Johannes Kepler Museum is housed in a building that dates from 1500, in which the famous mathematician and astronomer lived. Interesting displays describe his life and work.

Regensburg has numerous churches; those of interest are the Karmeliterkirche and the rococo Alte Kapelle next door. The Protestant Neupfarrkirche is noted for its fine Renaissance interior, while the Niedermünster parish church has interesting excavations, revealing remains from Roman, Merovingian, Carolingian and Ottonic times. The Scottish church of St Jacob has a Romanesque portal. The confessor of Mary, Queen of Scots, is buried here.

i   *Altes Rathaus (Old Town Hall), Rathausplatz 3*

▶   *From Regensburg drive east for 12km (7 miles) to Donaustauf.*

FOR HISTORY BUFFS

Regensburg can lay claim to two of the oldest constructions in Germany: the Porta Praetoria from AD 179 is the oldest city gate, and the stone bridge across the Danube is the earliest bridge of its kind in Germany.

---

4   **Donaustauf,** Bayern
The Walhalla, near Donaustauf, should definitely be seen if time allows. Surrounded by trees, it is a copy of the Parthenon in Athens, dedicated to men and women whose achievements benefited the German state. King Ludwig I of Bavaria had the temple built between 1830 and 1842, and laid an obligation upon his successors to add to it. The Bavarian government has

added nine more marble busts since 1945, and the number of dignitaries exhibited is now 122. Although the Walhalla is set in a charming site, visitors expecting an exact replica of the Athenian original will be disappointed.

▶   *From Donaustauf turn back to Regensburg and take the B16 south for 20km (13 miles) to Kelheim.*

5   **Kelheim,** Bayern
The Befreiungshalle (Liberation Hall), which stands above the town, was built in 1842 and commemorates the liberation of Germany from Napoleon. The rewarding views from the gallery of the circular temple make the trip worthwhile. Inside the temple are memorials to those who played a vital part in Napoleon's defeat.

stands right above the town, and there is an excellent view from the keep.

▶ *From Essing continue north-west for 8km (5 miles) along the Altmühl valley to Riedenburg.*

7 Riedenburg, Bayern
This is an area rich in castles, and one worth stopping for is Schloss Rosenburg, dating from the 12th century. The 16th-century part, which is well preserved, houses the local museum and the Bavarian centre for falconry. Displays of flying eagles, vultures and falcons are presented in medieval surroundings.

Perched on the top of a rock above the river is the nearby castle of Prunn, one of the best-kept knights' castles in Bavaria. The entry to this mighty build-ing is over a bridge, and there is a museum.

Schloss Eggersberg, situated a bit further away in a more remote setting, used to be a hunting lodge before its conver-sion into a hotel.

⌈i⌋ *Marktplatz 1*

▶ *From Riedenburg turn south and drive for 36km (22 miles) via Altmannstein and Demling to Ingolstadt.*

8 Ingolstadt, Bayern
Strategically located on the upper reaches of the Danube, Ingolstadt is an important industrial town, but reminders of its past make it attractive to visit. The Kreuztor (Cross Gate), with its seven small towers, is one of the most inter-esting remaining parts of the old city fortifications, and dates back to the 14th century. Other, later landmarks are the churches designed and built by the famous Asam brothers. The church of Maria de Victoria is a jewel of Bavarian rococo style, finished in 1736. Inside there is an enormous fresco on the ceiling and a richly ornate high altar.

The Kloster Weltenburg church near by stands on an ancient site, though the present structure dates back to the first half of the 18th century. Its two architects have left their own images inside – one looks down from a railing, and one is painted in a fresco. Clever use of light through a window draws attention to the statue of St Georg in front of the large high altar painting.

⌈i⌋ *Donaupark 13*

▶ *From Kelheim take a short drive of 8km (5 miles) west to Essing.*

6 Essing, Bayern
The ancient past is evident here, as Essing lies below rocky cliffs with many prehistoric caves. In the cave known as the Grosse Schulerlochhöhle, excavations have revealed

> **RECOMMENDED WALKS**
>
> A walk from the Kloster Weltenberg to see the Danube gorge along the cliffs is very rewarding. The gorge cannot be seen by car, but a boat trip provides another opportunity to see this phenomenon. Take the river boats from Kelheim or Schloss Weltenberg.

remains of a former hunting station from the Stone Age and early Bronze Age. In the nearby smaller cave, Kleine Schulerlochhöhle, drawings were found which date back to about the 15th century BC. One interesting sight is the old wooden bridge over the Altmühl river, its exit guarded by the Altmühltor (gate). The ruin of the fortress Randeck

The Liebfrauenmünster (Minster of Our Lady) is one of the larger Bavarian churches in the late Gothic period, dating from 1425. The altar stands 9m (29 feet) high and is decorated with 91 paintings. The centrepiece is the *Madonna of the Cloak*; the Virgin Mary is the patron saint of Bavaria.

The Bayerisches Armeemuseum (Bavarian Army Museum) is housed in a former Duke's Palace built by Ludwig the Bearded.

Street scene in Ingolstadt

i *Rathaus, Rathausplatz 4*

▶ *From Ingolstadt take the **A9** south to the junction with the **A93**. Continue on the **A93** northeast to exit Mainburg, drive 9km (6 miles) east towards Mainburg and take the Deutsche Ferienstrasse via Volkenschwand to Landshut.*

❾ Landshut, Bayern
Landshut provides perhaps the best picture of an elegant medieval city in Bavaria. The old town has hardly changed, and the houses in the main street, with their high gables and painted façades, are still dominated by St Martin's Church, with its 133m (436-foot) spire, which starts off square but becomes octagonal as it rises. The church was designed by Hans von Burghausen, and took 110 years to complete. One of the treasures inside is the larger-than-life woodcarving of the Virgin Mary. Called the Landshuter Madonna, this statue is renowned as an important example of late Gothic woodcarving. Stone was used as material for the high altar and the pulpit, both of which were built between 1424 and 1429.

Burg Trausnitz was the residence of the Dukes of Wittelsbach, and is one of the largest and most impressive castles in Germany. One of the Dukes, called Ludwig the Rich, arranged a magnificent wedding for his son Georg, so impressive that it has become part of local legend. The castle became a meeting place for artists and comedians, who enjoyed the generous hospitality of the wealthy Dukes.

The Stadtresidenz (Town Palace) consists of two wings: the 16th-century Italian Renaissance wing and the 18th-century German wing, which faces the Altstadt (Old Town).

i *Altstadt 315, Rathaus*

▶ *From Landshut take the **B299** southeast to Aich, turn left and continue on the **B388** east to Passau.*

SPECIAL TO...

Every four years, the wedding of Georg, the son of Ludwig the Rich, is re-created in Landshut. The original wedding took place in 1475 and was such a splendid occasion that it has passed into local history. For those interested, the next celebration is due in 2009.

Around Lake Chiem

& Berchtesgaden

Rosenheim is situated at the meeting point of the rivers Inn and Mangfall, and its position makes it an ideal base for touring the mountains and the lakes in the area. The focal point in town is Max-Josefs-Platz, surrounded by the houses of noteworthy residents of former times, with beautifully painted fronts and stucco ornaments.

2 DAYS • 248KM • 155 MILES

ITINERARY	
ROSENHEIM	▶ **Prien (27km–17m)**
PRIEN	▶ **Herrenchiemsee**
	(3km–2m)
HERRENCHIEMSEE	▶ **Seebruck (19km–12m)**
SEEBRUCK	▶ **Traunstein (31km–19m)**
TRAUNSTEIN	▶ **Bad Reichenhall**
	(25km–16m)
BAD REICHENHALL	▶ **Berchtesgaden**
	(21km–13m)
BERCHTESGADEN	▶ **Ruhpolding (45km–28m)**
RUHPOLDING	▶ **Reit im Winkl (23km–14m)**
REIT IM WINKL	▶ **Rosenheim (54km–34m)**

i Kufsteiner Strasse 4, Rosenheim

▶ *From Rosenheim go south and join the **A8** east towards Salzburg. Leave at exit Frasdorf northeast for Prien, 27km (17 miles).*

1 Prien, Bayern
The baroque parish church of Maria Himmelfahrt was built in 1653 and enlarged in 1736. The ceiling was painted by the locally renowned artist, Johann Baptist Zimmermann. The Heimatmuseum, located in a house built in 1681 has displays that illustrate what peasant life around the lake was like during times past.

> **FOR HISTORY BUFFS**
>
> The steam railway line from Prien to Stock on the lake shore dates back to the end of the 19th century. The delightful old train could well reside in a museum, but luckily for visitors, it is still in operation.

i Alte Rathausstrasse 11

Enjoying a refreshing glass of Bavarian beer

▶ *From Prien drive 2km (1 mile) to the lake shore at Prien Stock. The trip can also be done from the railway station by the historical Chiemsee Railway, built in 1887, using its original engine and coaches. Then take a boat to Herrenchiemsee.*

> **RECOMMENDED WALKS**
>
> The island of Fraueninsel near Prien is ideal for gentle strolls and pleasant views, and is a favourite spot for artists.

2 Herrenchiemsee, Bayern
The magnificent Schloss Herrenchiemsee was the idea of Ludwig II, the Mad King, who, following a visit to Versailles, decided to build a similar castle for himself here on the island. Work began in 1878, but in 1885 the project ran out of money, after an enormous amount had already been spent. It was eventually finished much later, and today houses a museum with rare antique furniture and many valuable artefacts. Guided tours are available through the

highly ornate rooms. The magnificent Gallery of Mirrors is about 77m (253 feet) long and the State Room is often used for candlelit concerts during the summer months.

The Altes Schloss, or Old Castle, built in 1700, was once part of a monastery, which explains the Herren ('men') in the name of the town. The library hall is beautifully decorated by the master of rococo, Dominikus Zimmermann; many churches and buildings in this area display his work.

The Fraueninsel ('Ladies Island') is much smaller but more romantic and intimate. The Benediktinerinnen Kloster, a convent founded in AD 782 by Duke Tassilo, is still used by nuns as a religious retreat, and is also a boarding school for girls. It is therefore closed to the public, although the little 13th-century church offers visitors the chance to write down their thoughts in a book which is located behind the altar. Brighten up your visit with a taste of the local spirit, *Klostergeist*. Each Kloster (convent) has its own traditional recipe.

▶ *After returning by boat to Prien drive along the lake in a northerly direction via Gstadt to Seebruck, 19km (12 miles).*

3 Seebruck, Bayern
Seebruck is worth a stop to see the Roman remains in the Heimathaus and, weather permitting, enjoy a swim in the lake in the large open-air enclosure called the Freibad.

A short northwesterly detour is recommended to visit the Kloster Seeon, situated on an island in the Klostersee. Of special interest are the combinations of architectural styles in the church, which dates from the 10th century. The wall paintings were rediscovered in 1911, having been lost for generations.

An attractive journey northwest from here, on the

Deutsche Ferienstrasse (German Holiday Road), leads to Wasserburg on the Inn river, about 25km (15½ miles) away. The Burg (castle), which gave the town its name, was first built in the early Middle Ages, but Herzog (Duke) Wilhelm IV

The baroque church of St Bartholomä, on the shores of the Königssee, near Berchtesgaden

ordered that it be dismantled, and in 1531 work began on the new castle. Step gables are a distinctive feature of the high roof and, inside, vaulted passages provide the link to the staircases and an attractive hall on the first floor. The chapel between the castle and the adjacent corn store was built in 1465, and stucco decorations were added in 1710.

The parish church of St Jacob was the work of architect and builder Hans Stethaimer; the main building was built between 1410 and 1445, with the tower added in 1478. The baroque pulpit was beautifully carved by the brothers Zürn in the 17th century. The Frauenkirche (Church of Our Lady) was built in the 14th century, but the light interior

and ornaments show all the characteristics of baroque, and date from the late 18th century. The Rathaus, with its tall gable, was built in the 15th century, when the town was earning its riches from a strategic position on the main salt trading route between Augsburg and Salzburg.

i Am Anger 1

▷ *Drive back to Seebruck and continue in a southeasterly direction to Traunstein.*

SPECIAL TO...

At Amerang, a few kilometres west of Obing between Seebruck and Wasserburg, is the Bauernhausmuseum (Museum of Farmhouses). Old farmhouses from the area between the Inn and Salzach rivers have been reconstructed to demonstrate the farming life of the past. The museum is open daily from the middle of March until November, except on Mondays.

---

4 Traunstein, Bayern
Traunstein calls itself the 'Green Town on the German Holiday Road', as it hosts a research centre for forestry, which has an international reputation.

On Easter Monday the Georgritt takes place here. Riders wearing historic armour and local costumes proceed on beautifully adorned horses to the little church at Ettendorf to receive a blessing for their horses.

i Kulturzertrum im Stadtpark, Haywards Heath-Weg 1

▷ *From Traunstein take the B306 south to the junction with the B21 and turn sharp left northeast to Bad Reichenhall, 25km (16 miles).*

5 Bad Reichenhall, Bayern
This is one of the main spas in

the area, well-known for the salt deposits in its mountains. The healing effects of the salts are used here to treat many ailments, including asthma, rheumatism and even pneumonia. The Münster (Minster) of St Zeno was destroyed by fire and rebuilt in 1512. Ironically, St Zeno is the patron saint who protects against the danger of water and flooding! This is the largest Romanesque church in Upper Bavaria, and the jewel of the town. The gate and the Gothic font are noteworthy and there is a woodcarving of the Coronation of the Holy Mary, which dates back to the early 16th century. As with many other Bavarian churches, there is a great deal of superb wood-carving.

King Ludwig I had the Alte Saline (Old Saltmine) built in 1834, and a visit today gives a good idea of what working in the salt-mines was really like. Visitors are provided with protective clothing. Salt was an important trading item during the Middle Ages and in the past brought enormous wealth to the owners of the mines.

i Wittelsbacherstrasse 15

▷ *From Bad Reichenhall take the B20 to Berchtesgaden.*

6 Berchtesgaden, Bayern
Berchtesgaden is surrounded by beautiful mountains along the Austrian border. Its environs make it a good base for day trips in the area. The town itself has a castle dating from 1410, which became the home of the ruling Wittelsbach dynasty in the 19th century. Crown Prince Rupert, son of the last King of Bavaria, lived here until his death in 1955. The castle is now a museum showing the many treasures which the Crown Prince collected during his lifetime. The Salzbergwerk (salt-mine) is also open to visitors. As the salt deposits in this area are exploited by both Austria and Bavaria, the mine tunnels often run between the two countries.

From the town one of the most rewarding trips is up to the Kehlsteinhaus, or Eagle's Nest, named because of its precipitous position on the mountain. Cars are only allowed as far as Obersalzberg, and the journey is then completed by bus, on foot and by lift. The lift rises 124m (407 feet) up into the mountain. The views are breathtaking. Allow plenty of time for the excursion: walkers may want extra time to enjoy some of the summit paths on the Kehlstein.

On the way down from the parking area you may wish to stop at the Hotel Türken to see something of the remains of the Third Reich, with which this area is so closely associated. The Berghof, Hitler's Alpine retreat, once stood close to the hotel. The air-raid shelter network under the houses belonging to Nazi leaders still remains, although there is not much left to see. After the war, the Bavarian government decided to destroy all traces of the buildings associated with the Third Reich; the ground-work had already been done by an RAF bombing raid on 25 April, 1945, when most of the buildings were left in ruins.

The area around the Obersalzberg is also served by the Rossfeld–Höhenringstrasse, a circuit often used for motor rallies. It is not unusual to see immaculately maintained vintage cars coping gracefully with the bends and steep gradients of this road. Another rewarding excursion leads from Berchtesgaden to the Königssee, a ride that takes only about five minutes, depending on the traffic. The Königssee is surrounded by steep mountain slopes descending to the lake, with no road around the shores. Motorboats are available, however, to make the journey around the lake. The picturesque chapel of St Bartholomä, perched on the eastern face of the Watzmann mountain, dominates the whole area with its formidable height and contours.

ℹ Maximilianstrasse 9

▶ Take the **B305** west for Ruhpolding.

SCENIC ROUTES

The road from Berchtesgaden to Ruhpolding is an experience in itself, through lush valleys and between mountains. But drive carefully! The river is often perilously close to the road.

The stretch between Ruhpolding and Reit im Winkl leads through more magnificent scenery, with small lakes on either side of the road.

7 **Ruhpolding,** Bayern
In Ruhpolding stands one of the most beautiful churches of the Alpine area – the parish church of St Georg, right in the middle of the town. Elaborately decorated, its main attraction is the Ruhpoldinger Madonna, dating back to the 13th century.

ℹ Hauptstrasse 60

RECOMMENDED WALKS

Take a left turn at Ramsau en route from Berchtesgaden and proceed to the Hintersee. Away from the busy tourist routes, you can enjoy a relaxing walk along the lake shore – or, if you prefer, take a boat to admire the scenery.

▶ From Ruhpolding go south and rejoin the **B305** southwest to Reit im Winkl, 23km (14 miles).

8 **Reit im Winkl,** Bayern
Reit im Winkl is a favoured destination for excursions from many surrounding areas. It is a perfect example of a typically delightful Alpine village. A short stroll up the hill called Grünbühel is worth it for the superb views of the nearby Kaiser Gebirge (Kaiser Mountains). From Reit im Winkl, a short detour northwest to Aschau is suggested; take the B305 via Bernau. The main attraction here is the castle

Looking out across an Alpine meadow near Berchtesgaden

Hohenaschau, which was built around 1100. The original complex was enlarged to include a brewery and iron foundry. The first beer was brewed in 1549 and it has kept its reputation ever since. A cable-car can take visitors to the top of the Kampenwand mountain, which reaches an altitude of 1,669m (5,575 feet). The views are breathtaking.

ℹ Dorfstrasse 38

▶ From Reit im Winkl join the **B305** north to Bernau and then west to Rosenheim.

FOR CHILDREN

An open-air park should keep children amused for a while at Ruhpolding. Among the attractions at Märchenpark are a mini railway, a playground and decorative models from fairy-tales.

The Bavarian
Lakes

München (Munich) owes its origins to the 12th-century Duke, Henry the Lion, who diverted the lucrative trade in salt via a new bridge over the Isar so that he could levy taxes. München today is not only the capital of Bavaria, but also one of Germany's major cultural centres.

2 DAYS • 200.5KM • 123 MILES

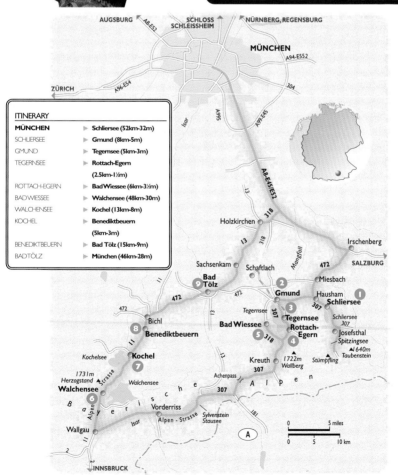

Marienplatz, Neues Rathaus

▷ *Leave München on the A8 southeast. Leave at exit Irschenberg and proceed southwest on the B472 to Miesbach and south on the B307 to Schliersee.*

❶ Schliersee, Bayern
Situated on the northern end of a lake of the same name, Schliersee lies in the centre of activities in this area. The village is in the foothills of the surrounding mountains, with a steep slope from the upper part of the village to the lake.

The 18th-century parish church in baroque style is worth visiting, as is the town hall. There is a cable-car connection to the peak of the Schlierberg, 1,256m (4,120 feet) high, which has a leisure park. Another worthwhile excursion takes you to the southern end of the lake, past the 1,000-year-old ruin of

SCENIC ROUTES

The toll road south of Josefsthal passes through magnificent Alpine scenery, with gradients of up to 1 in 7. Remote Alpine roads can sometimes face sudden closure for long periods. It is always advisable to check the road conditions at the local information office.
Another scenic mountain drive starts along a pleasant stretch on Lake Tegern. Continue in a southerly direction and face a 1-in-6 gradient up to the Achenpass, followed by a leisurely drive alongside Lake Sylvenstein to Walchensee.

Munich's Rathaus and the onion-domed Frauenkirche

Hohenwaldeck. Continue in a southerly direction, via Neuhaus and Josefsthal, to the Spitzingsee, a remote and beautiful Alpine lake. Rewarding panoramic views can be had by using the chair-lift to the 1,580m (5,180-foot) high Stümpfling, or the cable-car to the 1,640m (5,380-foot) high Taubenstein.

RECOMMENDED WALKS

It is possible to walk right around the Schliersee and when you feel you have had enough, there is a pleasant lake steamer to take the weight off your feet.

ⓘ *Bahnhofstrasse 11a*

▶ *From Schliersee head north to Hausham and turn west to Gmund.*

② Gmund, Bayern
Set on the northern end of the lake, Gmund is a small resort noted for its parish church of St Aegidius. The architects of the church were the ones who introduced the Italian baroque style that can be seen in many church buildings in Upper Bavaria dating from the late 17th and early 18th centuries. The church obtained its high altar from the Kloster at Tegernsee, after the rest of the building had been destroyed by fire.

ⓘ *Rathaus, Kirchenweg 6*

▶ *Go south on the east side of the lake to Tegernsee.*

③ Tegernsee, Bayern
Tegernsee town was founded by Benedictine monks, who came from St Gallen in Switzerland in the 8th century. The monastery was converted into a castle in 1803 and became a country home for royalty. Parts of the castle are open to visitors, especially the main hall (Kapitelsaal), which is also part of the local museum. Another attraction is the Bräustüberl in the northern part of the castle, formerly a brewery, now serving beer.

The castle also houses displays on the lives and works of various local celebrities, such as the satirist Ludwig Thoma. Steamer trips on the lake and the many cable-cars provide enjoyable excursions.

ⓘ *Hauptstrasse 2*

▶ *From Tegernsee continue south to Rottach-Egern.*

④ Rottach-Egern, Bayern
The mountains between the lakes prevent a more direct connection, but this small detour is worth it for the beautiful scenery.

The twin towns of Rottach and Egern have combined to form a health resort and winter sports centre on the southern end of Tegernsee. The 15th-century parish

---

SPECIAL TO...

Tegernsee has a special private railway, which runs to Schaftlach to connect with the main line to München. On some occasions, the old steam engine is used, to the delight of old and young alike.

---

church was formerly a centre for pilgrims who came to venerate a picture of the Madonna, called the *Egerner Gnadenbild*.

In the past Lake Tegern was popular with German writers and composers, a few of whom are buried here. A small detour south via a toll road, called the Wallbergstrasse, leads to the Moosalm, but the most magnificent views can only be enjoyed by continuing on foot to the Wallberghaus.

ⓘ *Rathaus, Nördliche Hauptstrasse 9*

▶ *From Rottach-Egern turn north on the west side of the lake to Bad Wiessee.*

⑤ Bad Wiessee, Bayern
This spa offers a thermal spring containing iodine and sulphur, with a water temperature of 27°C (77°F). The water is supposed to have healing effects on heart and circulatory diseases, as well as rheumatism and disorders of the skin. The resort is now one of the most elegant in Germany.

ⓘ *Adrian-Stoop-Strasse 20*

▶ *From Bad Wiessee go back south on the B318, joining the B307 to Vorderriss and continue west to Wallgau, then take the B11 north to Walchensee.*

BACK TO NATURE

Take the cable-car from Rottach-Egern up to the Wallberg. For those who wish to venture into more remote areas, a walk of about 45 minutes leads to the mountaintop, 1,722m (5,650 feet) high. From there the scenery is superb.
Look out for Apollo butterflies and colourful alpine flowers. Rock buntings and citril finches can also be seen, along with alpine accentors – birds which are characteristic of higher altitudes.

---

⑥ Walchensee, Bayern
After Wildbad Kreuth the road climbs steeply up to the Achenpass. The Alpenstrasse (Alpine Road) then leads to the Sylvenstein-See, an artificial lake which creates hydroelectric power, but also prevents

RECOMMENDED
WALKS

A short walk from Bad
Wiessee in a southerly direction leads to Abwinkl, from
where the route branches off
into the mountains to Bauer
in der Au, a popular resting
place. Along the way, the walk
passes through delightful
mountain scenery with serene
grazing cattle.

flooding when the winter snow
melts. The route crosses the
lake by bridge and then continues on a toll road to Wallgau, a
picturesque mountain village
where some of the farmhouses
have decorative frescoes dating
back to the 16th century. The
route then changes direction to
go north to the Walchensee,
Germany's biggest mountain
lake, which reaches a depth of
200m (656 feet). It is also the

highest Alpine lake in the
country, 800m (2,625 feet)
above sea level. An excursion
by chair-lift to Herzogstand
offers panoramic views of the
surrounding area. The journey
from the lake takes 11 minutes.

[i] *See Kochel (below)*

▶ *From Walchensee continue
north on the B11 to Kochel.*

7 Kochel, Bayern
As with other mountain lakes,
motorboats are not allowed
here on Kochelsee, but there is
ample opportunity for hiring
rowing and sailing boats as well
as paddlers. Swimming is also
possible, of course, but will
only appeal to the hearty, as the
water in the mountain lakes
tends to be chilly. Kochel also
has a modern leisure centre
called 'Trimini' to keep you
in trim.

[i] *Kalmbachstrasse 11*

The pretty village of Schliersee
lies on the shores of its lake

▶ *From Kochel drive north to
Benediktbeuern.*

8 Benediktbeuern, Bayern
The former Benedictine abbey
was founded as early as AD 740,
with the assistance of St
Bonifatius, but was partly

FOR HISTORY BUFFS

The monument to Balthasar
Mayr in Kochel was erected
in commemoration of his
attempt to liberate his
Bavarian homeland from the
Austrian Habsburgs in 1705.
He was killed as a result and
became a symbol of Bavarian
patriotism.

destroyed by marauding
Magyars from Hungary in the
10th century. It has survived

Mud, mud, glorious mud – the therapeutic value of mud baths is much appreciated in Bavaria

and been rebuilt twice, and the existing structure, completed in 1686, has frescoes by the Asam brothers. Apart from their religious duties, the monks also enjoyed painting and literary activities.

The abbey contains the Fraunhofer Glashütte (glassworks). Fraunhofer was a scientific researcher whose work rooms have been kept in their original state. The Fraunhofer firm continues a long tradition of glass-making, specialising in the preservation of medieval stained-glass windows in the churches of Europe.

i *Prälatenstrasse 3*

▶ *From Benediktbeuern continue on the B11 to Bichl and then on the B472 via Bad Heilbrunn to Bad Tölz, 15km (9 miles).*

9 Bad Tölz, Bayern
Bad Tölz, originally a fishing village, produces the highest output of iodine-containing water in Germany, and offers a variety of cures based on this element. The spa also has other amenities connected with the health springs, such as a Trinkhalle, where you can 'take the waters', and a Moorbad (mud bath). These establishments have become focal points in the recent past for social gatherings of the healthy and unhealthy alike. The parish church of Mariahilf is a centre for pilgrimages, and is adorned with a fresco by Mathias Günther, depicting the Tölz plague procession of 1634. A Kreuzweg (Way of the Cross) to the top of the Kalvarienberg (Calvary) leads past seven stations with seven chapels.

i *Max Höfler Platz 1*

▶ *From Bad Tölz take the B13 northeast via Holzkirchen to the A8 and return north to München.*

The bronze statue of a wild boar greets visitors to Munich's Hunting and Fishing Museum

The Alps South
of München

The München (Munich) museums appeal to all tastes and many happy days can be spent exploring their treasures. The Glyptothek exhibits Greek and Roman sculpture, including the famous figures from the Aegina temple. One of the great picture galleries of the world is the Alte Pinakothek, a large building in Venetian Renaissance style, built in 1836 to house the many paintings acquired by the Wittelsbachs from the early 16th century.

2 DAYS • 293KM • 182 MILES

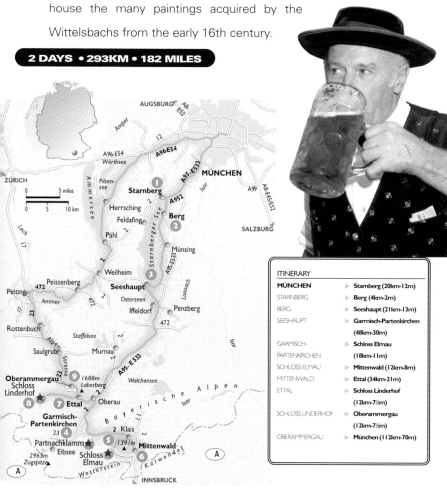

ITINERARY	
MÜNCHEN	▸ Starnberg (20km-12m)
STARNBERG	▸ Berg (4km-2m)
BERG	▸ Seeshaupt (21km-13m)
SEESHAUPT	▸ Garmisch-Partenkirchen
	(48km-30m)
GARMISCH-	▸ Schloss Elmau
PARTENKIRCHEN	(18km-11m)
SCHLOSS ELMAU	▸ Mittenwald (12km-8m)
MITTENWALD	▸ Ettal (34km-21m)
ETTAL	▸ Schloss Linderhof
	(12km-7½m)
SCHLOSS LINDERHOF	▸ Oberammergau
	(12km-7½m)
OBERAMMERGAU	▸ München (112km-70m)

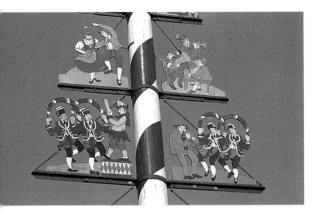

Part of the traditional maypole in Munich's Viktualienmarkt

_i_ *Marienplatz, Neues Rathaus, München*

▶ *From München take the **A95** south, then take the **A952** to Starnberg, 20km (12 miles).*

SPECIAL TO...

Munich's annual beer festival has to be mentioned, although it is very well advertised all around the world. The official title is Oktoberfest, but it takes place in the second half of September and ends at the beginning of October. Basically it is a popular carnival devoted to the consumption of large quantities of beer. Obviously, it is necessary to be in the right mood to enjoy this festival, and participants also need a strong stomach!

---

❶ Starnberg, Bayern
This is a very popular holiday resort, partly due to the excellent connections to and from München, and offers many leisure activities such as sailing, windsurfing, boating and diving. The adjoining villas, with their beautiful gardens, enhance the general holiday atmosphere around the Starnberger See.

The parish church of St Josef was built between 1764 and 1766 in the rococo style. The high altar built by Ignaz Günther is flanked by statues in white marble, and the interior seems filled with light, enhanced by its lofty position.

During the 16th and 17th centuries 'playgrounds of the rich' developed in Europe, and Starnberg claims to be one of the first. In 1663, the Elector Ferdinand invited 500 guests to a gondola party on the lake, with 100 oarsmen in charge of the boats. Now there is a yacht harbour, and more modest sailing regattas during the summer. A Heimatmuseum (local museum) advises on local activities during the past and present, and a notable picture gallery features works by painters of the Romantic period.

_i_ *Wittelsbacherstrasse 2c*

FOR HISTORY BUFFS

The former Austrian Empress Elisabeth, being Bavarian born, chose Feldafing on the western side of Starnberger See as her favourite summer retreat. Her former villa is now the luxury Kaiserin Elisabeth Hotel, and a commemorative statue stands in the hotel park.

▶ *Continue along the east side of the lake for 4km (2 miles) to the village of Berg.*

❷ Berg, Bayern
Berg is famous as the place where King Ludwig II met his tragic death in 1886. Having been certified insane and deprived of the throne, Ludwig was sent to Schloss Berg and kept under medical supervision. An outing in a small rowing boat proved fatal for him and his doctor: both bodies were found, next to their boat, in shallow water at Possenhofen, the lake's main bathing beach. The exact circumstances of their deaths remain a mystery. Ludwig drained Bavaria's coffers to build the extravagant castles which are a monument to him. A cross in the lake marks the spot where the bodies were found; a Memorial Chapel stands on the shore.

_i_ *Ratsgasse 1*

▶ *Continue south along the lake for 21km (13 miles) to Seeshaupt.*

❸ Seeshaupt, Bayern
Seeshaupt, on the southern end of the lake, is less crowded than the northern shores and is a good base to explore the nearby Osterseen, a group of numerous tiny lakes dating from the last Ice Age. It is of special interest to ornithologists because of the ideal nesting conditions in the tall reeds for all kinds of birds. Geologists find the soil and rock formations of interest.

_i_ *Weilheimer Strasse 1–3*

BACK TO NATURE

The Osterseen (lakes) south of Seeshaupt are in a designated nature reserve and their formation dates back to the last Ice Age. In all, 21 small lakes have been counted in the group. Bird-watchers should find it interesting – there are numerous species to be seen, including great crested grebes, spotted crakes and pochards.

Heraldic lion decorating the façade of a house in Garmisch-Partenkirchen

*Turning southward for 8km (5 miles), rejoin the **A95** at Penzberg/Iffeldorf and proceed to Garmisch-Partenkirchen, a total of 48km (30 miles).*

FOR CHILDREN

Skaters have the opportunity to enjoy an all-year ice rink at Garmisch-Partenkirchen. The Alpspitz Wellenbad in Garmisch provides plenty of entertainment for children and adults.
The leisure complex offers self-drive boats, a sauna, a solarium and swimming in a pool with artificial waves.

❹ Garmisch-Partenkirchen, Bayern

Two adjoining towns, united in a double name, are best known as the major German winter sports resort and host to the Winter Olympics of 1936. One of Germany's busiest resorts, it offers magnificent views of the surrounding mountain ranges, especially the massive Zugspitze, Germany's highest mountain – 2,963m (9,718 feet). King Ludwig's lodge is now a museum of local history. The German composer Richard Strauss lived here and met American troops when they occupied Garmisch-Partenkirchen at the end of World War II.

An excursion to the top of the Zugspitze should not be missed – first by cogwheel train to Eibsee, then by cable-car or by a more leisurely route, continuing by train to Schneefernerhaus, followed by a short ride by cable-car to the top. The latter route avoids the very sudden change in altitude of about 2,000m (6,600 feet) in 10 minutes.

Glacier skiing is practised on the top all year round, and if you wish to venture into Austria, there is a tunnel link between the two countries, with windows cut into the rocks so

BACK TO NATURE

Between Garmisch-Partenkirchen and the Austrian border, there are several forest tracks that can be explored on foot. Hazel hens and woodland grouse live on the wooded slopes, and unusual orchids grow beside the paths.

RECOMMENDED WALKS

A fascinating walk is from Garmisch-Partenkirchen in a southerly direction to the Partnachklamm (ravine). A well laid-out path leads on one side of the ravine through many tunnels. The walk is highly recommended.

that passengers may enjoy the views over the mountains.

☐ *Richard Strauss Platz 1a*

▶ *From Garmisch turn east on the B2 to Klais, 12km (7 miles) and then southwest on a toll road to Schloss Elmau.*

5 Schloss Elmau, Bayern
Still owned by the family who built it during World War I, this stately home offers a sort of English house-party atmosphere with a mixture of cultural and intellectual pursuits on a residential basis for paying guests. Meals are taken communally and guests can enjoy painting, music and dancing classes, concerts and music weeks, sometimes attended by famous musicians. A visit to the Schloss is worthwhile, even for day visitors who do not wish to stay. The feeling of space in the big halls and corridors, and the elegance of days gone by, are combined with modern comforts.

☐ *Elmau 10*

▶ *From Elmau return to Klais and 6km (4 miles) south to Mittenwald.*

6 Mittenwald, Bayern
This name, which means 'in the middle of the woods', describes the beautiful surroundings of this health and winter sports resort, situated in a valley between two massive mountain ranges, the Karwendel and the Wetterstein.

The town flourished in the Middle Ages, when it was a staging point for trade between Venice and northern Europe, and reminders of this boom-time can still be found in the market-place. In 1684, Matthias Klotz founded the town's specialist industry, which continues to this day: violins, violas, cellos, zithers and guitars are all made here, often using local wood. The descendants of Matthias Klotz continue the family business. The Geigenbau Museum and

A cable-car set against the back-drop of the Zugspitze, Germany's highest mountain at 2,963m (9,718 feet)

the Heimatmuseum offer more insights into local history and crafts. At the Geigenbau, it may even be a descendant of Matthias Klotz who demonstrates the art of violin-making. All the work is done by hand.

Numerous excursions can be taken from Mittenwald. The western peak of the Karwendel Mountains can now be reached by cable-car and offers a magnificent panorama of the Bavarian and Austrian Alps and beyond. Chair- and cabin-lifts take you to other peaks in the region.

☐ *Dammkarstrasse 3*

▶ *From Mittenwald drive north-west to Klais, take the B2 west to Garmisch, 12km (7 miles) and north to Oberau, 8km (5 miles), then turn left on the B23 to Ettal.*

7 Ettal, Bayern

Visitors are attracted to the Benedictine Abbey, a monastery founded in 1330 by the Holy Roman Emperor for his knights and monks. It is called 'Kloster', which means convent, although only monks live here. The Gothic building took 50 years to complete, and contains an enormous fresco 25m (82 feet) wide.

Today, the abbey houses a school and the monks distil a special liqueur, called Klosterlikör, which is made from health-giving herbs in accordance with a centuries-old recipe, which is, as you would expect, a secret.

Schloss Linderhof, the baroque fantasy of King Ludwig II, with its elegant park

[i] *Ammergauer Strasse 8*

▶ *From Ettal continue west for 12km (7 miles) to Schloss Linderhof.*

8 Schloss Linderhof,
Bayern

A charming, comparatively small castle built for Ludwig II, this is idyllically set, surrounded by woods, mountains and a small lake. The lavish interiors reflect the King's desire to emulate the grandeur of Louis XIV of France. The Hall

Oberammergau is famous for its delightful woodcarvings of religious scenes

of Mirrors is said to represent Ludwig's dream world. There is a collection of paintings portraying French celebrities during the reigns of Louis XIV and Louis XV. The extensive gardens are in harmony with the landscape, with waterfalls tumbling down rocks, fed by mountain streams. There is a grotto dedicated to Venus, and many fountains, notably the Neptune Fountain, its great jets of water rising higher than the top of the castle itself. A Moorish pavilion was brought here straight from the Paris Exhibition of 1867.

i *Schloss Linderhof*

▶ *From Schloss Linderhof return east for about 7km (4 miles), then take a left turn to Oberammergau.*

❾ Oberammergau, Bayern
Oberammergau is famous the world over for its Passion Plays, which have been performed since 1634, and in ten-year cycles since 1680. The houses in the main streets are decorated with colourful frescoes showing that woodcarving is the local industry here. The

Passion Play Theatre should be visited, even when no plays are taking place. The impressive auditorium seats around 5,000 and the stage is open-air, with remarkable acoustics.

Woodcarvers are at work at all times, and the variety of their

Entertaining the crowds in Munich's Viktualienmarkt

products, mainly religious objects, can be seen in shop windows all over the town. The parish church was built by the famous Josef Schmuzer and the frescoes are by Mathäus Günther.

Oberammergau also offers a variety of recreational facilities, including tennis, swimming, keep-fit, hang-gliding, canoeing and, of course, walks through the countryside. Or take the chair-lift to the Kolbensattel or the cable-lift to the Laberberg: both offer panoramic views over the countryside.

SPECIAL TO...

The Oberammergau Passion Play started during a plague epidemic, when the village councillors vowed that if God would halt the spread of the disease they would stage a play every ten years. The plague stopped suddenly, and the survivors put on the first performance in 1634. The next one is scheduled for the summer of 2010.

---

i *Eugen-Papst-Strasse 9a*

▶ *Take the B23 northwest to Peiting, and turn due east on the B472 to Peissenberg. After Peissenberg, take the left fork to Weilheim. Continue north on the B2 for about 8km (5 miles), then turn left for Pähl and the Ammersee. Drive along the eastern shore to Herrsching, then northeast along the Pilsensee for the A96 to München.*

Bavarian
Swabia

2 DAYS • 311KM • 193 MILES Augsburg prospered in the 15th and 16th centuries, mainly due to two wealthy merchant families: the Fuggers and the Welsers. The Fuggerhäuser, some of Augsburg's outstanding buildings, were destroyed in World War II, but were rebuilt by the present Fugger family.

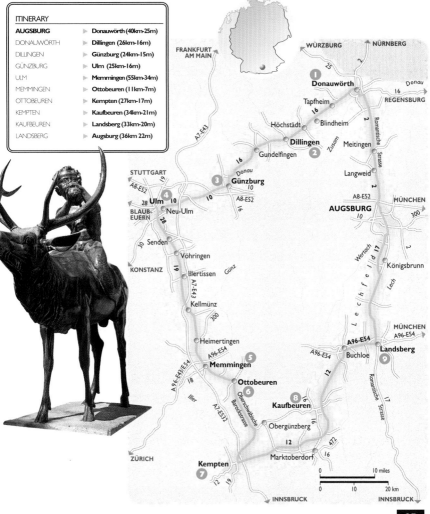

Bird's-eye view over Augsburg, the third biggest city in Bavaria, after Munich and Nürnberg

ℹ️ *Schiessgrabenstrasse 14, Augsburg*

▶ *Leave Augsburg north on the B2, the 'Romantic Road', for Donauwörth, 40km (25 miles).*

❶ Donauwörth, Bayern
Donauwörth lies at the point where the Wörnitz River enters the Danube. The Fuggers of Augsburg left their mark here, too, and the Fuggerhaus, built in 1539, has had many famous visitors, such as the Swedish King Gustavus Adolphus and Emperor Charles VI.

The Reichstrasse, with its parish church, dominates the town. The church was built in the 15th century and contrasts in style with Heiligkreuzkirche, which is in lavish baroque and was built much later, in about 1717. The builder was Joseph Schmuzer, who is known for many Bavarian churches of this period. Of special note inside is the high altar, which is richly decorated.

ℹ️ *Rathausgasse 1*

▶ *From Donauwörth take the B16 southwest for 26km (16 miles) to Dillingen.*

❷ Dillingen, Bayern
Dillingen was a university town for over 200 years from the 16th

century onwards. The university was founded by Cardinal Bishop Otto Truchsen von Waldburg, who had to request permission from the Emperor and the Pope. The Aula, or Goldener Saal (main hall), as it is called here, is a masterpiece of late rococo. It measures about 30m (98 feet) long, 12m (39 feet) wide and only 6m (19 feet) high, and the combination of design and ornament is truly magnificent.

The Schloss (castle), where the Bishop of Augsburg used to live, now has a more secular use: law courts, tax and forestry offices. The church of St Peter was founded in 1619, and the Königstrasse provides a good example of how the streets and their surrounding buildings looked between the 16th and 18th centuries.

ℹ️ *Rathaus, Königstrasse 37*

▶ *Continue on the B16 to Günzburg.*

❸ Günzburg, Bayern
Günzburg warrants a short stop to see the Frauenkirche, built between 1736 and 1741 by Zimmermann – a masterpiece of south German rococo. Another building worth visiting

---

FOR HISTORY BUFFS

At Höchstadt, 6km (4 miles) before Dillingen, stands a memorial commemorating the battle which took place on 13 August, 1704, between the 'allies' – Austria, Holland and England – and Bavaria and France. The battle was fought to decide the succession to the Spanish throne and was won by the allies. The English army was led by the Duke of Marlborough, who named his palace in England 'Blenheim' after the village of Blindheim, near the battlefield.

SCENIC ROUTES

Before and after leaving Dillingen, the route is particularly scenic as it follows the course of the Donau (Danube). From Obergünzburg onwards, the route takes you through memorable country landscapes until it reaches Kaufbeuren.

here is the castle of a former Austrian Margrave, which was started in 1579 and completed in 1609. Only the chapel, which was erected in 1754 by Zimmermann's pupil, Joseph Dossenberger, has survived in its original style. The rest of the castle was converted into government offices.

ⅰ *Schlossplatz 1*

▶ *Take the* **B10** *to Ulm.*

BACK TO NATURE

Blaubeuern lies 17km (10 miles) west of Ulm, and at the northern end of the town is the Blautopf (Blue Pot), the source of the River Blau. The crystal-clear water emerges from a depth of 22m (72 feet) and flows along rocks and ravines, which provide a perfect natural setting. The River Blau joins the mighty Danube a little later. You may see dippers here – little black-and-white birds that bob up and down.

4 Ulm, Baden-Württemberg
Ulm is really a border town: the new town of Neu-Ulm across the river is still in Bavaria, while Ulm is in Swabia. The Münster (Minster) is known for its high spire, 161m (528 feet) high, and is Germany's second largest Gothic church. The foundation stone was laid in 1377, but work extended over many centuries.

Many families of builders dedicated their working lives to the minster. The robust may decide to climb the 768 steps up the main spire, but the view is a reward – as far as the Alps on a clear day. The Rathaus (Town Hall) building was started in 1370 with a simple design but, like the minster, it became the work of many artists and took a long time to complete. The paintings on the walls and the figures date back to 1540. The interior was totally redesigned after the bomb damage of 1944.

The Schwörhaus (House of Swearing-In) is a reminder of the still-practised annual tradition, in which the Mayor and the Guilds swear their loyalty anew to the constitution of the town. Crossing the Danube into Neu-Ulm, there are some fine old gabled houses. The leaning tower of Ulm, the Metzgerturm (Butcher's Tower), is about 2m (6 feet) off balance. Part of the old city walls can be seen from here.

Ulm also prides itself on its fountains – the Brunnen – which were created in the

15th century in connection with the building of two waterworks. They all have names, and the Delphinbrunnen has 53 water jets. Lovers of

Right: detail of 15th-century carved choirstall inside Ulm's Gothic cathedral (below)

The archway in the old city walls at Memmingen

rococo style will want to visit the library at the Benediktiner-kloster, while the Klosterkirche St Martin is a baroque masterpiece. The German Bread Museum gives information on the manufacture of bread and on the ancient bakers' guilds, as well as the present world food situation.

i *Münsterplatz 50, Stadthaus*

▶ *From Ulm drive via Neu-Ulm and the B28 and B19 along the Bavarian/Württemberg border to Memmingen.*

5 **Memmingen,** Bayern
The Rathaus (Town Hall), built in 1589, with a façade of 1765, is the major attraction in the Old Town, which is preserved in its original state. An architectural

curiosity is the Sieben-dächer-haus (House with Seven Roofs), three either side and one on top. This former tanners' house was unfortunately totally destroyed by bombing during World War II, but rebuilt according to the original design.

Look out also for the Steuerhaus on the market square, which dates back to 1495; pretty arcades lead through to the market. The

Gothic style of architecture dominates in the town, but parts of this building, as well as the town museum, show baroque influence.

The old city gates are still standing, as are parts of the city wall, and the Gothic Martinskirche, with its 66m (216-foot) spire, is the symbol of the town. The choir is a masterpiece of local woodcarving. The Fugger dynasty also erected a building here in 1589: the Fuggerbau.

[i] *Marktplatz 3*

▶ *From Memmingen drive southeast to Ottobeuren, 11km (7 miles).*

6 Ottobeuren, Bayern
The church in Ottobeuren represents one of the most important buildings in baroque style in Germany, although there has been a church on this site since AD 764. This structure was begun in 1737, and while many craftsmen created different parts of the church, the end result shows a remarkable artistic harmony. The foundations for other parts of the Kloster were laid in 1711, and the Kaiser Bibliothek (library) and Theatersaal should also be seen.

[i] *Marktplatz 14*

The Abbey Church at Ottobeuren, a fine example of German baroque, has a superb organ and choirstalls

▶ *Continue south on the Oberschwäbische Barockstrasse south to Kempten.*

7 Kempten, Bayern
Kempten lies on the River Iller, and has a Celtic and Roman past, but like so many towns and cities in this area is now a living reminder of the exuberant architectural glories of the 17th and 18th centuries. The Residenzplatz is dominated by the palace of the former Prince Abbots. The lavishness of the interior reflects the worldly part of the Prince Abbots' role, rather than the spiritual. Purists may disagree about whether the style is really late baroque or early rococo, but to most visitors it will simply seem opulent.

The Basilika of St Lorenz adjoins the west wing of the Residenz and was erected at about the same time, in the mid-17th century. The basilica was built over a period of four years; the Residenz took 13 years to complete.

Kempten is also an important dairy farming centre.

The tower and entrance to the lovely hillside town of Landsberg

i *Rathausplatz 24*

▶ *From Kempten take the B12 east to Kaufbeuren.*

8 **Kaufbeuren,** Bayern
Kaufbeuren's old quarter dates back to the Middle Ages. Since 1945 it has been the home of the Gablonzer glass industry, the craftsmen and their families having been expelled from their former homes in Gablonz, now in the Czech Republic. They brought their craft here, and Neugablonz is the area in which they work. The St Blasien-Wehrkirche was built in 1436 on the city wall, thus adding to the defences of the town. Five towers of the wall still stand. The church altar is distinguished by wonderful 16th-century woodcarvings.

More woodcarvings can be found at the St Martinskirche in town. The local Stadtmuseum is worth a visit, and an exhibition celebrates the work of the famous local writer Ludwig Ganghofer, who died in 1920.

i *Rathaus, Kaiser-Max-Strasse 1*

FOR CHILDREN

The Tänzelfest takes place on the third Sunday in July, when the history of Kaufbeuren is presented by about 1,600 children in historical costume. The procession is led through the town and the evening is crowned by an exciting torchlit tattoo and fireworks display.

▶ *Continue on the B12, then the A96 north to Landsberg. 33km (20 miles)*

9 **Landsberg,** Bayern
Enter the town through a beautifully decorated gate, the Bayertor, erected in the 15th century. From the top of the tower, which formed part of the city's defences, there is a wide view over the town. On one side of the market-place, with its Maria Brunnen fountain, stands another tower, the Rathaus, built between 1699 and 1702. The architect Dominikus Zimmermann worked here and erected the exterior stucco façade of the Rathaus. He was also Lord Mayor of the town for five years from 1759. The interior of the parish church is decorated in rich baroque style and was built between the years 1458 and 1488. It contains several treasures, including a rosary altar by Zimmermann.

i *Rathaus, Hauptplatz 152*

▶ *Take the B17 north to Augsburg a distance of 36km (23 miles).*

FOR HISTORY BUFFS

West of the road from Landsberg to Augsburg lies the Lechfeld, where an important battle was fought in AD 955. The invading Magyars from Hungary, who had looted and destroyed throughout southern Germany and Austria, were finally defeated by Otto the Great, who became Emperor Otto I in AD 962.

The Alps East
of Lindau

Lindau is set on an island in the Bodensee (Lake Constance), connected to the mainland by a causeway. Cars are discouraged in the centre; there is free parking near the station. It is a place to wander around on foot – an enchanting maze of medieval streets, with the magic of the lake never too far away.

2 DAYS • 286KM • 177 MILES

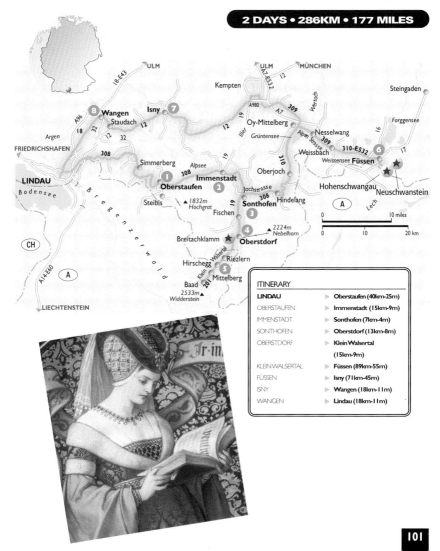

ITINERARY		
LINDAU	▶	**Oberstaufen** (40km-25m)
OBERSTAUFEN	▶	Immenstadt (15km-9m)
IMMENSTADT	▶	Sonthofen (7km-4m)
SONTHOFEN	▶	Oberstdorf (13km-8m)
OBERSTDORF	▶	Klein Walsertal
		(15km-9m)
KLEIN WALSERTAL	▶	Füssen (89km-55m)
FÜSSEN	▶	Isny (71km-45m)
ISNY	▶	Wangen (18km-11m)
WANGEN	▶	Lindau (18km-11m)

▶ *From Lindau drive a short stretch on the B12 before turning off for the B308 via Scheidegg to Oberstaufen, 40km (25 miles).*

❶ Oberstaufen, Bayern
In the 19th century a Silesian peasant made a useful discovery: a cure for the effects of over-eating and drinking! The cure involves fasting – although mulled wine is part of it – and Oberstaufen is always busy with customers for the 'Schrothkur'. An alternative cure might be a drive to Steibis near by, and a cable-car ride and walk to the summit of Hochgrat with its breathtaking views.

i Hugo-von-Königsegg Strasse 8

▶ *From Oberstaufen take the B308 east to Immenstad.*

❷ Immenstadt, Bayern
Immenstadt has the ideal Alpine setting – a lake encircled by mountains. It offers sailing, surfing and rowing on the lake, and plenty of walks through the attractive countryside. The

---

SPECIAL TO..

In September in Immenstadt is the Berglerfest, when cowherds drive their cattle down from the mountains back to their cowsheds. Traditionally, beards grown during the summer stay on the Alpine pastures are measured, with prizes given for the longest.

The ultimate fairy-tale castle. Neuschwanstein was built by King Ludwig II in the 1870s

parish church of St Nikolaus was built in late baroque style in 1707, and the Rathaus (Town Hall) slightly earlier in the 17th century. Two 17th-century ruins, the Laubenbergstein castle, north of the town, and the Schloss Königsegg in town, are worth visiting.

i Marienplatz 3

▶ *From Immenstadt take the B308 southeast for 7km (4 miles) to Sonthofen.*

❸ Sonthofen, Bayern
This well-known resort should be mentioned for the great variety of facilities it offers to sport

4 Oberstdorf, Bayern

The old village of Oberstdorf has grown into an excellent resort. It is very much associated with winter sports and well-known for its long ski-jump. Exciting summer sports are also available, such as hang-gliding and parasailing: enthusiasts can take advantage of the many cable-cars which travel to the mountain-tops.

The Nebelhornbahn cable-car goes from Oberstdorf – 828m (2,717 feet) above sea level – up to 1,933m (6,342 feet), a good starting point for hikes and mountain walks. To reach the summit of the Nebelhorn, just continue from the last station by chair-lift. The Fellhornbahn is a grander affair, the largest cable-car in Germany, the cabin taking 100 people at a time. A second stage goes to a point just beneath the summit. In winter, five ski-lifts provide the usual 'Skicircus' atmosphere. Lastly, the Sollereck-bahn rises 1,400m (4,593 feet) in 11 minutes to a superb area for walking and hiking.

Down in the valley, the sight to see is the Breitach-klamm – a ravine sometimes only 2m (6 feet) wide, so that in certain places the sky can hardly be seen. The curious rock formations along the way add to the impression of being inside a cave.

i Marktplatz 7

▷ From Oberstdorf drive on the **B19** southwest into the Klein Walsertal. The road becomes the **B201** when in Austria, 15km (9 miles).

5 Klein Walsertal,

Vorarlberg (Austria)

Geographically, this valley is in Austria, but as there are no rail or road links with that country, it is economically allied with Germany. Visitors who buy postcards will need Austrian stamps. Apart from these man-made peculiarities, nature has created a little paradise here. An abundance of alpine flowers, most of them protected, adorn the meadows.

There are four main villages in the valley: Riezlern, Hirschegg, Mittelberg and Baad. As there are no plans for any changes in the present status of the valley, it can be hoped that this special place will stay unspoilt for some time.

i Klein Walsertal, Austria; Hirschegg im Walserhaus

▷ Drive back on the **B201/ B19** to Sonthofen, then due east on the **B308** via Hindelang along the Jochstrasse. Turn left before the Austrian border at Oberjoch on the **B310** and along the Grüntensee. Turn

enthusiasts, including swimming, bowling, canoeing, tennis, squash and cycling. In winter there is an equal variety, with sports such as skiing, curling and skating. A camp site is also open all year round.

i Rathausplatz 1

▷ From Sonthofen proceed south on the **B19** for 13km (8 miles) to Oberstdorf.

One of Wangen's attractive old and narrow streets

rooms and salons feature designs inspired by old German sagas, including parts of the legends used by Richard Wagner for his operas. Wagner was a frequent visitor and his piano is still kept in tune. The castle was used as a summer residence, and its terraces offer tranquil views over the countryside and lakes – and to the castle of Neuschwanstein.

Neuschwanstein must be seen to be believed, but it is very difficult to get a good photo of it, and the best ones are usually done from the air. The castle was the brain-child of Ludwig II, and work began on it in 1869. The plans were drawn up by a stage designer to take the king's dream world into reality. The mythical world of Wagner's operas – heroic and magical – influences the interiors. It truly is a fairy-tale in stone and paint, and fascinating to visit. The castle took 17 years to build, but the tragic king only lived here for 102 days. Since his mysterious death (see page 90), millions of visitors have been enthralled by his living fantasy.

RECOMMENDED WALKS

A climb up the Widderstein mountain from Baad in the Klein Walsertal is a worthwhile experience for the energetic. An early rise followed by a 4½-hour climb is necessary to experience the beautiful scenery up at the top.

southeast to Füssen, 89km (55 miles).

6 **Füssen,** Bayern
The parish church of St Mang was erected between 1701 and 1717 in baroque style by the builder and painter Jakob Herkomer, who studied in Venice, and his work shows a strong Italian influence. The former Benedictine abbey now serves as the Rathaus (Town Hall); the Fürstensaal (Hall of the Princes) and the Papstzimmer (Room of the Pope) are also well worth visiting. The Hohes Schloss, built on a hill, has origins from around 1330, although the present building dates from the 15th century.

Near Füssen are two important castles: Hohenschwangau and Neuschwanstein. Hohenschwangau stands above the village of Schwangau; a steep walk leads up to the castle from the car-park. The architect was chosen by Crown Prince Maximilian of Bavaria for his theatrical connections, and he favoured the English Tudor style. The drawing

FOR HISTORY BUFFS

From Füssen drive the 22km (13½ miles) along the B17 to Steingaden, turn right after 3km (2 miles) and right again to Wies; here, the Wieskirche is a pilgrimage church designed and built by Dominikus Zimmermann. Work started in 1746 and was finished eight years later, and both the exterior and interior decorations are fine examples of baroque and rococo. On the return journey, stop in Steingaden to visit the former monastery church of St Johannes der Täufer, which dates from the mid-12th century, although the interior was extensively decorated in the 18th century.

[i] Kaiser-Maximilian-Platz 1, Füssen

BACK TO NATURE

The River Lech has to pass through a narrow ravine just south of Füssen, near the Austrian border. The nearby Lech waterfall completes this natural spectacle, which can be admired from a small bridge across the ravine. For the bird-watcher, the ravine by the castle at Neuschwanstein is a renowned haunt of the wallcreeper.

► *From Füssen take the* **B310** *northwest until it becomes the* **B309** *to the Kempten ring road, then turn left and take the* **B12** *to Isny, 71km (45 miles).*

7 Isny, Baden-Württemberg
Isny is a border town between Bavaria and Württemberg, and

The old lighthouse and the Lion of Bavaria guard Lindau's harbour

actually lies in the latter. The Rathaus prides itself on having a mighty stove, which reaches from floor to ceiling, and is decorated with coloured clay tiles. On the ground floor is a copy of a Roman milestone from AD 202.

The Romanesque St Nikolaus's Church has a library housed in its spire. The Gothic choir and font are also interesting. The church of St Georg was built in baroque style in 1661. However, the rococo decorations are mostly 18th-century. The climate around Isny, which is an officially desig-nated health resort, is known to be beneficial for many respira-tory illnesses, as well as heart and circulation problems.

[i] *Unterer Grabenweg 18*

► *Continue on the* **B12** *west-wards, but turn right before Staudach for Wangen.*

8 Wangen, Baden-Württemberg
Wangen's interesting past still shows through its buildings and

streets. Most of the houses were built after the great fire of 1539, and the fronts are painted with motifs in traditional colours. The end of the Herrenstrasse (Gentlemen's Road) runs most appropriately to the Frauentor (Ladies' Gate), again beautifully decorated, and built in 1608.

[i] *Marktplatz 1, Rathaus*

► *Return on the* **B32**, *then the* **B12** *to Lindau, 18km (11 miles).*

FOR CHILDREN

A tour of Hohenschwangau, the castle near Füssen where the Bavarian King Ludwig II, who as an adult retreated into a fairy-tale world, spent his happy childhood, is likely to be of interest to children. The special family tours need to be booked in advance at the Ticket Centre, Alpseestrasse 12, in Hohenschwangau village (not at the castle).

BADEN-WÜRTTEMBERG

Baden-Württemberg stretches across southwest Germany, with the Rhine forming a natural border to the west and the south where it joins the Bodensee (Lake Constance). Germany occupies by far the largest proportion of the lake shores, but this geographical advantage over neighbouring Switzerland and Austria does not upset the harmony of this relaxed lakeside community. Lake steamers ply from country to country and co-operation exists between the partners whose commerce, language and history have so much in common.

A street in Freiburg leading to the 13th-century Martins Gate, part of the old ramparts

The Rhine flows past the southern reaches of the Black Forest region. Here it should be mentioned that the term 'black' is something of a misnomer, as the forest is both brilliantly green and extremely beautiful. There seems to be a parallel here with the 'Blue Danube' which rises near Donaueschingen. Poetic licence transforms this great river, which is normally grey as it is fed by the melting waters from the Alpine glaciers, though occasionally – looked at from a certain angle – the river acts as a mirror and reflects the blue sky. The Black Forest also fails to live up to its name in winter, when it is inevitably cloaked in deep snow which transforms the area into a popular winter sports location. Traditional crafts such as clock-making and glass-blowing can still be seen in the Black Forest villages. The Deutsche Uhrenstrasse (German Clock Road) draws attention to the origins of the cuckoo clock deep in the heart of the forest. Modern industry is largely restricted to tourism. The area around Bodensee and the Black Forest is not only spectacularly beautiful, but the woods and hills are well supplied with enchanting hotels and inns.

The Romans discovered the joy of spa life centuries ago, but the Black Forest's natural hot springs suffered a long period of neglect before their restorative powers came back into fashion again at the end of the last century. Europe's ruling monarchs and carriage-loads of the aristocracy enjoyed their summer vacations in these spas. Now they are open to all and still very popular. Although the main attraction of the Black Forest region and Bodensee lies in their scenic beauty, there is no need to miss out on the sightseeing front, with magnificent castles and other works of art standing testimony to the generations of gifted architects and artists of times gone by.

The picturesque riverfront of the Neckar at Tübingen, one of Germany's oldest university towns

cent scenery are the main feature of this tour as it proceeds along the Rhine, takes a turn on the Hochschwarzwald (High Black Forest), and stops off at a Roman spa before circling back by way of the Hexental (Valley of the Witches).

Tour 20

The Romans were the first to stumble upon Baden-Baden, one of Germany's best-known spas and the starting point of this tour. Following a most attractive route through the Black Forest, the Mummelsee, near the Hornisgrinde mountain, is a popular stop-off about halfway along the outward journey. Approaching Stuttgart, be prepared for the traffic, which is very heavy around the town. In spite of its industrial suburbs, the centre is very pleasant, with pedestrian precincts. From Stuttgart, the tour proceeds to two extraordinary castles. At Gengenbach the tour picks up the popular Badische Weinstrasse (Wine Route) and wends its way out of the western end of the Black Forest range into the vineyards and on to Baden-Baden.

Tour 18

In ecological terms the Bodensee (Lake Constance) forms a reservoir for the Rhine. From the town of Konstanz, it is a pleasant drive along the southwestern shores of the peninsula which projects into the northern end of the lake, then southeast through a series of lakeside towns. A trip further inland leads through hilly countryside with plenty of stopping places and attractive scenery. A car ferry saves the long drive around the lake – regular lake steamer services provide good connections to all points around the shores. You can visit three countries in a day with perfect ease by just hopping on and off the steamers.

Tour 19

This tour begins in historic Freiburg im Breisgau, one of Germany's greatest cultural centres. From Freiburg, the road runs through the Höllental (Valley of Hell), one of the best-known valleys in the Black Forest, and then follows the Schwarzwälder Panoramastrasse (Black Forest Panoramic Road). Donaueschingen marks the spot where the two primary tribu-

taries of the Danube, the Breg and Brigach, unite to form one of Europe's major waterways. The might of the Danube is only evident much further on, when it is joined by rivers from the Alps. Small towns and magnifi-

Wall decorations at the spa centre in fashionable and popular Baden-Baden

Lakes & Shores
of Konstanz

Konstanz (Constance) is the largest town on Bodensee (Lake Constance). The Altstadt (Old Town) was fortunate to escape destruction during World War II, saved by its proximity to neutral Switzerland. It features lovely half-timbered houses, and the massive Konzilgebäude, a former warehouse, built in 1388 for the linen trade. The original Romanesque Münster (Minster) was started in 1052 and completed in 1089.

1/2 DAYS • 158KM • 97 MILES

ITINERARY	
KONSTANZ	▶ **Insel Reichenau (9km–6m)**
INSEL REICHENAU	▶ **Überlingen (41km–26m)**
ÜBERLINGEN	▶ **Unteruhldingen (7km–4m)**
UNTERUHLDINGEN	▶ **Salem (7km–4m)**
SALEM	▶ **Heiligenberg (7km–4m)**
HEILIGENBERG	▶ **Wilhelmsdorf (13km–8m)**
WILHELMSDORF	▶ **Weingarten (24km–15m)**
WEINGARTEN	▶ **Ravensburg (4km–2m)**
RAVENSBURG	▶ **Friedrichshafen (19km–12m)**
FRIEDRICHSHAFEN	▶ **Meersburg (20km–12m)**
MEERSBURG	▶ **Konstanz (7km–4m)**

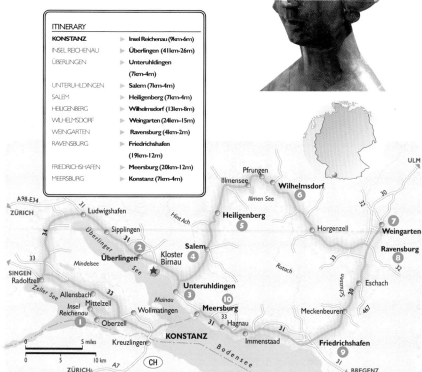

[i] *Bahnhofplatz 13, Konstanz*

FOR CHILDREN

At Allensbach, about halfway between Konstanz and Radolfzell, the local zoo features a great variety of European wild animals, and there is a Streichelzoo (petting zoo) especially for children, with goats, donkeys and deer.

▶ *From Konstanz head northwest on the **B33** for Insel Reichenau, 9km (6 miles), which is reached by a causeway.*

BACK TO NATURE

On the way to the island of Reichenau, just north of Konstanz, you will find the Wollmatinger Ried Bird Sanctuary. The most common inhabitants on these marshlands are waterfowl. Waterproof boots are recommended.

Richly decorated façade in Konstanz, a town with a very long history

❶ Insel Reichenau, Baden-Württemberg

Reichenau is also known as the 'Garden Island', and vegetables are the main crop, flourishing profitably in the rich soil and mild climate.

The first village over the causeway is Oberzell, which has one of the oldest Romanesque churches in Germany, dating back to about AD 888. The interior is decorated with several famous wall frescoes painted in the 10th and 11th centuries, which depict the *Miracles of Christ*. At Mittelzell, the 8th-century Münster (Minster) is dedicated to St Maria and St Markus. The original basilica, founded in AD 724, is typically Romanesque in style, but the main parts of the monastery were built later, in the 10th and 11th centuries. Take time to inspect the treasures of the Schatzkammer (Treasury), such as the five Gothic shrines housing religious relics, among them a 5th-century ivory goblet etched with details of the *Miracles of Christ*, and examples of 1,000-year-old stained glass.

The third church to visit is in Niederzell. Dedicated to St Peter and St Paul, the original Romanesque edifice was greatly altered and added to in the 15th century, but the highlight here is a series of Romanesque frescoes uncovered during restoration in 1990.

RECOMMENDED WALK

Passing through Radolfzell, on the way from the island of Reichenau to Überlingen, stop off for a walk along the elegant lakeside promenade and, if time permits, try a visit to the 14th-century Gothic Liebfrauenmünster.

[i] *Pirminstrasse 145*

▶ *Leave via the causeway, take the **B33** northwest, then turn right on to the **B34**, round the north end of the lake to meet the **B31** at Ludwigshafen. Take the **B31** southeast to Überlingen, 41km (26 miles).*

❷ Überlingen, Baden-Württemberg

This part of the lake is actually called the Überlinger See, as the northern end of Lake Constance is divided by the

FOR HISTORY BUFFS

A detour to Singen and the nearby ruins of the Hohentwiel fortress is recommended. Several parts of the fortress that are standing give a good idea of its size and magnificent position. The fortress was never conquered, but Napoleon felt compelled to have it destroyed between 1800 and 1801.

Bodanruck peninsula, with Konstanz at its southernmost tip.

The city centre is formed by Münsterplatz, with the Rathaus and the Münster (Minster). The basilica is very large for a comparatively small town, but the site on which it was constructed originally held two churches. The present Gothic-style building consists of five naves, erected between 1350 and 1562, and it is topped by two spires, one smaller than the other, which contains the Osannaglocke (bell). The fine Rathaus (Town Hall) is in late Gothic style, and you can visit the Ratsaal (Council Chamber) with its High Gothic decorations, wooden panelling and figures representing the member states of the Holy Roman Empire, among others.

Northwest of Münsterplatz, the Franziskanerkirche dates back to the 14th and 15th centuries. Across the way, in Krummerbergstrasse , the Reichlin von Meldegg Haus (1462) was originally the home of an important local family. It now houses the town's Stadtisches Museum, which uses a wide variety of interesting exhibits to illustrate the history of the town from its earliest origins.

i Landungsplatz 14

▶ Continue along the shore in a southeasterly direction for 7km (4 miles) to Unteruhldingen. Stop halfway to see the pilgrimage church at Kloster Birnau.

❸ Unteruhldingen, Baden-Württemberg
A unique insight into the early life of Man is provided here on the shore of Bodensee at the Pfahlbaumuseum. The museum has finds from local excavations and also has a re-creation of a lakeside village showing how the prehistoric inhabitants would have lived. It was created in 1922 by archaeologist Hans Reinerth.

i Schilstrasse 12

▶ Turn away from the lake, heading northeast for about 7km (4 miles) to Salem.

❹ Salem, Baden-Württemberg
Records of Salem's Münster date back to 1137. The abbey was created by the Cistercian order and was a substantial foundation, supporting 300 monks and novices within the walled precincts by the end of the 13th century. Although the foundation stone of the Münster was laid many years earlier, the abbey church was not consecrated until 1414, and is considered to have been the most important Gothic building in the region at its peak. The present monastery buildings date back to the 16th and 18th centuries and are largely baroque in style. A notable feature here is the wonderful Riepp-Organ, constructed in 1766. When the abbey was secularised it passed to the princes of Baden-Baden, and Prince Max of Baden founded a famous boarding school which still occupies part of the abbey complex. One renowned headmaster, Dr Kurt Hahn, later left Germany and founded Gordonstoun School in Scotland.

In 1700, part of the former Kloster (abbey) was rebuilt and renamed the Schloss (castle). Visitors should find the imposing Kaisersaal (Emperor's Hall) of particular interest.

i Schloss Salem

▶ Continue north for 7km (4 miles) to Heiligenberg.

❺ Heiligenberg, Baden-Württemberg
Although the counts of Heiligenberg are supposed to have had a residence here even earlier, the first records of the present castle do not appear until 1276. There is a fabulous carved wooden ceiling adorning the Rittersaal (Knights' Hall), which occupies two floors of the south wing. The Renaissance carvings have been hailed as some of the finest in Germany. The castle chapel also has beautiful carvings, several of which date back to the 13th century, and its coloured glass paintings exude a marvellous glow, especially on a sunlit day.

i Schulstrasse 5

▶ About 4.5km (2½ miles) north take a sharp right turn to Illmensee and drive via Pfrungen to Wilhelmsdorf.

❻ Wilhelmsdorf, Baden-Württemberg
The centre of the village is the square-shaped Saalplatz, formed by the intersection of the two roads and dominated by the church. There is a small museum located in the oldest house in town, which is dedicated to the history of the village, and can be visited by appointment.

i Bürgermeisteramt, Saalplatz 7

▶ From Wilhelmsdorf head due south, bypassing Ravensburg, to Weingarten, 24km (15 miles).

❼ Weingarten, Baden-Württemberg
The present church in Weingarten was erected between 1715 and 1724 on the site of a former Romanesque basilica. Two spires, each 58m (190 feet) high, dominate the façade, and the interior is especially interesting. One of Germany's largest baroque basilicas, the church was decorated and furnished by a distinguished collection of carefully selected artists.

Cosmas Damian Asam contributed the ceiling frescoes which, after more than 250 years, still shine as if they had been painted much more recently. Another impressive sight is the massive organ by Joseph Gabler; its appearance is almost as imposing as the magnificent sound it produces.

i *Münsterplatz 1*

▶ *From Weingarten continue south on the B30 for 4km (2 miles) to Ravensburg.*

FOR HISTORY BUFFS

Numerous Alemann graves were unearthed by archaeologists just outside Weingarten in the 1950s. These date back to the 6th and 8th centuries, and more information is provided by the Alemannenmuseum, which is housed in the Kornhaus, a former granary.

SPECIAL TO...

On the Friday after Ascension Day, Weingarten celebrates a historic ceremony involving the handing over of a relic of the Holy Blood of Christ, with a procession of horseback riders known as the 'Blutritt'.

---

8 Ravensburg, Baden-Württemberg

The historic town of Ravensburg grew up around its 11th-century castle, and served as the seat of the influential Welf dynasty. The castle enjoyed an advantageous military position, and the town's fortifications still present an imposing sight. The oblong Marienplatz forms the centre of the town. In the middle stands the 16th-century Bläserturm. Beautifully preserved medieval houses which belonged to the former Patriziers (patricians – the noble and wealthy citizens of the town) line Marienplatz and Marktplatz. Drei König Haus and Rad Haus are especially noteworthy.

Of particular historic interest for their commercial connections are the Waaghaus (Weighing Office), the elongated Kornhaus (Corn Exchange)

and the Lederhaus, which was the Leatherworkers' Guildhouse, decorated with beautifully coloured frescoes. The Rathaus (Town Hall), which was started in the second half of the 14th century and not finished until the 16th, has a 15th-century Lord Mayor's office which is well worth a visit. By far the most significant building in Ravensburg, and the emblem of the town, is the Mehlsack, which translates to the 'bag of flour', so called because of its light colouring. A sort of spy post which allowed the town watchmen to keep an eye on the neighbouring settlements, the 50m (164-foot) high tower still affords a terrific view, and on a clear day it is worth the effort of climbing up the 240 steps to see right over Bodensee to the Alps.

i *Kirchstrasse 16*

▶ *From Ravensburg turn southwest on the B30 for Friedrichshafen, 19km (12 miles).*

Baroque-style ornaments on the abbey church in Weingarten

⑨ Friedrichshafen, Baden-Württemberg

Friedrichshafen was not as fortunate as Konstanz in World War II, and suffered heavy bomb damage. During World War I, the famous Zeppelin airships were constructed here, and in the 1920s and 1930s the Dornier flying boats were built here. The lake, whose calm waters had proved to be such an ideal base for the Zeppelin's floating hangers, was also a natural testing ground for the flying boats. The Zeppelin Museum Friedrichshafen is housed in the former harbour railway station – itself a notable example of Bauhaus architecture – and contains the world's largest exhibit on the history and technology of airships.

A shoreside promenade leads to the Schloss Hofen, once the residence of the kings of Württemberg. Its church, with two distinctive 55m

(180-foot) high spires, can be seen from far away. The castle is now privately owned and is not open to the public.

☐ *Bahnhofplatz 2*

▶ *From Friedrichshafen head northwest along the lakeshore to Meersburg.*

⑩ Meersburg, Baden-Württemberg

Meersburg celebrated its 1,000th birthday in 1988, though its origins are said to go back much further. In AD 628, Dagobert, King of the Franks, is supposed to have laid the foundation stone of the Altes Schloss (Old Castle). Today, the Schloss, with its mighty Dagobert Tower, is one of the oldest remaining German castles, really more a fortress than a castle. It remains in private hands having been saved from demolition by Baron Joseph von Lassberg in the early 19th century. He made parts of the castle available to

sympathetic artists, the most famous of whom was his sister-in-law, the celebrated German poet Annette von Droste-Hülshoff (1797–1848). Her living quarters, the Knights' Hall, Minstrels' Gallery and dungeons can all be visited.

The Neues Schloss, opposite the original one, was built around 1750 as a residence for the Fürstbischöfe (Prince-Bishops) of Konstanz. Balthasar Neumann and Franz Anton Bagnato both worked on the project and the grand double staircase is one of Neumann's

Meersburg – one of the prettiest towns on the lake

The magnificent floral gardens
on Insel Mainau

masterpieces. Other features are
the Spiegelsaal (Hall of Mirrors),
and the Dornier Museum, on
the top floor, which exhibits
items relating to the German
aviation industry. Do not miss
the Weinbaumuseum, with its
enormous barrel with a capacity
of 50,000 litres (11,000 gallons).

i   *Kirchstrasse 4*

▶   *From Meersburg take the car*
ferry back to Konstanz.

SCENIC ROUTES

From the island of Reichnau,
there is a lovely drive along
the shores of Lake Constance
to Radolfzell. The first part of
the road is called the Swabian
Poets Road, and is followed
by a Green Road.
Between Salem and
Heiligenberg, the Ober-
schwäbische Barockstrasse
(Upper Swabian Baroque
Road) leads through some
enchanting country.

BACK TO NATURE

From Meersburg take a trip by
lake steamer to Mainau, which
belongs to the Swedish
Bernadotte family. The island's
famous arboretum contains
hundreds of superb trees not
normally seen so far north.
Look out for banana trees,
bougainvillaea and hibiscus
among others. In spring the
whole island is in bloom with a
multitude of brilliant, sweet-
scented flowers.

The Southern
Black Forest

Freiburg im Breisgau enjoys one of the most enviable settings, on the rim of the Black Forest. Centuries of Austrian Habsburg rule have also left a gentle lifestyle amid many attractive historical buildings.

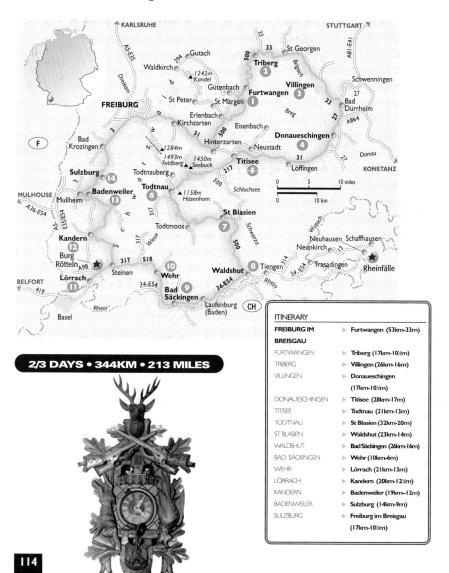

2/3 DAYS • 344KM • 213 MILES

ℹ️ *Rathausplatz 2–4, Freiburg*

▷ Take the **B31** southeast for 27km (17 miles), turn north at Hinterzarten and then drive 26km (16 miles) west on the **B500** to Furtwangen.

FOR CHILDREN

En route from Freiburg to Furtwangen, turn right at Kirchzarten and make a short detour (11km/7 miles) to the Steinwasen Park. The two 800m (2,623-foot) long summer toboggan runs and the animal enclosures are huge favourites with young visitors.

Freiburg's attractive Rathaus

❶ Furtwangen, Baden-Württemberg

Furtwangen is the home of Germany's watchmakers' school, founded in the middle of the 19th century. Its first head-master, Robert Gerwig, began to collect watches and the result of his labours, the Deutsches Uhrenmuseum (Horological Museum), now exhibits more than a thousand timepieces. A reconstructed workshop shows how clocks were made by hand. The finished products on display range from the first Black Forest clocks made in the 17th century, and driven by stone weights, to more elaborate clocks and, of course, the local speciality – cuckoo clocks. The Planetarium, an astronomical clock driven by a pendulum, shows the movements of the sun and its planets.

The River Breg, one of the first tributaries of the Danube, starts near 12th-century St Martin's Chapel in Furtwangen.

ℹ️ *Lindenstrasse 1*

▷ Take the **B500** north for 17km (10½ miles) to Triberg.

❷ Triberg, Baden-Württemberg

Triberg's main attraction is its Wasserfall (waterfall), an easy half-hour walk from the main

---

SCENIC ROUTES

The main attraction of the Schwarzwald (Black Forest) is its scenery and there is an abundance of scenic drives. A circular trip from Furtwangen leads west via Gütenbach through the Simonswald forest and the Wilde Gutach Valley towards Gutach. Turn left, and after about 3km (2 miles) turn left again at Waldkirch. The road now climbs in serpentine bends to the Kandel mountain and on to St Peter. After numerous bends it reaches St Märgen, then changes direction from southeast in a sharp swing around to the northeast at Erlenbach, then due north to Furtwangen. The stretch of road between Waldkirch and Erlenbach is popularly known as the Schwarzwälder Panoramastrasse (Black Forest Panoramic Road).

---

road. The water cascades 162m (531 feet) down over seven steps. On the Schönwald road, the pilgrimage church of Maria in der Tanne (Our Lady of the Fir Tree) was already a little chapel in 1645, with an altar painting of the Madonna reputed to work miracles. Later the painting was found fastened to a fir tree, which gave the church its name. It was one of the few buildings to survive a devastating fire in 1826, which completely destroyed Triberg. The present church was erected between 1699 and 1702, and a sculptor from nearby Villingen, Anton Joseph Schupp, designed the high altar with its famous Madonna.

ℹ️ *Wallfahrtstrasse 4*

▷ From Triberg take the **B33** east to Villingen.

❸ Villingen, Baden-Württemberg

Villingen was founded by Duke Berthold III of the Zähringen dynasty, and much of the town's original defensive walls and the gate towers are still standing. In fact, the wall was so well built that it withstood two attacks by the Swedes in 1525 and 1625 and another by the French in 1703. In the centre of Villingen stands 12th-century Münster Unser Lieben Frau (Minster). Most of the original Romanesque architecture was replaced after a fire in 1271.

Villingen's Altes Rathaus houses a museum displaying works of art dating back to the 13th century, and its former Kloster (abbey) was founded by the Franciscans in 1268. The Franziskanermuseum in the abbey exhibits archaeological finds from the tomb of a Celtic nobleman.

The twin city of Schwenningen was incorporated in 1972, providing industry and commerce to the newly formed double-barrelled metropolis of Villingen-Schwenningen.

[i] *Rietgasse 2*

▶ *Take the **B33/27** south to Donaueschingen.*

❹ Donaueschingen, Baden-Württemberg

The rivers Breg and Brigach

unite here and form the original source of the Danube. A pond in the Schlosspark marks the meeting point. Donaueschingen was the seat of the Princes of Fürstenberg. The baroque Schloss was founded in 1723, but considerably altered in the 19th century, and the interior is the most interesting part. Exquisite Renaissance, baroque and rococo furniture is exhibited in luxuriously appointed halls, their walls hung with fine Gobelin tapestries and paintings. Displayed in a gallery on Karlsplatz, the Fürstenberg-Sammlungen (Princes' Collections) contain paintings from the 15th- and 16th-century Swabian and Franconian schools.

[i] *Karlstrasse 58*

▶ *Take the **B31** west for 28km (17 miles) to Titisee.*

❺ Titisee-Neustadt, Baden-Württemberg

Together with its sister town of Neustadt, Titisee is a well-situated centre in the southern Black Forest region. The picturesque lake provides all the usual recreational and water sports facilities, and there are numerous hiking and driving excursions to be made using the town as a base.

[i] *Strandbadstrasse 4, Titisee*

▶ *From Titisee take the **B317** southwest for 21km (13 miles) to Todtnau.*

Huge ornamental clocks are typical of the Black Forest region

The old wooden bridge across
the Rhine at Bad Säckingen

FOR CHILDREN

The Schwarzwaldbahn (Black
Forest Railway) makes a short
trip from Titisee to Schluchsee
rather more interesting. The
Schluchsee is the largest lake in
the region and offers plenty of
opportunities for bathing and a
variety of watersports.

---

6 Todtnau, Baden-
Württemberg
Todtnau is surrounded by
mountains on every side, all
of which reach a height of over
1,000m (3,280 feet), and is
officially classified as a health
resort.

Situated between Todtnau
and its neighbouring village of
Todtnauberg, there is a large
waterfall, where the water pelts
down from a height of about
100m (328 feet) with a deafen-
ing noise. One of the nearby
mountain peaks, the
Hasenhorn, can be reached by
chair-lift, and it is well worth the
trip for a great view over the
southern Black Forest.

i Meinrad Thoma Strasse 21

BACK TO NATURE

A 10-minute walk or short
drive north of Todtnau leads
to the Hangloch Wasserfall
(waterfall). In the forest, look
for birds such as Bonelli's
warblers, nutcrackers, black
woodpeckers and collared
flycatchers.

SPECIAL TO...

At Todtnau-Aftersteg you can
visit the Glasbläserhof where
handblown glass is still being
made in the time-honoured
fashion, using processes and
techniques that have remained
the same for centuries.

▶ *From Todtnau drive 3km
(2 miles) south, turn left for
Todtmoos, then east to St
Blasien, 32km (20 miles).*

7 St Blasien, Baden-
Württemberg
Benedictine monks built the
old Kloster (abbey) here
between 1772 and 1783, though
it is believed that previous
buildings have stood on this site
for over a thousand years. It is

---

always a surprise to find a building of this size in a small village,
and the dome of the abbey
church is one of the largest in
Europe. The interior of the
dome is interesting as the architect cleverly created the illusion
of the cupola being supported
by 20 columns, whereas, in fact,
it rests on another hidden structure which bears the full weight.

i Kurgarten 1

▶ *Take the eastern exit from
St Blasien in the direction of
Häusern, then due south on
the B500 for Waldshut,
23km (14 miles).*

8 Waldshut-Tiengen,
Baden-Württemberg
This small market town lies on
the banks of the Rhein (Rhine)
right by the Swiss border. The
main street, Kaiserstrasse,
boasts some fine examples of
16th-, 17th- and 18th-century
architecture.

Although it means crossing
into Switzerland, there is one
excursion from here that should
not be missed, the Rheinfälle
(Rhine Falls) just outside
Schaffhausen on the other side
of the border. Europe's most
powerfull waterfall thunders
down at an average rate of

700cu m (25,000 cubic feet) per second in a dazzling mist of spray and sound.

ℹ️ *Wallstrasse 26*

▶ *From Waldshut drive west for 26km (16 miles) on the B34 to Bad Säckingen.*

9 Bad Säckingen, Baden-Württemberg
As the name suggests, Bad Säckingen is a natural spa with thermal springs recommended for the treatment of rheumatic pains. Its most notable feature, however, is a 200m (655-foot) long, 400-year-old wooden pedestrian bridge over the Rhine, which links Germany with Switzerland. How many people must have looked longingly across to the freedom of neutral Switzerland, especially during World War II. It is a memorable crossing between the two countries. A happier story made Bad Säckingen famous, the epic romance of a young trumpeter and the daughter of the local lord of the manor. The episode occurred over 300 years ago, but it earned Bad Säckingen the nickname 'The Trumpet Capital', and in Schloss Schönau, a little palace in town, the legend is celebrated by a trumpet museum.

Do not miss the Fridolinmünster (St Fridolin's), the basilica of the former Kloster (abbey) founded in the 13th century. Its two spires can be seen from many parts of the town.

ℹ️ *Waldshuter Strasse 20*

▶ *Continue on the B34, then take the B518 to Wehr, 10km (6 miles).*

10 Wehr, Baden-Württemberg
Two former fortresses, both of them in ruins, can be found near Wehr. The first, Werach, was probably built in the early Middle Ages to house and protect refugees from other war-torn areas. There is a fine view

across the southern Wehrtal (valley) from a pavilion erected above the foundations of the old watch tower. The other fortress, Bärenfels, dates back to the 12th and 13th centuries.

At the subterranean caves, known as the Haseler Tropfsteinhöhle, located 4km (2½ miles) north of Wehr, there is an interesting and professional presentation of life inside a mountain over the centuries.

ℹ️ *Hauptstrasse 14*

▶ *Take the B518 northwest to join the B317, then head west for 21km (13 miles) to Lörrach.*

11 Lörrach, Baden-Württemberg
Four kilometres (2½ miles) north of Lörrach, Burg Rötteln was destroyed by the French when they invaded the area towards the end of the 17th century. It was one of the largest fortresses in southwest Germany, and the origins of the complex can be traced back to the 12th century, when it was the seat of the Nobles of Rötteln. You can still identify the basic layout of the fortress, including the main tower which is still standing, and also the Romanesque keep. The Museum am Burghof (local museum) provides information on the history of Burg Rötteln and of Lörrach, and there are exhibits concerning the lifestyles of people through the ages.

ℹ️ *Herrenstrasse 5*

▶ *From Lörrach drive 5km (3 miles) east on the B317, then turn sharp left at Steinen and head northwards to Kandern.*

Dark trees reflected in dark waters give the Black Forest its name

⓬ Kandern, Baden-Württemberg

Kandern is a pleasant holiday resort with a small, but perfectly formed baroque palace, Schloss Bürgeln. It offers superb views and also includes a museum. Near by, the old Sausenberg fortress was another victim of French artillery in 1678. However, its tower is still standing, and affords a panoramic view over neighbouring Switzerland.

ℹ️ *Hauptstrasse 18*

▶ *Drive north via the Kandertal, then turn left to Badenweiler.*

⓭ Badenweiler, Baden-Württemberg

The Romans were the first to appreciate the potential of Badenweiler, and they built a baths complex around the natural spring in the 1st century AD, during the reign of Emperor Vespasian. After the withdrawal of the Roman garrison the spa fell into obscurity until 1784, when the baths were rediscovered, and careful excavations have revealed a great deal about the highly civilised Roman lifestyle. Badenweiler now offers all the modern facilities for those seeking a cure. Apart from the Roman baths, another historic ruin occupies a place in the modern Kurpark, the Burgruine, a ruined fortress which once belonged to the Zähringer dynasty.

ℹ️ *Ernst-Eisenlohr-Strasse 4*

▶ *Continue west to Müllheim, then turn right in a north-easterly direction to Sulzburg.*

⓮ Sulzburg, Baden-Württemberg

Sulzburg is renowned for its Kloster, a convent in this case. None of the original buildings are still standing, except the Klosterkirche (abbey church) which dates back to AD 1000. The important segments of the church have been preserved and can still be admired.

In 1980 the government of Baden-Württemberg opened a mining museum in Sulzburg, which portrays the history of mining in the province.

ℹ️ *Am Marktplatz*

▶ *Continue north to join the main road (B3) leading north, the 'Badische Weinstrasse'. Follow this through the Hexental (Valley of the Witches) to Freiburg, a total distance of 17km (10.5 miles).*

ITINERARY	
BADEN-BADEN	▶ Freudenstadt (60km-37m)
FREUDENSTADT	▶ Herrenberg (52km-32m)
HERRENBERG	▶ Stuttgart (39km-24m)
STUTTGART	▶ Tübingen (40km-25m)
TÜBINGEN	▶ Reutlingen (13km-8m)
REUTLINGEN	▶ Lichtenstein (12km-7m)
LICHTENSTEIN	▶ Hechingen (47km-29m)
HECHINGEN	▶ Balingen (15km-9m)
BALINGEN	▶ Alpirsbach (46km-29m)
ALPIRSBACH	▶ Gutach (39km-24m)
GUTACH	▶ Gengenbach (29km-18m)
GENGENBACH	▶ Offenburg (11km-7m)
OFFENBURG	▶ Baden-Baden (42km-26m)

Spas & the
Northern Black
Forest

3 DAYS • 445KM • 275 MILES

Baden-Baden is one of Europe's top spas, and its double-barrelled name not only distinguishes it from other 'Baden' (spas), but it also denotes that this is the Baden of the province of Baden. The actual spa, known as the Caracalla Therme, after its Roman patron, is today a luxuriously appointed complex with several pools. To enjoy Baden-Baden, take time to linger and savour the atmosphere.

⌐i⌐ *Kaiserallee 3 (Trinkhalle)*

▷ *From Baden-Baden take the **B500/B28** (Schwarzwald Hochstrasse) south for 60km (37 miles) to Freudenstadt.*

❶ Freudenstadt, Baden-Württemberg
Founded by Duke Friedrich von Württemberg as a silver-mining town in 1599, Freudenstadt was flattened by Allied bombs in 1945. The large square in the centre of town was part of the original plans drawn up by the duke, whose chess-board layout allowed all the houses around it and those in adjoining streets behind to be interconnected by passages. The Stadthaus and Post Office are situated in the Marktplatz (Market Square), and the Protestant parish church takes up one corner. An interesting

---

SCENIC ROUTES

The Schwarzwaldhochstrasse (Black Forest High Road) from Baden-Baden to Freudenstadt skirts the rim of the hills and mountains and runs through magnificent scenery. There are numerous opportunities for scenic drives in the Black Forest region, not just on the Hochstrasse, but remember when planning a trip it can take rather longer to drive these winding roads than the actual distances would suggest.

---

feature is the L-shaped nave which segregates men and women attending the same service.

On the opposite corner of the square, the Rathaus (Town Hall) tower affords superb views over the town and the surrounding countryside. Back at street level, take the time for a stroll through the charming shopping arcades built into the houses surrounding the square.

⌐i⌐ *Marktplatz 64*

▷ *Take the **B28** northeast for 52km (32 miles) to Herrenberg.*

Spectacular views from The Batter rock, above Baden-Baden

Atmospheric, old timber-framed buildings in Herrenberg

2 **Herrenberg,** Baden-Württemberg

Herrenberg lies on the western border of the Naturpark Schönbuch and the 750-year-old Schlossbergturm (Castle Tower) gives a good view of the whole town, dominated by the Stiftskirche's mighty tower. The Gothic church, which was built between 1275 and 1294, features a late Gothic font, a 16th-century carved pulpit and a heavily decorated choir section dating from 1517.

[i] *Marktplatz 5*

▶ *Follow the B14, A81 and B14 again northeast to Stuttgart.*

3 **Stuttgart,** Baden-Württemberg

Capital of the province of Baden-Württemberg, Stuttgart is situated at the bottom of a wide valley surrounded by hills, bordered to the northeast by the River Neckar and the adjoining town of Bad Cannstatt.

Duke Liutolf set up a stud here in around 950. The town's name is derived from *Stute*, the German word for mare, and *Garten*, literally 'mare's garden'. The city's coat of arms bears a black horse.

The most impressive and important square in town is Schlossplatz (Castle Square), across which the Altes Schloss (Old Castle) and the Neues Schloss (New Castle) face each other. The old castle is a massive Renaissance building,

erected in the second half of the 16th century. The arcaded castle yard is particularly attractive and the castle houses the Landesmuseum collections of medieval artworks, Württemberg's crown jewels, examples of historic costumes and archaeological finds. Adjoining the castle, Schillerplatz is notable for the historic buildings that surround it. There is the oldest church in Stuttgart, the Stiftskirche, which was founded in the 12th century; the Fruchtkasten, a wonderful medieval building of 1393; and the Prinzenbau (Dukes' Building), designed to contain the living quarters of the Erbprinz Friedrich Ludwig. At the centre of the square stands a monument to the poet Schiller.

Back on Schlossplatz, the Neues Schloss was built along the lines of a French baroque castle between 1746 and 1807; it was all but destroyed in World War II. The façade was restored between 1959 and 1962, and the interior converted to house government offices as well as to host receptions.

The west side of the Schlossplatz borders Stuttgart's

SPECIAL TO...

A visit to the Mercedes Benz Museum in Stuttgart-Untertürkheim is a must for motoring enthusiasts. Like Rolls and Royce, Daimler and Benz were – and the companies still are – pioneers in the development of motor vehicles. Exhibits range from the early days of motor transport right through to the most recent models, and modern demonstration techniques make this a fascinating visit. Another famous maufacturer, Porsche, is based at Zuffenhausen, just north of Stuttgart. The business was started here in 1931, and all Porsche models are pure sports and high-perfomance cars.

main thoroughfare. A pedestrian zone, it is lined with all the best shops and businesses.

ℹ️ *Königstrasse 1a*

▶ *From Stuttgart take the B27 south, via Waldenbuch, to Tübingen, 40km (25 miles).*

4 Tübingen, Baden-Württemberg
There is a very good view of Tübingen's Altstadt (Old Town) from Platanenallee on the right bank of the River Neckar. The Old Town rises steeply from the Neckar, sandwiched between the green knoll of the castle hill and the Hölderlin tower.

In Holzmarkt (Timber Market) the late Gothic Stiftskirche is a church dating

Enjoying the view of baroque-style Neues Schloss in the Schlosspark at Stuttgart

from the 15th century. It houses several beautifully decorated tombs created for members of the House of Württemberg. When the great German poet Goethe visited the church, he described the stained-glass windows as 'items of supreme glory'.

The 15th-century Rathaus (Town Hall) is a really magnificent building on the market square. Its astronomical clock was added in 1511. The Neptune market fountain in front of the Rathaus was erected in 1615 and the whole market square is surrounded by marvellous medieval houses.

RECOMMENDED WALKS

The Black Forest region extends from Baden-Baden southwards to the Rhine and the Swiss border. It provides a staggering number of suggestions for walks, plus maps and information, including the approximate duration of each route.
Local information offices usually provide village maps and many offer to introduce visitors to the innovative Wandern Ohne Gepäck (hiking without luggage) concept. Certain villages and small hotels co-operate in the scheme by transporting your luggage from one stop to the next.

[i] *An der Neckarbrücke*

▷ *Take the B28 east for 13km (8 miles) to Reutlingen.*

5 Reutlingen, Baden-Württemberg
Reutlingen's Tübinger Tor (gate) is one of the old city gateways built in the 13th century. Its timber-framed upper storey was added in the 16th century to provide a better lookout and it somehow survived the great fire of 1726.

Another landmark is the Marienkirche, a particularly beautiful example of early Gothic style. The Holy Sepulchre in the choir section is late Gothic.

The main artery of the town is Wilhelmstrasse, a pedestrian precinct that is ideal for strolling along and admiring the interesting architecture. The Nikolaikirche overlooks a charming fountain erected by the tanners' and dyers' guild, while the mighty Spendhaus, built in 1518, now houses the town's art museum.

[i] *Listplatz 1*

FOR HISTORY BUFFS

Three beautiful 16th-century fountains can be admired in Reutlingen: the Lindenbrunnen, erected in 1544; the Kirchbrunnen, with a statue of Emperor Friedrich II, built in 1561; and the 1570 Marktbrunnen, adorned by a statue of Maximilian II.

▷ *From Reutlingen take the B312 south to Lichtenstein.*

6 Lichtenstein, Baden-Württemberg
In the heart of the mountainous Swabian Jura, three villages joined together to form the town of Lichtenstein. In 1826, author Wilhelm Hauff published *Lichtenstein*, a novel about the town's old fortress

which had been demolished in 1802. This novel inspired Count Wilhelm von Württemberg to make plans for a new castle to be built on the same spot, and so the present edifice took shape from 1840 to 1842. It looks like an image from a fairy-tale and the design must have been influenced by Hauff's works.

Following a scramble up to the belvederes above the castle, there is an excellent detour to be made to the Nebelhöhle cave in nearby Unterhausen. The main part of the cave complex was discovered in 1920 and a 380m (1,246-foot) long walkway has been constructed for easy access. The view of the stalagmites and stalactites is superb, and the formations are brilliantly enhanced by well-placed illuminations.

[i] *Rathausplatz 17*

BACK TO NATURE

Almost anywhere in the Schwarzwald is a good habitat for birds. Look for woodpeckers, collared flycatchers, Bonelli's warblers and red kites. Plants include coralroot orchids and yellow wood violets.

▷ *From Lichtenstein take the B313 south for 21km (13 miles) to Gammertingen, then the B32 for 26km (16 miles) to Hechingen.*

7 Hechingen, Baden-Württemberg
From fairy-tale castle to historic fortress, the imposing Burg Hohenzollern, seat of the kings of Prussia, perches on an 856m (2,808-foot) rocky outcrop. Plans for the old fortress were used for the new building, constructed between 1850 and 1867, but only the 15th-century Catholic Chapel of St Michael remains from the original site. The fortress treasury contains memorabilia of Friedrich der

Grosse (Frederick the Great), decorations and insignia belonging to Wilhelm II, the crown of the Prussian kings and many works of art. On Schlossplatz (Castle Square), the Altes Schloss (Old Castle), former seat of the Dukes of Hechingen, now houses the local Heimatmuseum.

In 1976 the ruins of a Roman villa were discovered about 3km (1¾ miles) north-west of Hechingen. The remains date back to the 1st to 3rd centuries AD. Parts of the villa have been reconstructed.

[i] *Kirchplatz 12*

▷ *From Hechingen take the B27 for 15km (9 miles) to Balingen.*

8 Balingen, Baden-Württemberg
Balingen's Protestant parish church is in the market square. It was erected between 1443 and 1516, and the ceiling of the pulpit and the crucifix are the work of local sculptor Simon Schweitzer. Also of interest is the chapel in the cemetery, which is decorated with late Gothic wall paintings. An attractive corner of town is the 'Little Venice' district, so named for the millstream which flows down past the old tanneries and remnants of the city wall.

The Museum für Waage und Gewicht (Scales and Weights Museum) pays tribute to local priest Philipp Matthäus Hahn, who invented a simple scale that could be used in the home, a precursor of the more modern appliances.

[i] *Färberstrasse 21*

▷ *From Balingen continue due west via Oberndorf to Alpirsbach.*

9 Alpirsbach, Baden-Württemberg
The abbey church of the former Benedictine Kloster Alpirsbach dates back to the 12th century. The basilica, with its three

naves, has undergone several enlargements and attempts at restoration, but has remained largely intact.

South of the church are the cloister buildings where international orchestras perform in summer. The candlelit surroundings and excellent acoustics create an unforgettable atmosphere.

☐ *Hauptstrasse 20*

▶ *Take the **B294** south to Schiltach and continue on the **B462** to Schramberg. Turn right to Hornberg, then right again on the **B33** to Gutach, 39km (24 miles).*

🔟 Gutach, Baden-Württemberg

North of Gutach, sited on the Hausach road, the Freilichtmuseum Vogtsbauernhof is a fascinating open-air museum illustrating life in the Black Forest. Typical 16th- and 17th-century houses have been re-created with original furnishings and traditional artefacts and utensils to give the visitor a real insight into local lifestyles in former times. There are even old water-powered saw-mills shown in full working order.

A monument to the 'Mourning Lady of Gutach' is a popular subject for snapshots. It portrays a grieving girl in front of a small rock, crying for those lost in the wars.

☐ *Im Bahnhof Bleibach*

▶ *Take the **B33** north, then west via Hausach for 29km (18 miles) to Gengenbach.*

11 Gengenbach, Baden-Württemberg

Gengenbach fulfils all one's expectations of a small, romantic German town. It has been placed under a preservation order and its timber-framed houses, gates and towers linked by sections of the old walls exude a timeless charm. There is a remarkable market-place edged by the Rathaus

(Town Hall) built in 1784, the Kauf und Kornhaus of 1696 and numerous well-preserved 17th-to 18th-century patrician houses.

☐ *Winzerhof, Höllengasse 2*

▶ *From Gengenbach continue northwest for 11km (7 miles) to Offenburg.*

12 Offenburg, Baden-Württemberg

Offenburg lies on the outskirts of the Black Forest, between sloping vineyards and the plains of the Rhine Valley. The Marktplatz is the centre of the town, bordered by the Rathaus (Town Hall), which was built in 1741. Northwest of Marktplatz, the interior of the Heilige Kreuzkirche (Church of the Holy Cross) is dominated by an imposing high altar. Other historic sights include the Fischmarkt (Fish Market), St Andreas' Kirche, the Löwenbrunnen (Lion Fountain) and the Hirschapotheke (Pharmacy).

☐ *Fischmarkt 2*

Tübingen's old Rathaus (note the *trompe-l'oeil* paintings)

▶ *Return to Baden-Baden on the **B3**, 42km (26 miles).*

FOR CHILDREN

The Europa-Park at Rust is one of the largest and most successful amusement parks in Europe. To get there, drive south from Offenburg on the A5 in the direction of Lahr, then take the Rust 57b exit, and turn west for 3.5km (2 miles) to Rust. Follow signs to Europa-Park. A trip on the suspended monorail around the grounds gives a good overview of what is in store. Children will enjoy Chocoland, a so-called 'chocolate laboratory', where they can make their own chocolates. Other attractions include wild torrent rides, trips on the Swiss Bobsleigh, Acapulco 'death divers', high-wire acts and dolphin and sea-lion performances.

THE FIVE RIVER VALLEYS

Rivers play an important part in this region, and many towns were created using them for transport; Köln on the Rhine, Trier on the Mosel, Koblenz at the confluence of the Mosel and Rhine, Frankfurt on the Main and Heidelberg on the Neckar. The most prominent of all is the Rhine. Hilly woodlands and the lower-lying vineyards put their pleasant mark on the countryside. This is the centre of the German wine-growing area, and the famous labels of the distinctive Rhine and Mosel wines are internationally known.

History has been made here since Roman times, but credit must be given to the Emperor Charlemagne who, in the 9th century, united the people of the former Roman provinces of Gaul and Germania and made Aachen (Aix-la-Chapelle) the capital of his new Empire of the West. Christianity then brought further cultural advancement and the most remarkable expressions of human creativity and effort can be seen in the magnificent cathedrals of this region.

The River Mosel at Zell, a charming wine-town whose round tower was part of its medieval defences

Thanks to centuries of skirmishing and warring between medieval knights for power and wealth, the process that Charlemagne began at Aachen took 1,000 years to complete. One of the most famous aggressors of history, Napoleon Bonaparte, finally provided the impetus for the new empires of the 19th century.

The region has special appeal for those who want to be active on their vacation. There is an abundance of walks on offer for serious hikers, all well mapped out. The constant flow of the rivers provides the backdrop for tours here and visitors may choose to become part of the busy river traffic, or just enjoy it from afar. There is always something new round every bend in the mountain roads. Nature also plays a big part in this area with many nature parks and wild deer roaming about the forests. The evenings are something to look forward to, sitting on the banks of the Rhine or Mosel rivers watching the world go by, trying a sample of the delicious local produce. Touring in this part of Germany promises to be both interesting and enjoyable.

Approaching the town of Cochem along the Mosel River

Tour 21

This tour starts in an area of large coal deposits, but with a difference. Pleasant mountainous countryside and a zest for culture among the population make it a fascinating part of Germany. The river has a deep green colour here, and is all the more startling when one of the enormous coal-carrying ships suddenly comes into view.

Tour 22

The starting point of this tour is difficult to leave as it is so full of historical interest. But a treat is in store – one of the most pleasant and enjoyable drives in Germany, along the Mosel River, surrounded by vineyards. An unconquered fortress offers an exciting visit before Koblenz is reached. Wine and the Rhine accompany the tour until it turns back into hiking country and the Mosel.

Tour 23

Heidelberg is at the start of this tour, but it then leaves the Neckar Valley to take in some of the forests and attractive towns to the north. One of Germany's most treasured towns is on the itinerary. The tour then turns back to the long-awaited Neckar, with many pleasure boats plying up- and down-stream. Before returning there is a short interlude in the woods off the Neckar which provides an interesting diversion.

Tour 24

Skyscrapers and finance put their stamp on the starting point of this tour. Then the route skirts along the 'Limes', the Roman border against the Germanic tribes. A famous spa and historic town are passed before the river is met again, further north. Ruins, castles and vineyards form the surroundings, and there are always ships on the Rhine. One of Germany's most elegant spas and a retreat from the business of the nearby financial world – Wiesbaden – is the last town before returning.

Tour 25

Perhaps the most magnificent of all Gothic churches stands at the start of this tour. Turning south, it takes in an eminent schloss and continues to what was once a sleepy little town on the Rhine, but made important through music and politics. The pleasant countryside around makes this a very attractive route to follow. Before returning to the start, the tour visits one of the oldest historical towns in Germany.

Aachen's cathedral was founded by Charlemagne in AD 800

The Tranquil
Saar Valley

2/3 DAYS • 438KM • 273 MILES Although Saarbrücken has a Celtic and Roman past, this 'bridge over the Saar' came into its own in the 19th century with the discovery and exploitation of its iron ore and coal deposits. St Johann is the hub of the town. From Schlossplatz walk to the Alte Brücke (Old Bridge) and stroll across to the other side of the river.

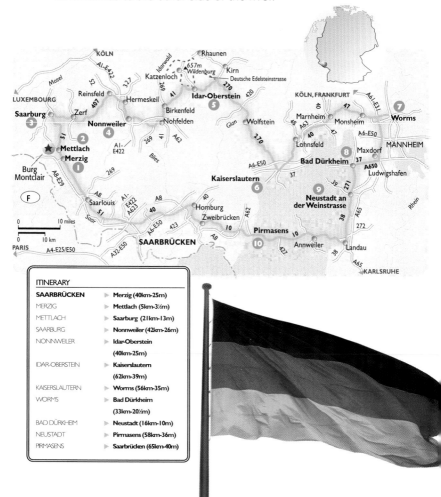

ITINERARY

SAARBRÜCKEN	▶ **Merzig (40km-25m)**
MERZIG	▶ **Mettlach (5km-3½m)**
METTLACH	▶ **Saarburg (21km-13m)**
SAARBURG	▶ **Nonnweiler (42km-26m)**
NONNWEILER	▶ **Idar-Oberstein**
	(40km-25m)
IDAR-OBERSTEIN	▶ **Kaiserslautern**
	(62km-39m)
KAISERSLAUTERN	▶ **Worms (56km-35m)**
WORMS	▶ **Bad Dürkheim**
	(33km-20½m)
BAD DÜRKHEIM	▶ **Neustadt (16km-10m)**
NEUSTADT	▶ **Pirmasens (58km-36m)**
PIRMASENS	▶ **Saarbrücken (65km-40m)**

▶ *From Saarbrücken take the*
B51 northwest for 40km
(25 miles) to Merzig.

❶ Merzig, Saarland
The Stiftskirche in Merzig can
perhaps claim a record for the
time it took to be built – started
in the 12th century and only
completely finished in the 19th.
As a result it is a mixture of
styles. Among the elaborate
decorations inside is a crucifix
from 1300, one of the best-

SCENIC ROUTES

The stretch from Merzig to
Mettlach along the Saar river is
very scenic. The following trips
are also worth making: from
Idar-Oberstein northwest into
the Idar mountains, and a
round trip taking the B422 to
Katzenloch, then northeast to
Rhaunen, south to Kirn and
back to Idar-Oberstein.

---

preserved items of this period.
The Rathaus (Town Hall) was
originally built between 1647
and 1650 as a hunting lodge for
the Elector of Trier, but was
later remodelled several times.

i *Poststrasse 12*

▶ *From Merzig take the B51*
north for 5km (3½ miles)
to Mettlach.

❷ Mettlach, Saarland
On the east side of the Saar
river, Mettlach has many attractions. The former Benedictine
abbey, built in the 18th century,
is in baroque style. Today it
houses one of the largest ceramics factories in the world
(Villeroy & Boch). The modern
town is dominated by ceramics
and the Keramisck Museum, in
the former Benediktinerabtei
(abbey), displays several
centuries worth of ceramics.
The restored Schloss
Ziegelberg (1878) houses an
elegant restaurant. One of the
main attractions in the area is

The Altfels rock formations
near Saarburg

the Saarschleife, a loop in the
Saar river, which can best be
seen from the ruins of the Burg
(fortress) Montclair, about 2km
(1½ miles) to the west.
    The original fortress was
built around the 9th century,
but existing remains are from
the 15th century. Later, the
fortress fell into gradual decay,
and the rocks and cliffs now
provide an ideal observation
platform.

i *Freiherr-vom-Stein-Strasse 64*

▶ *From Mettlach continue*
north along the Saar via the
B51 for 21km (13 miles)
to Saarburg.

❸ Saarburg, Rheinland-Pfalz
Saarburg is the centre for wine-
growing in the Saar region. The
town lies on both sides of the
river and the Leukbach, a small
stream with its noisy waterfall,
flows through the middle.

Marks on the houses still bear witness to the flooding of the Saar in former times.

Saarburg's other claim to fame is the casting of church bells, an industry here since the 17th century. The foundry is open to the public.

Also worth a visit are the ruins of the Saarburg fortress and the church of St Marien, which has attracted many generations of pilgrims.

ⓘ *Graf-Siegfried-Strasse 32*

▶ *From Saarburg take the **B407** east and turn left at Reinsfeld for the **B52** to Nonnweiler.*

4 **Nonnweiler,** Saarland
Surrounded by woods, Nonnweiler prides itself on its healthy climate and offers many relaxing walks through the countryside, especially round its large man-made lake.

On the slopes of the Dollberg (mountain) in Otzenhausen is the Hunnenring – a ringed wall which is up to 10m (33 feet) high in some places. It is estimated to be some 2,000 years old.

ⓘ *Triererstrasse 5*

▶ *Continue east to Nohfelden, turn left, then take the **B41** north to Idar-Oberstein, 40km (25 miles).*

5 **Idar-Oberstein,**
Rheinland-Pfalz
A most striking sight here is the Felsenkirche (Church in the Rock), built in a grotto in the rocks that soar high above the town. The church is in Gothic style and dates from 1482. A painted, winged altar of the 15th century has been incorporated into the building. Although it looks quite small when viewed from the Marktplatzbrücke, the church can hold 500 worshippers at a time. The town is known for its precious stones and diamond industry. The Deutsches Edelsteinmuseum (Precious

FOR HISTORY BUFFS

From Idar-Oberstein take the B422 northwest to Katzenloch, then turn right to Kempfeld. Up on a rocky hill stands the ruin of the fortress Wildenburg, whose origins date back to the Celts. Parts have been reconstructed to demonstrate the original design.

Stones Museum) exhibits samples from all over the world, in their raw and polished state.

At the historic working museum Weiherschleife, stones are polished in the old way, by using water power. Of course the industry now uses more modern methods. The Idar-Oberstein Museum also has interesting displays of raw materials, and fluorescent and precious stones.

SPECIAL TO...

A well-mapped-out circular route from Idar-Oberstein passes through a number of villages on the Deutsche Edelsteinstrasse (German Gems Road). There are about 60 traditional factories that transform raw stones from all over the world into gems. The sign of a cut diamond on the road shows directions to these places, and also denotes factories that can be visited. Lapidary seminars are offered and a master goldsmith arranges courses for those who wish to make their own jewellery.

Also recommended is a visit to the former copper mine, the Besucherbergwerk, at Fischbach, where green- and turquoise-coloured seams contain copper deposits. The

historic Edelsteinminen (Precious Stones Mine) in the Steinkaulenberg is open to the public and offers a fascinating insight into this industry.

ⓘ *Hauptstrasse 419*

BACK TO NATURE

Near Ruin Wildenburg is a memorable animal park with indigenous wildlife (deer, stags and wild boar). There are also enclosures housing animals from Asia and colourful birds (peacocks, wild geese, wild ducks and pheasants).
If you drive into the Idar Mountains, be sure to keep your eyes open for birds such as red kites, sparrowhawks, hobbies, Bonelli's warblers and middle-spotted woodpeckers, which live in the forests, as do wild boar.

▶ *From Idar-Oberstein continue on the B41 northeast, then turn sharp right for the B270 to Kaiserslautern.*

6 Kaiserslautern,
Rheinland-Pfalz
Kaiserslautern has great historic associations with the 12th-century Emperor Friedrich Barbarossa (Redbeard). There are only a few remnants left of the old castle, which are incorporated in the Rathaus. The Stiftskirche is an important church in early Gothic style and was built in the 13th and 14th centuries. An ante-room displays a monument erected in 1883 to commemorate the union of the Lutheran and Calvinist branches of Protestantism.
   The Fruchthalle, formerly the fruit and vegetable market, was built in Renaissance style between 1843 and 1846 but

The River Saar loops through the countryside near Dreisbach

now functions as a banqueting hall for official receptions. The Pfalzgalerie in Museum-platz shows the work of local painters, sculptors and graphic artists.

ⓘ *Fruchthallstrasse 14*

▶ *From Kaiserslautern take the B40 northeast to Marnheim, then turn right for the B47 to Worms, 56km (35 miles).*

7 Worms, Rheinland-Pfalz
The curiously named Worms is one of the oldest towns in Germany. Religion has played an important part in its turbulent history, and the number of churches testifies to that. There was a bishopric here from the 4th century. The Dom of St Peter and St Paul is a Catholic cathedral known to be one of

the finest constructions in late
Romanesque style in the
Rheinland. The high altar is by
the famous Balthasar Neumann,
and the late Gothic sandstone
reliefs from the demolished
cloisters are also worth noting.
The Gothic Liebfrauenkirche
(Church of Our Lady) stands
amongst vineyards which
produce the famous wine called
Liebfraumilch. There is a
monument to Luther on
Lutherplatz.

[i] *Neumarkt 14*

▶ *From Worms join the A61*
west of town, drive due
south to the exit west of
Ludwigshafen and follow
the B37 via Maxdorf to the
B271 and Bad Dürkheim,
33km (20½ miles).

8 Bad Dürkheim,
Rheinland-Pfalz
This officially designated spa is
in the middle of a major wine-
producing region. The warm
spa waters are used to cure a
variety of ailments. There is

also a casino for those seeking
financial cures.
    The ruin of the Kloster
Limburg was bought by the
council in 1847 and the gardens
were developed in the English
style. Concerts and open-air
performances take place here
in the summer.
    For those who enjoy
wandering round ruins, try
Burgruine Hardenburg, 4km
(2½ miles) west of the town.
This building was first
mentioned in 1093, but met
with misfortune later. In 1692
it was blown up, and in 1794
burnt down.

[i] *Kurbrunnenstrasse 14*

▶ *Continue south on the B271*
to Neustadt.

9 Neustadt, Rheinland-Pfalz
The town's full name is
Neustadt-an-der-Weinstrasse
(Neustadt-on-the-Wine-Road),
which gives a strong hint as to
the major activity around here.
As the centre of the largest
German wine-growing area, the

Balthasar Neumann's extravagant
high altar, a masterpiece of craftsmanship in Worms' Cathedral

town is also called the 'Wine
Capital'. The centre has well-
preserved houses with old interior courtyards. The Stiftskirche
is 600 years old and still has the
town watchman's apartment in
the southern tower, occupied
until only a few years ago. The
church claims to have the
largest church bell in the world,
which is housed in the tower.
    Schloss Hambach is noted
for a meeting that took place on
27 May, 1832, when 25,000
democratically orientated
people supported a call from 34
citizens of Neustadt to demand
German unity. It was here that
the black, red and gold flag as a
symbol of a united Germany
was hoisted for the first time.

[i] *Hetzelplatz 1*

▶ *From Neustadt take the B38*
south towards Landau, then
turn right for the B10 west to
Pirmasens, 58km (36 miles).

FOR CHILDREN

Take the children to the Hassloch Holiday Park about 9km (6 miles) east of Neustadt. Apart from the usual fun runs there are several special shows for entertainment: the water-ski show, 'The Treasure of the Seven Seas', 'The Wonders of Radscha', and the 'Sun Tseng Hai Show'.

RECOMMENDED WALKS

There are pleasant walks just off the Deutsche Weinstrasse (German Wine Road). Stop at Annweiler, about halfway between Neustadt and Pirmasens, and walk up to the Burg Trifels, about 1km (½ mile). Here you can see the dungeon where Richard the Lionheart of England was imprisoned in 1193. He was finally released after a huge ransom had been paid.

❿ Pirmasens, Rheinland-Pfalz

The lively town centre is built around the wide Schlossplatz (Castle Square) which forms a well-designed pedestrian precinct. Shoe manufacture is the major industry in town – the German college for shoe manufacture is also housed here. Nearly all the historic buildings in the town were destroyed during bombing raids in World War II. Of interest, however, are the attractive dual staircases, the so-called Ramba-Treppen, which have water cascading down between them.

🛈 *Exerzierplatzstrasse 3*

▶ *Take the B10, then the B423 to Homburg. Turn left and return on the B40 west to Saarbrücken.*

The dual Ramba-Treppen staircase, a prominent feature in Germany's footwear capital, Pirmasens

The Enchanting
Mosel Valley

Long before Rome was founded – legend says around 2050 BC – there was a settlement at Trier. The city blossomed under the Romans, but later was repeatedly attacked by invading Vandals. It is now a major tourist attraction.

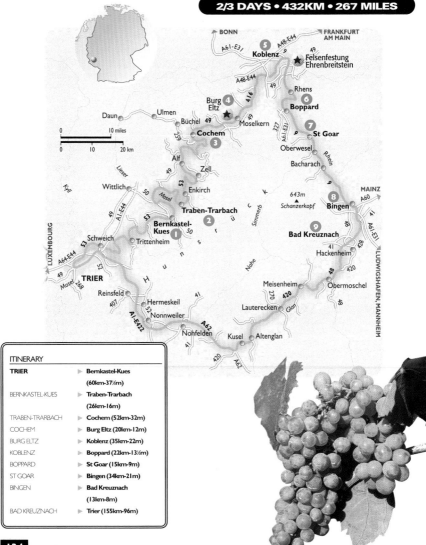

2/3 DAYS • 432KM • 267 MILES

i̇ *Porta Nigra, Trier*

▶ *From Trier join the **B53** north-east to Bernkastel-Kues, 60km (37½ miles).*

FOR CHILDREN

The Spielzeugmuseum (Toy Museum) in Hauptmarkt in Trier should amuse children, and will probably arouse childhood nostalgia in adults. Three floors contain a selection which includes metal toys, model railways, dolls' houses, cuddly toys and rocking horses.

❶ Bernkastel-Kues,
Rheinland-Pfalz

The square of this picturesque town is surrounded by timber-framed houses, with the fountain of St Michael in its centre, and the Rathaus (Town Hall) which was built in 1608. Fascinating but not quite so picturesque are the iron chains of the Pranger (stocks), the public punishment of the Middle Ages, preserved here. The parish church of St Michael dates from the 14th century and contains interesting works by a

View of the Mosel Valley and the wine centre of Bernkastel-Kues

local sculptor, Hans Ruprecht Hoffmann. Bernkastel-Kues has a wine museum, and the Bernkastler wine is well-known.

South of Bernkastel stands the ruin of the Landshut, the second fortress to be built on the same site, in 1280.

i̇ *Gestade 6*

▶ *Continue on the **B53** for 26km (16 miles) to Traben-Trarbach.*

FOR HISTORY BUFFS

St Nikolaus-Hospital in Bernkastel-Kues dates back to a donation in 1447 by scientist and philosopher Cardinal Nikolaus Krebs. He dedicated the hospital to 33 poor men of the village. Krebs died in 1465 and his tombstone lies in the hospital chapel. Of special interest in the chapel are the high altar paintings which show the *Passion of Christ* and are the work of an artist from Köln (Cologne).

SPECIAL TO...

En route from Bernkastel-Kues to Traben-Trarbach, branch off after crossing the Mosel past Zeltingen and drive for about 11km (6½ miles) to Wittlich. Every year in mid-August the town celebrates a festival called the Saubrenner-Kirmes (Festival of the Burnt Sows). The story goes that one evening, when the town was under attack, the gatekeeper could not find the bolt to lock up the gates so he used a turnip in its place. A sow looking for food ate the turnip and thus opened the gate for the conquerors. As punishment, the citizens drove all the pigs to the marketplace and burnt them.

❷ Traben-Trarbach,
Rheinland-Pfalz

A trip to the ruins of the fortress Grevenburg above Traben-Trarbach offers rewarding views over the town and the picturesque Mosel Valley. Between 1520 and 1734 the fortress was besieged six times and then blown up, so it is small wonder that only a fragment of a wall with window holes is left.

The little town of Zell, on the other side of the river, should not be missed. It appears to be built into the landscape with vineyards all around it. The castle is now a hotel. Emperor Maximilian lived here at one time and it contains many treasures. Zeller Schwarze Katz (Black Cat) is a popular wine from the local grapes.

ⓘ *Am Bahnhof 5*

▶ *Continue on the **B53**, then the **B49** to Cochem.*

❸ Cochem, Rheinland-Pfalz
A real centre for tourism in the Mosel Valley is Cochem, which also lies in an important wine-growing area. The former Reichsburg, (imperial castle), was rebuilt in 1874, using plans from 1576. It affords splendid views over the Mosel Valley and

Cochem, with its romantic castle, the former Reichsburg, overlooking the Mosel

its vineyards, which stretch from the river's edge and up into the hills.

ⓘ *Endertplatz 1*

▶ *From Cochem continue on the **B49/B416** and turn left at Moselkern for Burg Eltz.*

BACK TO NATURE

Take the B259 south of Cochem uphill via Buchel to Ulmen for 21km (13 miles) and turn left for the B257 to Daun. The area around Daun is called the Vulkaneifel (Volcanic Eifel) after the Eifel mountain range. The craters hereabouts were formed 10,000 years ago and have since filled with water.

They are located south of Daun and are called Maaren. Their depths range from 38 to 74m (75 to 242 feet) and some offer bathing, boat hire and fishing. In some places you can still see bubbles of gas rising from the bottom of the crater.

Boppard, a large, pleasant resort, especially at wine-festival time, has many Rhineside cafés

❹ Burg Eltz, Rheinland-Pfalz
High above the wine-producing village of Moselkern stands the

burg or fortress of Eltz, one of the most rewarding attractions in the area. Numerous oriels and towers and a superb position made this fortress unconquerable for centuries. Even now, cars find the ascent difficult. The road stops at the Antonius Chapel, and the last few hundred metres have to be covered on foot or by shuttle bus. The knights of Eltz were called the Eisenköpfe (Iron Heads), a tribute to their stubbornness as well as to the numerous skirmishes in which they took part. The guided tour around the fortress is accompanied by many entertaining stories and anecdotes.

▶ *From Burg Eltz return to Moselkern, then turn left on the B416 to Koblenz.*

5 Koblenz, Rheinland-Pfalz
Where the Mosel enters the mighty Rhine lies Koblenz. Its unique situation has made it a place of great importance from Roman times. Koblenz's name is derived from the Roman *castrum ad confluentes*, the 'camp at the confluence'. It is not known when the Romans actually established their outpost here, but it must have been

before the reign of Emperor Tiberius (AD 14–37).

After almost total wartime destruction, part of the old centre of Koblenz has been meticulously restored. The actual point of land where the Mosel and Rhine meet is called the Deutsches Eck (German Corner), marked by a monument to German unity.

The Festung Ehrenbreitstein (Rock Fortress) dominates the Rhine and Mosel and is supposedly the largest fortress in Europe. It is best reached by chair-lift. The view from the fortress's terrace is spectacular, down to Koblenz and in the distance to the Eifel and Hunsrück mountain ranges. The fortress was always a thorn in the flesh of the French, and Napoleon destroyed it in 1801. It was subsequently rebuilt, but a clause in the Treaty of Versailles after World War I stated it must never again be used for military purposes. It now houses the Rhine Museum.

The former Kurfürstliches Schloss, or Residenzschloss as it is also known, was once the seat of Prince Wilhelm von Preussen and until 1918 it was owned by the Prussian kings. It now

SCENIC ROUTES

The drive from Trier through the Mosel Valley is an enjoyable one but bear in mind that the many twists and turns of the road should dictate a careful speed. Allow ample time for the bends, but also stop to enjoy the views. The route from Koblenz to Bingen along the Rhine Valley is full of dramatic scenery.

belongs to the state and is used for administrative purposes.

Schloss Stolzenfels, which was built in 1242, is a former royal castle. It was destroyed by the French in 1688 and rebuilt after 1836. Its interior is worth seeing, especially the large Rittersaal (Knights' Hall) and the King's quarters.

ℹ *Bahnhofplatz 17*

▶ *From Koblenz take the B9 south for 22km (14 miles) to Boppard.*

6 Boppard, Rheinland-Pfalz
At a bend in the Rhine lies Boppard, a very old settlement which the Celts called

Bandobriga. Later the Romans erected fortifications here around AD 400, and parts of the 8m (26-foot) high walls can still be seen. St Severuskirche (Church of St Severus) is late Romanesque. The Karmeliterkirche is interesting; it has no tower, which is very rare for a Gothic church. The Alte Burg (Old Castle), dating from the 14th century, now houses the Museum der Stadt Boppard.

[i] *Marktplatz, Altes Rathaus*

▶ *Continue south on the B9 for 15km (9 miles) to St Goar.*

7 St Goar, Rheinland-Pfalz
In the Middle Ages, many knights living in fortresses on narrow stretches of river supplemented their incomes by collecting tolls from passing ships – or just simply robbing them. They were the so-called Raubritter (robbing knights). One such fortress was 13th-century Burg Rheinfels, just before St Goar. This former royal castle is now a pleasant hotel. The Stiftskirche in St Goar is a delightful mixture of styles. The church itself is 15th-century, the crypt is Romanesque and the marble tombs are from the 16th and 17th centuries.

[i] *Heerstrasse 86*

▶ *From St Goar continue south on the B9 to Bingen, 34km (21 miles).*

8 Bingen, Rheinland-Pfalz
The Burg Klopp fortress, which overlooks Bingen, was built on a Roman site with a deep well of 52m (170 feet), which probably goes back to the same period. The fortress was destroyed in 1689, and the remnants blown

Castle ruins on the hillside above the village of St Goar

up in 1711, but between 1875 and 1879, it was totally rebuilt. The town has an interesting Heimatmuseum (local museum) which contains pre-historic exhibits.

On an island in the river stands the Mäuseturm (Mice Tower). This stone construction dates from 1208 and replaced a wooden Roman tower erected in 8 BC under the Roman military leader Drusus. Legend has it that when Bishop Hatto was thrown into the tower as a punishment for his cruelties, he was eaten alive by mice.

[i] *Rheinkai 21*

▶ *From Bingen continue due south on the B48 to Bad Kreuznach, 13km (8 miles).*

❾ Bad Kreuznach,
Rheinland-Pfalz

This sizeable spa lies on the River Nahe, and its thermal springs are used as the basis for well-organised treatments for rheumatism, gout and similar ailments. Unique to the town are the well-preserved Brücken-hauser (Bridge Houses). These date from the 15th century, and have been chosen as the town

The main market square in Trier, probably the oldest city in Germany

emblem. In the Römerhalle Museum, Roman mosaics and remains from the military camp are on view.

ℹ *Kurhausstrasse 22–24*

▶ *From Bad Kreuznach take the **B48**, then the **B420** south to Kusel. Join the **A62** and travel northwest towards Nonnweiler. Continue on the **A11/E422** north to exit Moseltal, then southwest to Trier on the **A602/B49**, 155km (96 miles).*

RECOMMENDED
WALKS

Drive to one of the Wanderparkplätze, car-parks usually marked with a green 'W' and the starting point for a hike. From the Rotenfels car-park there is a good brisk walk up to the Schanzenkopf. After a short drive to Hackenheim, walk to the nearby recreation area of Schloss Rheingrafenstein.

The Romantic
Neckar

Heidelberg is a charming and picturesque town. It is also ancient. 'Heidelberg Man', evidence of the earliest human life in Europe, is in fact a 500,000-year-old jawbone found near here. More recently, Heidelberg was completely rebuilt in the 17th-century baroque style after Louis XIV had destroyed much of the city.

2 DAYS • 459KM • 286 MILES

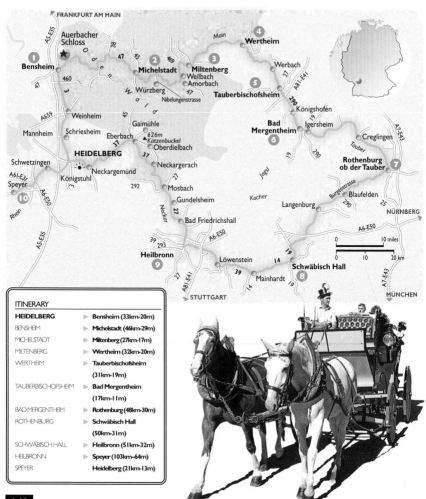

ITINERARY

HEIDELBERG	▶ Bensheim (33km-20m)
BENSHEIM	▶ Michelstadt (46km-29m)
MICHELSTADT	▶ Miltenberg (27km-17m)
MILTENBERG	▶ Wertheim (32km-20m)
WERTHEIM	▶ Tauberbischofsheim
	(31km-19m)
TAUBERBISCHOFSHEIM	▶ Bad Mergentheim
	(17km-11m)
BAD MERGENTHEIM	▶ Rothenburg (48km-30m)
ROTHENBURG	▶ Schwäbisch Hall
	(50km-31m)
SCHWÄBISCH HALL	▶ Heilbronn (51km-32m)
HEILBRONN	▶ Speyer (103km-64m)
SPEYER	▶ Heidelberg (21km-13m)

i   *Willy-Brandt-Platz 1*

▶ *From Heidelberg take the*
 B3 north to Bensheim.

1 Bensheim, Hessen
About 5km (3 miles) from the
town, the former fortress
Schloss Auerbach is protected
by an encircling wall and two
high watch-towers. Although
the fortress is now really only a
well-preserved ruin, it is a very
popular spot in the area. Built in
the 13th century on the slopes
of the Schlossberg (Castle
Mountain), it could at that time
only be entered by the draw-
bridge. It is now used for
medieval and other events.

Landgrave Count Ludwig
erected a small manor house,
called the Schlösschen, near
mineral springs between 1790
and 1795, and in the garden is
possibly the highest Mammut
tree in Europe, 53m (173 feet)
high and 5m (16 feet) thick.

i   *Hauptstrasse 39*

▶ *From Bensheim take the*
 B47 northeast for 46km
 (29 miles) to Michelstadt.

2 Michelstadt, Hessen
There are delightful medieval
timber-framed buildings here,
none so delightful as the fine
Rathaus (Town Hall), built in

The stone bridge across the
Neckar at Heidelberg, with its
castle in the background

1484. Its two upper storeys are
supported by columns, creating
an open space at ground level.
The second floor is built high
into the roof, and two spires on
oriels provide an attractive
front. The parish church behind
the Rathaus is in Gothic style
and was built in the 15th and
16th centuries with a mighty
elongated steeple. The
Carolingian Einhardsbasilika is
interesting as it is a rare and
well-preserved building dating
from the 9th century.

i   *Einhardspforte 3*

FOR CHILDREN

Take the children to see the
Odenwald-und-
Spielzeugmuseum in
Michelstadt. Dolls' houses and
toys from France and Mexico
are on display, together with
model farms, railways and
dolls of all sizes.

▶ *Take the **B47** east, turn north*
 *on the **B469** towards the*
 Main River near Weilbach,
 then turn sharp right to
 Miltenberg.

FOR HISTORY BUFFS

Southeast of Michelstadt, in the
village of Würzberg, remnants
of two Roman towers can be
seen and also an excavated
Roman bath, now surrounded
by woods.

BACK TO NATURE

South of the village of
Würzberg, near Michelstadt,
visitors can watch the feeding
of the boar, which are kept in
an enclosure in the woods. If
you take a walk in the woods
locally, you may also come
across them living wild.
Although normally shy – they
are hunted – sows and families
of striped piglets are occasionally seen by quiet strollers.

3 Miltenberg, Bayern
A stop at Amorbach is worthwhile to see the abbey church
and its organ. It has 5,000 pipes
and 63 registers and is said to be
the largest baroque organ in
Europe.

In Miltenberg the market-
place exudes the unspoilt
medieval atmosphere of the
town. It is called the Stadt in
Holz (Town in Timber) because

of the well-preserved timber-framed houses which line the main street. The Haus zum Riesen (House of the Giant) dates back to the 12th century. It was altered in 1590 and is supposed to be the oldest country inn in Germany. Boat trips on the River Main are available – and make a relaxing way to enjoy this pleasant area.

i *Engelplatz 69, Rathaus*

▶ *From Miltenberg drive north along the River Main for 32km (20 miles) to Wertheim.*

4 **Wertheim,** Baden-Württemberg
Wertheim has managed to retain the character of an old Franconian town. Tiny passageways between the timber-framed houses and many historic buildings all contribute to the charm of this small town, which lies at the confluence of two rivers, the Main and the Tauber.

In the market square are the Engelsbrunnen (Angel's Well) and the Zobelhaus, the

The great castle of the Teutonic Knights at Bad Mergentheim

narrowest house in the town. High above is the Burg, a ruined fortress which provides visitors with fine views over the old town.

i *Am Spitzen Turm*

SCENIC ROUTES

The following routes are especially noted for their scenic beauty, and will be enjoyed by visitors; from Bensheim through the nature park to Michelstadt, then on the Nibelungenstrasse to Miltenberg; from Wertheim along the Tauber Valley to Tauberbischofsheim; and from Heilbronn through the Neckar Valley.

▶ *Drive southeast along the Tauber River to Tauberbischofsheim.*

5 **Tauberbischofsheim,** Baden-Württemberg
The Kurmainzisches Schloss is a very attractive castle, completed in the 15th and 16th centuries. Interestingly asymmetrical and made up of several separate buildings, it resembles a village rather more than a castle. The Türmersturm is a massive round tower of 13th-century origin which gives superb views of the village below. The parish church of St Martin was built in 1910 and displays work from the art school of the famous sculptor and woodcarver, Tilman Riemenschneider. Picturesque timber-framed houses in the Hauptstrasse (Main Street) and on the market square make for a relaxing and pleasant atmosphere.

i *Marktplatz 8, Rathaus*

▶ *Continue southeast on the B290 to Bad Mergentheim.*

6 **Bad Mergentheim,** Baden-Württemberg
On the Deutschordensplatz stands the Deutschordens-

Rothenburg ob der Tauber, a classic example of a medieval town

schloss, the castle of the Order of the Teutonic Knights. It was the residence of the Grand Master from 1525 to 1809, when the old order was dissolved. The buildings now standing were erected between 1525 and 1570. Today, part of the castle is a museum dedicated to the order, and in the castle's church are the tombs of former members. The market square is dominated by the gabled Rathaus (Town Hall) which was built in 1564. In the middle of the square stands a fountain with a monument to Wolfgang Schutzbar, one of the members of the Order of the Teutonic Knights, holding a flag and a shield.

In 1826 a shepherd discovered the natural springs which now offer cures for internal health problems.

i *Marktplatz 3*

▶ *Leave Bad Mergentheim on the **B10** east to Igersheim. Turn right and continue east along the Tauber on the Romantische Strasse (Romantic Road) to Rothenburg, 48km (30 miles).*

7 Rothenburg ob der Tauber, Bayern

Few towns in Germany have been able to preseve their history and beauty as well as Rothenburg. It seems only once to have been in major trouble. That was in 1631 during the Thirty Years' War when the Imperial troops under General Tilly were about to destroy the conquered town. But a brave ex-Mayor, Nusch, won a bet with the General by drinking 3.5 litres (5.75 pints) of wine in one go and thus saved the town. This occasion is commemorated in the centre of the town, where the former Ratsherrntrinkstube (Councillors' Tavern), built in 1446, houses the clock which reminds the citizens and visitors of Nusch. The Rathaus is next door and shows an interesting combination of two main styles, older Gothic (between 1250 and 1400) and the later Renaissance, which includes the oriel. The view from the top of the tower is especially rewarding because of the attractive buildings in the town and the gentle Tauber Valley beyond.

St Jacob's Kirche, a Gothic structure started in 1373, is worth visiting for its wonderful 'sacred blood' altar by Tilman Riemenschneider and some good stained glass. The old Wehrgang is a passageway along the old city walls which provides an interesting walk. The Weisser Turm (White Tower), Markusturm and Röderbogen (Röder's Arch) are all parts of the first city walls from the 12th century and are still standing. The Klingenbastei is also a covered walkway within the fortifications, dating back to 1587. The square tower once served as a water tower. In the Burggasse there is the Mittelalterliches Kriminalmuseum, a museum of law and punishment in the Middle Ages. The fortifications encircle the Burggarten, a relaxing park entered by the Burgtor, a fortified medieval gate.

ⓘ *Rathaus, Marktplatz 2*

▷ *Drive southwest on the Burgenstrasse (Castle Road) via Langenburg to Schwäbisch Hall, 50km (31 miles).*

8 Schwäbisch Hall, Baden-Württemberg

The impressive Benediktinerkloster Comburg (Benedictine abbey) dominates the town. The town's prosperity, as well as the origins of its name, is derived from salt. In medieval times salt was often used instead of money, and its merchants inevitably became prosperous. The medieval market-place of this former Free Imperial City is claimed to be one of the most picturesque in Germany. It is surrounded by St Michael's Church and the baroque Rathaus. In the middle stands the Fischbrunnen (Fish Fountain) and the Pranger (Stocks).

Originally a fortress, Comburg was transformed into a Kloster (abbey) of the Order of St Benedict in 1079. The surrounding wall with the watch towers makes this complex resemble a fortified castle rather than an abbey. It is now a teachers' training college. Features of note inside include a Romanesque chandelier in the abbey church. This is called the Radleuchter (wheel-shaped chandelier), made of iron, copper-plated and then gilded. It was made in 1130.

ⓘ *Markt 9*

SPECIAL TO...

Every year at Whitsun Schwäbisch Hall celebrates the town's saltmakers' traditional Kuchen-und-Brunnenfest (Cake and Fountain Festival). Salt manufacturing here dates back to Celtic times and the town flourished as salt was a valuable commodity.

▷ *Take the B14, then the B39 west to Heilbronn, 51km (32 miles).*

9 Heilbronn, Baden-Württemberg

Heilbronn is a very busy town which relies heavily on river traffic for commercial and leisure purposes. Wine is also an important product of the region. Unfortunately the old town was destroyed in 1944.

In the Marktplatz (Market Square) stands the Rathaus, which was constructed in Renaissance style and has a beautiful astronomical clock. Try to see the clock when it shows multiples of 4 (4am, 8am, noon, 4pm etc) – it comes alive with a wonderful display of carved figures. The Gothic St Kilian's Church dates from the 13th century and has a remarkable 62m (203-foot) high tower,

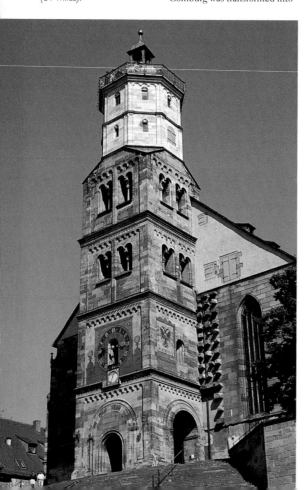

The tower of St Michael's Church in Schwäbisch Hall has an octagonal dome which dates from 1573

Timber-framed houses above the River Kocher in Schwäbisch Hall

completed in 1529. The church has been selected as the town's emblem. Opposite the church is the well (Brunnen) which gave the town its name.

[i] *Kaiserstrasse 17*

▷ *Before returning to Heidelberg, go north on the B27, then the B37, following the Neckar to Speyer, 82km (51 miles).*

[10] **Speyer,** Rheinland-Pfalz
Eight emperors and three empresses have been buried here in the majestic and inspiring Kaiserdom (cathedral), founded in AD 1030. The Krypta (crypt), impressive in itself, provides the entrance to the tombs. The tomb of Rudolf von Habsburg, who died in 1291, is of special note.

[i] *Maximilianstrasse 13*

▷ *Return to Heidelberg, 82km (51 miles).*

RECOMMENDED WALKS

En route from Heilbronn to Heidelberg stop at Neckargerach from where there is a fine walk through the Margentenschlucht ravine. Turn right at Eberbach in the Neckar Valley (en route to Heidelberg) for Gaimühle, then right again for Waldkatzenbuckel mountain and enjoy the view from the tower.

The River Main
& East of the Rhine

Frankfurt chose not to spend much on restoring old buildings after the last war, but opted instead to create an ultra-modern city, functional and efficient. The centre of Frankfurt is, however, a restored baroque-style building, the Hauptwache, once used to house the city's guards.

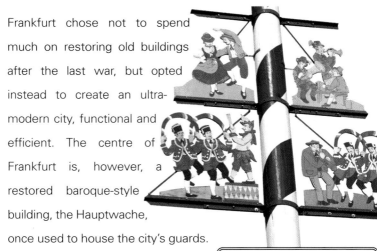

2 DAYS • 395KM • 245 MILES

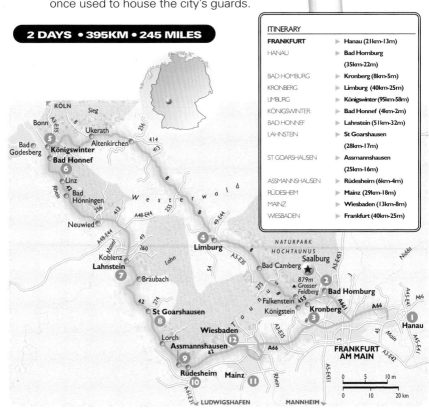

ITINERARY		
FRANKFURT	►	**Hanau** (21km-13m)
HANAU	►	**Bad Homburg** (35km-22m)
BAD HOMBURG	►	**Kronberg** (8km-5m)
KRONBERG	►	**Limburg** (40km-25m)
LIMBURG	►	**Königswinter** (95km-58m)
KÖNIGSWINTER	►	**Bad Honnef** (4km-2m)
BAD HONNEF	►	**Lahnstein** (51km-32m)
LAHNSTEIN	►	**St Goarshausen** (28km-17m)
ST GOARSHAUSEN	►	**Assmannshausen** (25km-16m)
ASSMANNSHAUSEN	►	**Rüdesheim** (6km-4m)
RÜDESHEIM	►	**Mainz** (29km-18m)
MAINZ	►	**Wiesbaden** (13km-8m)
WIESBADEN	►	**Frankfurt** (40km-25m)

i *Am Römerberg 27, Frankfurt am Main*

▶ *Take the **A66** east for 21km (13 miles) to Hanau.*

BACK TO NATURE

The Enkheimer Marsh near Frankfurt is an excellent spot for wildfowl, herons and waders, as are Westerwald and the Vogelsberg lakes. In particular, look for greylag geese, black terns, bitterns, grey herons, redskank and pochard.

---

❶ **Hanau,** Hessen
Hanau is the beginning of the German 'Fairy Tale Road', and the birthplace of the Brothers Grimm. Apart from their universally known stories, the chief trade is gold – master goldsmiths have worked here for centuries. The Goldschmiedehaus (House of the Goldsmiths) is an unsual timber-framed structure with a large gabled roof typical of this architectural style. The entrance is reached by an outside staircase to a raised ground floor, for security reasons. Inside, there are international exhibitions of jewellery from the past and present. It also houses the oldest German college for metalworking.

The Schloss Philippsruhe (castle) near Hanau functions in part as a museum for works of art, and the entrance gate is a creation in wrought iron from Paris. There are many objects relating to Hanau porcelain manufacture, brought here by Dutch refugees.

Schloss Steinheim, built between the 13th and the 16th centuries with a mighty belfry, houses a museum exhibiting objects of pre- and early history, from the Stone Age to Roman times.

i *Markt 14–18*

Frankfurt's cobbled Römerberg Square was once the setting for royal ceremonies

▶ *Take the **A66** west back towards Frankfurt and turn right for the **A661** north to Bad Homburg, 35km (22 miles).*

❷ **Bad Homburg**, Hessen
Bad Homburg, in the Taunus mountain range, is a modern spa with a Roman history . The restored Römerkastell (Roman Fort) at Saalburg is about 5km (3 miles) north and has been restored to its original design. It was part of the Roman Limes fortification line, which formed the northern frontier of the Roman Empire. The museum inside allows an interesting glimpse back to Roman times. The original fort was built in AD 120, and could accommodate a contingent of 500 soldiers. The inside looks as though the Romans have just left it: catapults, armouries, shops, houses, temples and baths are all there.

The Schloss (castle) in its present form was built between 1680 and 1685 on the same piece of land as an older fortress. The medieval fortress

is remembered only by one surviving tower, called the Weisse Turm (White Tower). The castle was the residence of the Counts of Hesse-Homburg and later the summer residence of the Prussian Emperor Wilhelm II. The Schloss is open to the public, and has valuable paintings and furniture from the 17th and 18th centuries. The Schlosspark is well cared for and has some exotic plants.

A curiosity to visit in the centre of Bad Homburg is the Siamtemple, donated by a Siamese king in gratitude for a successful cure at the spa. There is also a Russian chapel, and no less than seven health-giving springs in the attractively named Brunnenallee (Alley of the Springs).

FOR HISTORY BUFFS

In Bad Homburg there are mementoes of the famous men and women who visited this spa in its heyday. These include King Edward VII, Emperor Wilhelm II of Prussia, the Russian writer Dostoevsky and the last Tsarina of Russia, who, before her marriage, had been a Princess of Hessen.

---

i Louisenstrasse 58, Kurhaus

▶ Turn south to Oberursel and west to Kronberg on the B455.

FOR CHILDREN

The Opel Zoo, near Kronberg, has elephants, apes, giraffes, zebras and camels, along with other exotic and indigenous animals. Altogether over 950 species are kept here. Play areas and a special petting zoo attract children. Camel riding is also on offer.

---

3 Kronberg, Hessen
On a rock in the middle of the town stands the fortress of the Knights of Kronberg, which dates from 1220. The town has been popular with painters because of its picturesque winding streets and timber-framed houses. In the 19th century it became the home of the Kronberger school of artists, thus making its contribution to German art.

i Rathaus, Katherinenstrasse 7

BACK TO NATURE

Hessen's oldest falconry can be visited on the Grosser Feldberg, north of Kronberg. Weather permitting, eagles and vultures can be observed in free flight.

▶ From Kronburg drive west to Königstein, and turn right for the B8 to Limburg, 40km (25 miles).

4 Limburg, Hessen
On the way to Limburg, the ruins of Falkenstein and Königstein make good stopping places. Königstein is an interesting old town, with the Altes Rathaus (Old Town Hall) now housing the museum.

In the valley of the River Lahn, Limburg is an attractive medieval town with a cathedral dating from the 13th century, a masterpiece in late Romanesque style with seven towers. Inside, its original colours have been restored, and 13th-century frescoes revealed. This restoration work was completed in 1973, and the visitor is given a unique flavour of a real medieval cathedral.

The Domschatz (Treasury) is located in the bishop's residence and exhibits sacred works of art which also have great historic value. Special mention should be made of the Staurothek, a cross created by Byzantine craftsmen in the second half of the 10th century and the gem of the collection.

In the centre of the old town, around the fish market, there are many timber-framed houses, among them the Rathaus (Town Hall). Another building from 1296, claimed to be the oldest timber-framed house in Germany, is still occupied today.

i Hospitalstrasse 2

▶ Head northwest on the A8 for 68km (42 miles), then take the road leading west to Königswinter.

5 Königswinter, Nordrhein-Westfalen
Königswinter lies on the banks of the Rhine, and one of the most popular ruins in this area is the fortress Drachenfels, which was destroyed in 1634. There are several ways of getting up there to enjoy the wide view over the Rhine Valley and the countryside around: on foot, by donkey, by horse-drawn carriage or by cogwheel railway. The walk takes about half an hour, the railway eight minutes.

i Drachenfelsstrasse 11

▶ Take the B42 south for 4km (2 miles) to Bad Honnef.

6 Bad Honnef, Nordrhein-Westfalen
Bad Honnef offers mineral springs, a 30°C (86°F) swimming pool and a modern therapeutic institution. A visit is also recommended to the parish church of St Johann, which dates from the 12th century. In the section of town called Rhondorf there is a memorial to Konrad Adenauer, the late German statesman.

i Bahnhofstrasse 3

▶ Continue on the B42 for 51km (32 miles) to Lahnstein.

7 Lahnstein, Rheinland-Pfalz
Lahnstein lies on twin sites at the meeting of the rivers Lahn and Rhine. The left bank is called the Oberlahnstein, with Niederlahnstein opposite. Near Oberlahnstein, on a hill above

the Rhine stands the fortified castle of Burg Lahneck, erected in the 13th century and typifying the charm of the Rhine Valley. The interior furnishings and decorations are remarkable. There are attractive views from the castle down to the Rhine, but the best view of the castle and its setting can be obtained down below from the Alte Lahnbrücke.

In Niederlahnstein, there remain a few of the old manor houses which belonged to the aristocracy as well as the Wirthaus an der Lahn (Inn on the Lahn), which features in many German songs.

[i] *Kirchstrasse 1*

▶ *From Lahnstein continue on the B42 south for 28km (17 miles) to St Goarshausen.*

8 St Goarshausen,
Rheinland-Pfalz

This is also known as Loreleystadt (town of Loreley) because of its proximity to the famous rock known as the Loreley Rock. Above the town stands the fortress of Katz, crowning the rock on which it was built by the Counts of Katzenelnbogen. They controlled this area and the traffic on the Rhine through strategically sited fortresses, exacting what they believed were their 'dues' from passing ships. The fortress was built around the end of the 14th century and after its destruction rebuilt in 1806. It is not open to the public.

8 *Bahnhofstrasse 8*

▶ *Continue on the B42 south to Assmannshausen.*

Assmannshausen's chair-lift provides a good opportunity to view the Rhine Valley

---

SCENIC ROUTES

The route from Bad Homburg to Königswinter is particularly beautifu.
The delightful scenery from St Goarshausen along the Rhine is enhanced by the numerous castles and ruins on the hills, and the more graceful traffic of the river.

---

9 Assmannshausen,
Hessen

The route passes the Loreley Rock, 132m (433 feet) high, where the legendary Rhine maiden, the beautiful Loreley, would sit and lure passing ships to disaster.

Not many districts in Germany produce red wine, but Assmannshausen is known for its blue Burgundy grapes, which produce an excellent red.

East of the town, in Niederwald, stands a monument to German unity. The figure of Germania on top of the monument is 10m (33 feet) high with a 7m (22-foot) long sword in her hand.

[i] *See Rüdesheim*

▶ *Continue on the **B42** south to Rüdesheim.*

The Drosselgasse, in Rüdesheim, is an excellent place to enjoy the local taverns

10 Rüdesheim, Hessen

In this wine centre on the banks of the Rhine, Drosselgasse in the centre is a popular meeting place with one tavern after another, and entertainment and music that goes on until the early hours of the morning.

Schloss Brömserburg, a castle dating back to the 10th century, is now an important wine museum. The Adlerturm (Eagle's Tower) is a remnant of the town's 15th-century fortifications. It is only 20m (66 feet) high, but the walls are 1m (3 feet) thick. A cable-car from here travels up to the Niederwald monument.

[i] *Geisenheimer Strasse 22*

RECOMMENDED WALKS

Take the cable-car from Rüdesheim and ride over the vineyards to the hilltop. Pleasant walks through the vineyards lead down to the valley and the town.

SPECIAL TO...

Close to the famous Drosselgasse in Rüdesheim, the historic Brömserhof houses a large collection of self-playing mechanical musical instruments.

▶ *Continue on the **B42** towards Wiesbaden, turn right at Schierstein Kreuz for the **A643** and turn left for Mainz after crossing the Rhine.*

11 Mainz, Rheinland-Pfalz

The cathedral of Mainz is not far from the banks of the Rhine. The St Martins Dom, as it is called, belongs to a group of Romanesque cathedrals that show the mastery of German religious architecture in the Middle Ages. This enormous building project began in 975. The western part of the cathedral is meant to symbolise the spiritual world. After several fires the cathedral was finished in 1239 in its present form. It has been used for coronations and festive banquets.

One of 47 copies of the Gutenberg Bible, printed 1452–1455, is exhibited in the Gutenberg Museum.

The Kurfürstliche Schloss (Electoral Palace) was finished in 1678 and now houses collections of the Römisch-Germanisches Zentralmuseum (Romano-German Central Museum). The history of Mainz goes back to a Roman stronghold called *Monguntiacum*, which was erected close to a former Celtic settlement.

ⓘ Brückenturm am Rathaus

▶ From Mainz proceed to the ring road and drive north across the Rhine to Wiesbaden, 13km (8 miles).

⓬ Wiesbaden, Hessen

On the right bank of the Rhine, between the foothills of the Taunus mountain range and the river, lies Wiesbaden, capital of the province of Hessen. The Romans first discovered the healing spring here, and called it *Aquae Mattiacorum*, after the Germanic tribe resident here. It probably became a Roman fort between AD 41 and 50, was abandoned in AD 406 and taken over by the Franks, who made it a local capital. The name of Wiesbaden is first recorded as Wisbada in AD 829, which in German translates as 'bath in the meadows'.

It became prosperous in the 19th century, when the rich and famous of Europe rediscovered the hot springs. The English had a special liking for the spa, even building their own church here in 1863. Wiesbaden was also the summer home of

The onion-domed roof of the Russian Orthodox church in Wiesbaden

Emperor Wilhelm II, and its popularity peaked around the turn of the century. The Wilhelmstrasse, the town's elegant main street, is a reminder of those affluent days.

ⓘ Marktstrasse 6

▶ From Wiesbaden take the **A66** for around 40km (25 miles) back to Frankfurt am Main.

Along the Left
Bank of the Rhine

Köln (Cologne) is the undisputed capital of the Rhineland. Founded by the Romans, it was an important medieval trading city and is now a major industrial and commercial centre. On the approach to the city, the skyline is dominated by the soaring twin spires of the Dom.

2 DAYS • 305KM • 194 MILES

ITINERARY

KÖLN	► **Brühl** (13km-8m)
BRÜHL	► **Bonn** (19km-12m)
BONN	► **Bad Godesberg** (7km-4m)
BAD GODESBERG	► **Remagen** (14km-9m)
REMAGEN	► **Andernach** (22km-14m)
ANDERNACH	► **Maria Laach** (13km-8m)
MARIA LAACH	► **Nürburgring** (33km-20m)
NÜRBURGRING	► **Bad Münstereifel** (48km-30m)
BAD MÜNSTEREIFEL	► **Aachen** (71km-44m)
AACHEN	► **Köln** (65km-45m)

---

i *Unter Fettenhennen 19, Köln*

▶ *From Köln take the B51 south for 13km (8 miles) to Brühl.*

1 Brühl, Nordrhein-Westfalen
The castle of Brühl, popularly known as the Augustusburg, is the combined effort of three noted architects: Johann Conrad Schlaun, François Cuvilliés and Balthasar Neumann. The earlier castle had been blown up in 1689. Cuvilliés was responsible for the new rococo design of the castle, and Neumann designed the staircase, with pillars shaped in the form of male and female figures.

The hall, with its ornate staircase, is now used for concerts and receptions. The gardens are laid out in formal French style.

i *Uhlstrasse 1*

▶ *From Brühl drive east and join the B9 south to Bonn, 19km (12 miles).*

FOR CHILDREN

The Phantasialand amusement park at Brühl is open from April to October. The programme includes breathtaking rides through 'Hollywood' film sets and the Grand Canyon, and a trip on a monorail. Shows in 3-D, laser and the 'Western Saloon' are a few examples of what is on offer. Allow about six hours for a visit.

---

2 Bonn, Nordrhein-Westfalen
Until the re-unification in October 1990, Bonn was the federal capital of the former West Germany. Although the focus in German politics has shifted to Berlin, this elegant city has its own attractions. Before it became federal capital in May 1949, Bonn was a tranquil town on the Rhine, internationally known as the birthplace of the great composer Ludwig van Beethoven. The house

Vineyards cling to the slopes overlooking the Rhine Valley

where he was born in 1770 is now a museum, showing paintings from his time in Bonn and Vienna, his last piano, stringed instruments and manuscripts. Beethoven lived in Bonn until he was 22, when he left for the capital of music, Vienna.

The Altes Rathaus (Old Town Hall) was built by the French architect Michel Leveilly in 1737. It has all the features of a French castle, including richly decorated façades and large windows. It is the official seat of the Mayor, and hosts many official receptions. The splendid Münster (Minster) is 900 years old and was erected on an early Christian site during Roman times. It is a fine example of the 12th-century Rhenish-Romanesque transitional style, although the nave shows the advance of the Gothic influence which replaced it. The Rheinisches Landesmuseum exhibits collections from

Roman and medieval times, as well as the head of a prehistoric man found in the village of Neandertal, 40km (25 miles) north of Cologne, and estimated to be 60,000 years old.

i Windeckstrasse 1
(at Münsterplatz)

FOR HISTORY BUFFS

The Poppelsdorfer Schloss in Bonn used to be the summer residence of the Electors of Cologne, who lived in Bonn after losing a battle against Cologne's burghers in the 13th century. It was originally designed in baroque style by the French architect de Cotte.

▶ Continue south for 7km (4 miles) to Bad Godesberg.

⑧ Bad Godesberg,
Nordrhein-Westfalen
Its pleasant position on the Rhine has made this former spa town a popular residential area. The Rheinpromenade offers relaxing strolls along the river, and is especially attractive at the end of the day, when the sun sets over the surrounding castles and ruins. The ruin of the Godesburg, blown up in 1583, offers wonderful views from the surviving tower. The ruin has been incorporated into a restaurant.

i Ria-Maternusplatz 1

▶ From Bad Godesberg take the **B9** south for 14km (9 miles) to Remagen.

The house in Bonn where Ludwig von Beethoven was born is now a museum

④ Remagen, Rheinland-Pfalz
Remagen was originally a Celtic settlement and then a Roman fort. Of interest is the parish church of St Peter and St Paul, rebuilt in late Romanesque style. Near the Rathaus (Town Hall) are reminders of the old Roman fort, which was known as *Ricomagus*.

The bridge at Remagen achieved fame in World War II. American soldiers captured it intact in March 1945, but it collapsed three days later under the weight of their military equipment, killing 18 soldiers. By the side of the Rhine, appropriately, is a Friedensmuseum (Peace Museum).

⑧ Bachstrasse 5

FOR CHILDREN

En route from Remagen to Andernach, children can enjoy the Märchenwald at Bad Breisig. A fairy-tale atmosphere prevails, with scale models and moving and speaking figures which add to the entertainment.

SPECIAL TO...

Brohl-Lützing, just to the north of Andernach, is the terminus of a narrow-gauge railway called the Brohltalbahn. The line, which passes through some very pleasant countryside, was built to transport phonolith, a rare volcanic mineral used for the manufacture of glass, to the port or main railway terminal on the Rhine. A timetable gives information about trains and special treats are availanble on Sundays and public holidays, when a steam engine pulls the carriages.

▶ From Remagen continue travelling on the **B9** to Andernach.

The Romanesque church of Maria Laach, with its pretty six towers

5 Andernach, Rheinland-Pfalz

Once a Roman fort, Andernach was still heavily fortified in medieval times and was the scene of many battles. The medieval gates are still intact. The Runder Turm (Round Tower) is a former watch-tower, 56m (184 feet) high, and solid enough to have survived an attempt to blow it up in 1689.

[i] *Läufstrasse 4*

▶ *From Andernach go west via Nickenich for 13km (8 miles) to Kloster Maria-Laach.*

6 Kloster Maria-Laach, Rheinland-Pfalz

The Kloster Maria-Laach is a Benedictine abbey on the southwestern shores of the Laacher See (lake). The well-preserved Romanesque basilica, with its six towers, is a notable building. It was donated by Heinrich II in 1093 and in the western part of the choir section

is the colourful tomb of its founder. The church has three aisles, similar to the cathedrals of Mainz, Speyer and Worms and, in accordance with Romanesque style, the interior looks bare. The stained-glass windows were replaced after World War II. The altar has a baldachin-style roof, and the oldest part of the church is the triple-aisled crypt. The church-yard is called Das Paradies (Paradise) and in its centre stands the 'fountain of life'.

[i] *Klosterverwaltung*

▶ *Drive south to Mayen, turn right and take the B258 west to Nürburgring, 33km (20 miles).*

7 Nürburgring, Rheinland-Pfalz

Nürburgring provides a change of diet from the history of the area. One of the most famous motor-racing circuits in the world, it was built in the 1920s in the wooded countryside, where the first powerful motor cars were tested. The northern

sector is over 20km (13 miles) long, but the new Formula 1 track which opened in 1984 was extended in 2002 to 5.2km (3.2 miles). The German Grand Prix now alternates between the Nürburgring and Hockenheim, south of Heidelberg. On days when there is no racing or training going on, visitors may test their own cars on the circuit.

[i] *Nürburgring*

FOR CHILDREN

If you follow the B257 just west of Nürburgring about 20km (12 miles) north to Altenahr, you can take the children to the 500m (1,640-foot) long summer toboggan run. A drag-lift takes visitors up to the starting point.

▶ *From Nürburgring take the B258 northwest to Blankenheim, then turn right for the B51 northeast to Bad Münstereifel, a total distance of 48km (30 miles).*

Printen, a spicy gingerbread, is one of Aachen's specialities

8 Bad Münstereifel,
Nordrhein-Westfalen
Bad Münstereifel's old town is surrounded by a massive 13th-century wall, 1.5km (1 mile) long, with four gates and 18 watch-towers, and one of the best-preserved medieval fortifications in Germany.

The restored Romanesque abbey dates back to the 10th century. A stroll round the Marktplatz reveals some interesting historic houses. Look out for the gabled Windeckhaus in a nearby street. Near the Effelsberg stands the radio telescope of the Max Planck Institute. This is one of the largest fully rotating telescopes in the world, with a disc 100m (328 feet) in diameter.

i Kölner Strasse 13

▶ *From Bad Münstereifel continue on the B51 north towards Euskirchen, then turn left for the B56 to Düren, and left again on the B264 west to Aachen.*

9 Aachen, Nordrhein-Westfalen
The fall of the Roman Empire plunged Europe into chaos. The man who eventually united what is now basically Germany and France and ruled as King of the Franks was Charlemagne, and Aachen (Aix-la-Chapelle in French) was one of his centres of power. The Dom (Cathedral) was a chapel founded by Charlemagne in 800. His throne and his crown arehere, and his tomb, the Karlschrein, is a beautifully ornate work of art. From 936 to 1531, 32 German emperors were crowned here, and each one followed the custom of making a donation to the cathedral. The result is one of the most valuable collections of art objects in Germany. A bust of Charlemagne, cast in gold and silver and encrusted with jewels, was donated by Charles IV in 1349. Outside the cathedral, the Rathaus (Town Hall) is a 14th-century building on the site of Charlemagne's palace. The frescoes in the Krönungsaal depict his life, while the fountain in the market square is dedicated to the Emperor.

i Elisenbrunnen, Friedrich-Wilhelm-Platz

▶ *From Aachen take the A4/E40 f or 65km (40 miles) back to Köln.*

An equestrian statue in front of Köln's Cathedral, one of the world's great Gothic structures

MOTORING IN GERMANY

ACCIDENTS

As a general rule you are required to call the police when individuals have been injured or considerable damage has been caused. Failure to give aid to anyone injured will render you liable to a fine. (See also **warning triangles**.)

BREAKDOWNS

If your car breaks down, try to move it to the side of the road so it obstructs the traffic flow as little as possible. Place a warning triangle to the rear of the vehicle at a suitable distance and switch on your hazard warning lights.

The motoring club ADAC operates a breakdown service. The cost of any materials must be reimbursed.

In the event of a breakdown on a motorway a patrol can be summoned from an emergency telephone. A small arrow on the marker posts on the verges indicates the direction of the nearest one. When calling, ask specifically for 'Strassenwachthilfe' (road service assistance). (See also **warning triangles**.)

CAR HIRE

If you are not taking your own car you can make arrangements to hire one before departure. Many package holidays include car hire as an option. Car hire is available at most airports, main railway stations and in larger towns. You must be over 21, and have driven for at least a year.

CHILDREN

Children under 12 years of age and/or under 1.5m (4 feet 11 inches) in height must not travel as front-seat passengers unless they are wearing a suitable seat restraint. They must also wear restraints, if fitted, in the back of a car. Note: under no circumstances should a rear-facing restraint be used in a seat with an airbag.

CRASH (SAFETY) HELMETS

Visiting motorcyclists and their passengers must wear crash or safety helmets.

DIMENSIONS AND WEIGHT RESTRICTIONS

Private cars and trailers or caravans are restricted to the following dimensions – height 4m; width 2.5m; length 12m. The maximum permitted overall length of vehicle/trailer or caravan combination is 18m. A fully-laden trailer without an adequate braking system must not weigh more than 37.5kg, plus 50 per cent of the weight of the towing vehicle. A fully-laden trailer with an adequate braking system must not weigh more than the towing vehicle.

DOCUMENTS

A valid UK or Republic of Ireland licence is acceptable in Germany. The minimum age at which visitors from the those countries may use a temporarily imported car or motorcycle is 17 years. You also require the vehicle registration document, plus a letter of authorisation from the owner, if not accompanying the vehicle, and the current insurance certificate (a green card is not mandatory but is internationally recognised and can be helpful). Also, a nationality plate or sticker is required.

DRINKING AND DRIVING

The laws in Europe regarding drinking and driving are strict and the penalties severe. The best advice is, as at home, if you drink don't drive.

DRIVING CONDITIONS

Drive on the right, pass on the left. On-the-spot fines are imposed for speeding and other offences. Wearing seat belts is compulsory in both front and rear seats.

Germans are fast drivers, and popular resistance to a compul-

sory speed limit on the *autobahn* has succeeded in preventing one from being introduced. Note, however, that speed limits may apply to some stretches of *autobahn* which are particularly heavy with traffic or are curved.

On straight stretches the suggested maximum speed of 130kph (80mph) is often exceeded by cars travelling at more than 200kph (125mph), so overtaking or lane switching requires particular concentration. Most drivers are aware of what they are doing and respect the rules of the road, having passed the country's particularly rigorous driving test. Once you have become used to conditions, you will find the behaviour of fellow road-users fairly predictable.

Some additional rules of the road:

• On roads without priority signs, give way to traffic from the right.

• Seat belts must be worn by all occupants of the car.

• Children under 12 must use an appropriate safety seat.

• Halt at tram stops where there is no central reservation and allow passengers to cross the road to embark and disembark.

• Give way to trams and buses as they leave stops.

• Give way to pedestrians when turning right or left at uncontrolled junctions.

• Insulting behaviour to other drivers or the police is an offence.

FIRST-AID KIT AND FIRE EXTINGUISHER

The German authorities recommend that visiting motorists equip their vehicles with a fire extinguisher; having a first-aid kit in the vehicle is compulsory.

FUEL

You will find comparable grades of petrol in Germany, with familiar brand names along the main routes. You will normally have to buy a minimum of 5 litres, but it is wise to keep the tank topped up, particularly in more remote areas. Only lead-free fuel is now being sold at the pumps in grades Normal 91, Super 95, Super Plus 98 and Diesel. Fuel will normally be more expensive on the motorways, but is generally available 24 hours a day.

INSURANCE
Fully comprehensive insurance, which covers you for some of the expenses incurred after a breakdown or an accident, is advisable.

LIGHTS
Dipped headlights or fog lamps must be used in poor daytime visibility. Driving with sidelights only is prohibited. A spare set of bulbs is recommended.

Deflectors have to be fitted to the headlights of all right-hand-drive vehicles to avoid blinding oncoming traffic.

MOTORING CLUBS
The Allgemeiner Deutscher Automobil Club (ADAC) has offices in the larger towns. Office hours are 9–6 Monday to Friday. The ADAC also has offices at major frontier crossings. Information: tel: 01805 101-112, Breakdown Service: tel: 01805 222-222.

PARKING
There are strict rules for when and where you may not park. Parking is forbidden within 5m (5.5 yards) of a pedestrian crossing or road junction, or within 15m (16.5 yards) of a tram or bus stop. Do not park on a main road in the countryside, or where parking restrictions may be indicated by the standard sign (which you may have to look for).

Competition for parking spaces can be acute in densely built-up residential areas, as well as in the middle of cities. In the former, many spaces will be reserved for residents, while in the latter you will usually have to pay a fee, and the time you

may park on the street is likely to be limited to two hours or less.

POLICE FINES
There are on-the-spot fines for speeding and other offences.

ROADS
The *Bundesstrassen*, or state roads, vary in quality. In the north and west, and in the touring areas of the Rhine Valley, Black Forest and Bavaria, the roads are good and well-graded.

Germany has a comprehensive motorway (*Autobahn*) network which dominates the road system and takes most of the long distance traffic. They are identified by a white letter 'A' and a number on a blue background. Emergency telephones are sited every 2km (1.2 miles), the direction of the nearest telephone is indicated by the point of the black triangle on posts alongside the motorway. Traffic at weekends increases considerably during the school holidays, which are from July to mid-September.

In order to ease road congestion, heavy lorries are prohibited on all roads at weekends from approximately mid-June to the end of August and generally on all Sundays and public holidays.

Note: outside special built-up areas motor vehicles to which a special speed limit applies, as well as vehicles with trailers with a combined length of more than 7m (23 feet), must keep a sufficient distance from the preceding vehicle so that an overtaking vehicle may pull in. Anyone who is driving so slowly that a line of vehicles has formed behind must permit the following vehicles to pass, even if this means stopping at a suitable place.

ROUTE DIRECTIONS
Throughout the book the following abbreviations are used for German roads:
A – Autobahnen
B – Bundesstrasse (federal/national roads)*
*figures only on maps as B roads are numbered only.

SPEED LIMITS
Car
Built-up areas: 50kph (31mph)
Other roads: 100kph (62mph)
Dual carriageways: 130kph (80mph).
Motorway *(autobahn)*: no legal limit; the suggested limit is 130kph (80mph).

Car/caravan/trailer
Built-up areas: 50kph (31mph)
Other roads: 80kph (49mph)
Motorways/dual carriageways: 80kph (49mph)
In bad weather 50kph (31mph) on all roads when visibility is restricted to 50m (55 yards). Note that minimum speeds are also applied to some roads; these are indicated by a number on a blue circular sign.

TOLLS
All motorways are toll free for private cars.

UNFAMILIAR ROAD SIGNS
Abblenden Dip headlights
Alle Richtungen All directions
Anfang Start
Anlieger frei Except residents
Ausfahrt Exit
Baustelle Works
Einbahnstrasse One-way street
Einfahrt Entrance
Ende End
Gefahr Danger
Links/Rechts Left/Right
Radweg Bicycle path
Raststätte Service Area
Rollsplitt Loose chippings
Stau Hold-up, traffic jam
Steinschlag Falling rocks
Umleitung Diversion
Unfall Accident
Vorrang/Vorfahrt Priority
Zentrum Central city

WARNING TRIANGLES
The use of a warning triangle is compulsory in the event of an accident or breakdown. The triangle must be placed on the road behind the vehicle to warn of any obstruction; 100m (110 yards) on ordinary roads and 200m (220 yards) on motorways. Vehicles over 2,500kg (2 tons, 9cwt, 24lbs) must also carry a yellow flashing light.

ACCOMMODATION AND RESTAURANTS

Following is a selection of hotels (⬦) which can be found along the routes of each tour, along with suggestions for restaurants (⑩) to take a break.

Hotel Prices
The hotels listed are grouped into three price categories based on a nightly rate for a double room with breakfast:

€ up to €100
€€ €100–€200
€€€ over €200

Restaurant Prices
The restaurants listed are also grouped into three price bands, which are based on a three-course meal, without drinks, for one person:

€ up to €20
€€ €20–€40
€€€ over €40

TOUR 1
HAMBURG
⬦ **Wedina €€**
Gurlittstrasse 23
(tel: 040 2808900;
www.wedina.de).
59 rooms.

⑩ **Fischküche €€**
Kajen 12
(tel: 040 365631).
Seafood specialist where taste matters more than style.

SCHWERIN
Mecklenburg–Vorpommern
⬦ **Intercity €€**
Grunthalplatz 5–7
(tel: 0385 59500;
www.intercityhotel.com).
Also ⑩ €.
180 rooms.

WISMAR Mecklenburg
⬦ **Seehotel €€**
Seestrasse 12, Nakenstorf
(tel: 03842 225445).
Also ⑩ €€.
16 rooms.

LÜBECK Schleswig-Holstein
⬦ **Jensen €€**
An der Obertrave 4
(tel: 0451 702490;
www.hotel-jensen.de).
Also ⑩ €€.
42 rooms.

⬦ **Mövenpick €€**
Willy-Brandt-Allee 1–5
(tel: 0451 15040;
www.moevenpick-hotels.com). Also ⑩ €€.
197 rooms.

⑩ **Das Schabbelhaus €€**
Mengstrasse 48–52
(tel: 0451 72011).
North German and Italian cuisine in a traditional Lübeck setting.

KIEL Schleswig-Holstein
⬦ **Wiking €€**
Schützenwall 1–3
(tel: 0431 661090;
www.hotel-wiking.de).
42 rooms.

TOUR 2
HANNOVER
Niedersachsen
⬦ **Körner €€**
Körnerstrasse 24–25
(tel: 0511 16360;
www.hotelkoerner.de).
96 rooms.

⑩ **Clichy €€**
Weissekreutzstrasse 31
(tel: 0551 312447).
An elegant yet unfussy celebration of French cuisine.

BRAUNSCHWEIG
Niedersachsen
⬦ **Mercure Atrium €€**
Berliner Platz 3
(tel: 0531 70080;
www.mercure.com). Also ⑩ €.
130 rooms.

⑩ **Brodocz €€**
Stephanstrasse 1–2
(tel: 0531 42236).
Vegetarian and vegan with Mediterranean influence.

CELLE Niedersachsen
⬦ **Blumlage €**
Blumlage 87
(tel: 05141 974470;
www.blumlage.de). Also ⑩ €.
32 rooms.

⬦ **Schifferkrug €**
Speicherstrasse 9
(tel: 05141 374776;
www.schifferkrug.de).
Also ⑩ €.
12 rooms.

⑩ **Historischer Ratskeller €**
Markt 14
(tel: 05141 29099).
German and international food in a rustic décor.

TOUR 3
BERLIN Berlin
⬦ **Art'otel Berlin Kudamm €€**
Joachimstalerstrasse 28–29
(tel: 030 884470;
www.artotel.de).
133 rooms.

⬦ **Kempinski Bristol Berlin €€€**
Kurfürstendamm 27
(tel: 030 884340;
www.kempinski.com).
301 rooms.

⑩ **Lutter & Wegner €€**
Charlottenstrasse 56
(tel: 030 2029540).
A flair for traditional German and Austrian cuisine.

POTSDAM Brandenburg
⬦ **Bayrisches Haus €€€**
Im Wildpark 1
(tel: 0331 55050;
www.bayrisches-haus.de).
33 rooms.

⬦ **relaxa Schlosshotel Cecilienhof €€€**
Neuer Garten
(tel: 0331 37050;
www.relaxa-hotels.de).
41 rooms.

⌖ Juliette €€
Jägerstrasse 39
(tel: 0331 2701791).
*International and traditional
French cuisine.*

LÜBBENAU Brandenburg
◊ Spreewaldeck €
Dammstrasse 31
(tel: 03542 89010;
www.spreewaldeck.de).
27 rooms.

**TOUR 4
LEIPZIG** Sachsen
◊ Novotel €€
Goethestrasse 11
(tel: 0341 99580;
www.novotel.com).
200 rooms.

⌖ Thüringer Hof €
Burgstrasse 19
(tel: 0341 9944999).
*Thuringian, Franconian and
other regional specialities.*

MEISSEN Sachsen
**◊ Mercure Grand Hotel
Meissen €€**
Hafenstrasse 27–31
(tel: 03521 72250;
www.mercure.com).
97 rooms.

⌖ Vincenz Richter €€
An der Frauenkirche 12
(tel: 03521 453285).
German and Saxon specialities.

DRESDEN Sachsen
**◊ Mercure Dresden
Albertbrücke €€**
Melanchtonstrasse 2
(tel: 0351 80610;
www.mercure.com).
132 rooms.

**⌖ Italienisches
Dörfchen €€**
Theaterplatz 3
(tel: 0351 498160).
*An elegant mix of Saxon and
Italian cooking.*

MORITZBURG Sachsen
**⌖ Restaurant
Laubenhöhe €**
Köhlerstrasse 77
(tel: 035242 36186).
*Unpretentious but delicious local
cooking.*

BAD SCHANDAU
Sachsen
**◊ Zum Roten
Haus €**
Marktstrasse 10
(tel: 035022 42343;
www.hotel-zum-roten-
haus.de).
10 rooms.

**TOUR 5
WEIMAR** Thüringen
◊ Dorint €€
Beethovenplatz 1–2
(tel: 03643 8720;
www.dorint-hotels.com).
Also ⌖ €€
143 rooms.

FRIEDRICHRODA
Thüringen
◊ Friedrichroda €€
Burchardtsweg 1
(tel: 03623 3520;
www.ramada-treff-
friedrichroda.de).
153 rooms.

EISENACH Thuringen
**◊ Best Western Hotel
Kaiserhof €€**
Wartburgallee 2
(tel: 03691 88890;
www.kaiserhof-eisenach.de).
64 rooms.

MÜLHAUSEN Thüringen
◊ Mirage €
Karl-Marx-Strasse 9
(tel: 03601 4390;
www.mirage-hotel.de).
76 rooms.

⌖ Zum Nachbarn €
Steinweg 65
(tel: 03601 812513).
*A cosy place for good local
cooking.*

ERFURT Thuringen
**◊ Mercure Hotel Erfurt
Altstadt €€€**
Meienbergstrasse 26–27
(tel: 0361 5949502;
www.mercure.com).
141 rooms.

**◊ Radisson SAS Hotel
Erfurt €€**
Juri-Gagarin-Ring 127
(tel: 0361 55100).
282 rooms.

**TOUR 6
GOSLAR** Niedersachsen
◊ Sonnenhotel Kreuzeck €€
Am Kreuzeck 1–3
(tel: 0180 516 167 781 700;
www.sonnenhotels.de).
104 rooms.

◊ Der Achtermann €€€
Rosentorstrasse 20
(tel: 05321 70000; www.hotel-
der-achtermann.de).
152 rooms.

◊ Kaiserworth €€
Markt 3
(tel: 05321 7090;
www.kaiserworth.de).
Also ⌖ €€.
66 rooms.

WERNIGERODE Sachsen-
Anhalt
◊ Am Anger €
Breite Strasse 92–94
(tel: 03943 92320; www.hotel-
am-anger.de).
29 rooms.

⌖ Ratskeller €
Am Marktplatz 1
(tel: 03943 632704).
*A mix of traditional German and
Continental cuisine.*

HERZBERG Niedersachsen
◊ Landhaus Schulze €
Osteroder Strasse 7
(tel: 05521 89940;
www.landhaus-schulze.de).
20 rooms.
Also ⌖ €.

**TOUR 7
GÖTTINGEN**
Niedersachsen
◊ Central €€
Judenstrasse 12
(tel: 0551 57157;
www.hotel-central.com).
51 rooms.

◊ Gebhards €€
Goethe Allee 22–23
(tel: 0551 49680;
www.gebhardshotel.de).
Also ⌖ €€
61 rooms.

🍽 **Ratskeller €€**
Markt 9
(tel: 0551 56433).
German cooking in the town hall cellar.

HILDESHEIM
Niedersachsen
◇ **Bürgermeisterkapelle €€**
Rathausstrasse 8
(tel: 05121 179290;
www.hotelbuerger
meisterkapelle.de).
41 rooms.

HAMELN Niedersachsen
◇ **Mercure Hameln €€**
164er Ring 3
(tel: 05151 7920;
www.mercure.com).
105 rooms.

◇ **Hotel zur Börse €€**
Osterstrasse 41A
(tel: 05151 7080;
www.hotel-zur-boerse.de).
31 rooms.

◇ **Hotel zur Post €**
Am Posthof 6
(tel: 05151 7630,
fax: 05151/7641).
31 rooms.

🍽 **Klütturm €€**
Auf dem Klütberg
(tel: 05151 61644).
Traditional German cuisine.

🍽 **Rattenfängerhaus €€**
Osterstrasse 28
(tel: 05151 3888).
German cuisine, popular with tourists.

PADERBORN Nordrhein-
Westfalen
◇ **Ibis €**
Paderwall 1–5
(tel: 05251 1245;
www.ibishotel.com).
90 rooms.

🍽 **Zu den Fischteichen €€**
Dubelohstrasse 92
(tel: 05251 33236).
An extensive menu, including fish, steaks and vegetarian dishes, in a rambling villa setting.

HANN-MÜNDEN
Niedersachsen
◇ **Schmucker Jäger €**
Wilhelmshäuser Strasse 45
(tel: 05541 98100. Also 🍽 €.
30 rooms.

TOUR 8
KASSEL Hessen
◇ **Mark Hotel Hessenland €**
Obere Königsstrasse 2
(tel: 0561 91810; www.
markhotelhessenland.de).
48 rooms.

🍽 **Restaurant Park Schönfeld €€**
Bosestrasse 13
(tel: 0561 22050).
French cuisine in a country manor.

WALDECK Hessen
◇ **Schloss Waldeck €€**
Am Schlossberg
(tel: 05623 5890, fax: 05623
589289). Also 🍽 €€/€€€.
40 rooms.

MARBURG/LAHN
Hessen
◇ **Rosenpark €€–€€€**
Rosenstrasse 18
(tel: 06421 60050;
www.vilavitahotels.com).
138 rooms.

🍽 **Zur Sonne €**
Markt 14
(tel: 06421 17190).
German and international cooking.

BAD HERSFELD Hessen
◇ **Romantik Hotel Zum Stern €**
Linggplatz 11
(tel: 06621 1890;
www.zumsternhersfeld.de).
Also 🍽 €€.
45 rooms.

TOUR 9
HAGEN Nordrhein-
Westfalen
◇ **Mercure €€**
Wasserloses Tal 4
(tel: 02331 3910;
www.mercure.com).
Also 🍽 €€.
146 rooms.

MESCHEDE Nordrhein-
Westfalen
◇ **Hennedamm €**
Am Stadtpark 6
(tel: 0291 99600;
www.hennedamm-hotel.de).
Also 🍽 €/€€.
34 rooms.

BRILON Nordrhein-
Westfalen
◇ **Waldhotel Klaholz €**
Hölsterloh 1
(tel: 02961 3473; www.
waldhotel-klaholz.de).
20 rooms,

FREUDENBERG
Nordrhein-Westfalen
◇ **Hotel Zur Altstadt €**
Oranienstrasse 41
(tel: 02734 4960, fax: 02734
49649). Also 🍽 €.
42 rooms.

TOUR 10
WÜRZBURG Bayern
◇ **Mercure Hotel Würzburg am Mainufer €€**
Dreikronenstrasse 27
(tel: 0931 41930;
www.mercure.com).
Also 🍽 €€.
129 rooms.

COBURG Bayern
◇ **Stadt Coburg €**
Lossaustrasse 12
(tel: 09561 8740; www.hotel-
stadt-coburg.de). Also 🍽 €/€€
44 rooms.

BAYREUTH Bayern
◇ **Bayerischer Hof €€**
Bahnhofstrasse 14
(tel: 0921 78600;
www.bayerischer-hof-de).
50 rooms.

🍽 **Bürgerreuth €€**
An der Bürgerreuth 20
(tel: 0921 78400).
Wide-ranging Italian menu.

BAMBERG Bayern
◇ **Barock Hotel am Dom €€**
Vorderer Bach 4
(tel: 0951 54031;
www.barockhotel.de).
41 rooms.

◇ **National €€**
Luitpoldstrasse 37
(tel: 0951 509980; www.hotel-national-bamberg.de).
41 rooms.

🍽 **Romantik Restaurant-Weinhaus Messerschmitt €€**
Lange Strasse 41
(tel: 0951 297800).
Franconian and international cooking.

TOUR 11
NÜRNBERG Bayern
◇ **Ramada Nürnberg Park €€**
Münchener Strasse 25
(tel: 0911 47480;
www.ramada.com). Also 🍽 **€€**.
200 rooms.

◇ **City Hotel €**
Königstrasse 25–27
(tel: 0911 225638).
20 rooms.

◇ **Dürer €€**
Neutormauer 32
(tel: 0911 2146650;
www.altstadthotels-nuernberg.de).
107 rooms.

◇ **Ibis Nürnberg Centrum €**
Steinbühler Strasse 2
(tel: 0911 23710;
www.ibishotel.com). Also 🍽 **€**.
155 rooms.

🍽 **Weinhaus Steichele €**
Knorrstrasse 2–8
(tel: 0911 202280)
Franconian and Bavarian specialities.

WEIDEN Bayern
◇ **Europa €**
Frauenrichter Strasse 173
(tel: 0961 670710;
www.hoteleuropaweiden.de).
Also 🍽 **€€**.
24 rooms.

EICHSTÄTT Bayern
◇ **Adler €€**
Marktplatz 22
(tel: 08421 6767;
www.adler-eichstaett.de).
28 rooms.

🍽 **Domherrenhof €€**
Domplatz 5
(tel: 08421 6126).
Regional cuisine in a refined setting.

TOUR 12
PASSAU Bayern
◇ **Altstadt €€**
Bräugasse 23–29
(tel: 0851 3370;
www.altstadt-hotel.de).
54 rooms.

CHAM Bayern
◇ **Randsberger Hof €**
Randsbergerhofstrasse 15–19
(tel: 09971 85770, fax: 09971 20299). Also 🍽 **€**.
101 rooms.

REGENSBURG Bayern
◇ **Orphée €€**
Untere Bachgasse 8
(tel: 0941 596020;
www.hotel-orphee.de).
24 rooms.

◇ **Münchner Hof €**
Tändlergasse 9
(tel: 0941 58440;
www.muenchner-hof.de).
Also 🍽 **€€**.
53 rooms.

◇ **Park Hotel Maximilian €€€**
Maximilianstrasse 28
(tel: 0941 56850;
www.maximilian-hotel.de).
52 rooms.

◇ **Sorat Insel-Hotel €€**
Müllerstrasse 7
(tel: 0941 81040;
www.sorat-hotels.com).
75 rooms.

🍽 **Zum Neuen Gänsbauer €€€**
Keplerstrasse 10
(tel: 0941 57858).
Bavarian/international cuisine.

INGOLSTADT Bayern
◇ **Bavaria €**
Feldkirchener Strasse 67
(tel: 0841 95340; www.bavariahotel-ingolstadt.de).
40 rooms.

LANDSHUT Bayern
◇ **Romantik Hotel Fürstenhof €€**
Stethaimer Strasse 3
(tel: 0871 925502). Also 🍽 **€€**
24 rooms.

TOUR 13
ROSENHEIM Bayern
◇ **Parkhotel Crombach €€**
Kufsteiner Strasse 2
(tel: 08031 3580;
www.parkhotel-crombach.de).
62 rooms.

BAD REICHENHALL Bayern
◇ **Parkhotel Luisenbad €€**
Ludwigstrasse 33
(tel: 08651 6040; www.parkhotel.de). Also 🍽 **€€**
89 rooms.

BERCHTESGADEN Bayern
◇ **Krone €**
Am Rad 5
(tel: 08652 94600; www.hotel-krone-berchtesgaden.de).
21 rooms.

◇ **Vier Jahreszeiten €€**
Maximilian Strasse 20
(tel: 08652 9520).
59 rooms.

◇ **Wittelsbach €€**
Maximilian Strasse 16
(tel: 08652 96380).
29 rooms.

🍽 **Panorama Restaurant €€**
In Alpenhotel Kronprinz, Am Brandholz
(tel: 08652 6070).
German/international cooking.

TOUR 14
MÜNCHEN Bayern
◇ **Eden-Hotel-Wolff €€€**
Arnulfstrasse 4
(tel: 089 551150;
www.ehw.de).
210 rooms.

◇ **Bayerischer Hof €€€**
Promenadeplatz 2–6
(tel: 089 21200;
www.bayerischerhof.de).
Also 🍽 **€€€**.
395 rooms.

◇ **Exquisit €€**
Pettenkoferstrasse 3
(tel: 089 5519900; www.hotel-exquisit-de).
50 rooms.

◎ **Austernkeller €€€**
Stollbergstrasse 11
(tel: 089 298787).
Seafood in a cellar, especially oysters.

◎ **Ratskeller €/€€**
Marienplatz 8
(tel: 089 2199890).
Bavarian and Franconian dining in the town hall cellar.

ROTTACH-EGERN
Bayern
◇ **Bachmair am See €€€**
Seestrasse 47
(tel: 08022 2720; www.bachmair.de). Also ◎ **€€€**.
288 rooms.

◇ **Gästehaus Haltmair am See €€**
Seestrasse 35
(tel: 08022 2750; www.haltmair.de).
42 rooms.

BAD TÖLZ Bayern
◇ **Tölzer Hof €€**
Rieschstrasse 21
(tel: 08041 8060; www.toelzer-hof.de).
Also ◎ **€€**.
83 rooms.

TOUR 15
MÜNCHEN see **TOUR 14**.
◇ **Advokat €€€**
Baaderstrasse 1
(tel: 089 216310; www.hotel-advokat.de).
50 rooms.

◎ **Boettner's €€€**
Pfisterstrasse 9
(tel: 089 221210).
Top-class international cuisine.

GARMISCH-PARTENKIRCHEN
Bayern
◇ **Mercure €€**
Mittenwalder Strasse 2
(tel: 08821 7560; www.mercure.com).
112 rooms.

OBERAMMERGAU
Bayern
◇ **Alte Post €**
Dorfstrasse 19
(tel: 08822 9100; www.ogau.de). Also ◎ **€**.
32 rooms.

TOUR 16
AUGSBURG Bayern
◇ **Intercity Hotel €€**
Halderstrasse 29
(tel: 0821 50390; www.augsburgintercityhotel.de).
120 rooms.

◇ **Ibis Augsburg Beim Königsplatz €**
Hermanstrasse 25
(tel: 0821 50310; www.ibishotel.com).
Also ◎ **€**.
104 rooms.

◎ **Die Ecke €€–€€€**
Elias Holl Platz 2
(tel: 0821 510600).
Swabian and Bavarian cooking, with a touch of Mediterranean flair.

DONAUWÖRTH Bayern
◇ **Posthotel Traube €**
Kapellstrasse 14–16
(tel: 0906 706440; www.posthoteltraube.de).
43 rooms.

ULM Baden-Württemberg
◇ **Intercity Hotel €€**
Bahnhofplatz 1
(tel: 0731 96550; www.ulmintercityhotel.de).
Also ◎ **€€**.
135 rooms.

◇ **Maritim €€€**
Basteistrasse 40
(tel: 0731 9230; www.maritim.de).
287 rooms.

◎ **Zur Forelle €€**
Fischergasse 25
(tel: 0731 63924).
Swabian and German cooking as it used to be.

KEMPTEN Bayern
◇ **Parkhotel €€**
Bahnhofstrasse 1
(tel: 0831 25275;

www.parkhotelkempten.de).
Also ◎ **€€**.
42 rooms.

TOUR 17
LINDAU Bayern
◇ **Lindauer Hof €€€**
Seepromenade (tel: 08382 4064). Also ◎ **€€€**.
32 rooms.

◎ **Zum Sünfzen €€**
Maximilianstrasse 1
(tel: 08382 5865).
Bavarian, with focus on freshwater fish.

FÜSSEN Bayern
◇ **Hirsch €€**
Kaiser Maxmilian Platz 7
(tel: 08362 93980; www.hotelhirsch.de). Also ◎ **€€**.
53 rooms.

◎ **Schlossgasthof zum Hechten €€**
Ritterstrasse 6
(tel: 08362 91600).
Bavarian restaurant or self-service buffet.

TOUR 18
KONSTANZ Baden-Württemberg
◇ **Bayrischer Hof Konstanz €€**
Rosgartenstrasse 30
(tel: 07531 13040; www.bayrischer-hof-konstanz.de).
23 rooms.

◇ **Riva Konstanz €€€**
Seestrasse 25a
(tel: 07531 363090).
52 rooms.

◎ **Konzil-Gaststätten €€**
Hafen Strasse 2
(tel: 07531 21221).
Cuisine from the Bodensee district and lake.

SALEM Baden-Württemberg
◇ **Salmannsweiler Hof €**
Salmannsweiler Weg 5
(tel: 07553 92120; www.salmannsweiler-hof.de).
Also ◎ **€**.
10 rooms.

RAVENSBURG Baden-Württemberg
◇ **Romantik Hotel Waldhorn** €€
Marienplatz 15
(tel: 0751 36120;
www.waldhorn.de).
Also ⑩ €€/€€€.
30 rooms.

MEERSBURG Baden-Württemberg
◇ **Gasthof zum Bären** €€
Marktplatz 11
(tel: 07532 43220;
www.baeren-meersburg.de).
20 rooms.

⑩ **Residenz am See** €€€
Uferpromenade 11
(tel: 07532 80040).
Regional dishes and lake fish.

TOUR 19
FREIBURG IM BREISGAU
Baden-Württemberg
◇ **Central** €€
Wasserstrasse 6
(tel: 0761 31970;
www.central-freiburg.de).
49 rooms.

⑩ **Wolfshöhle** €€
Konviktstrasse 8
(tel: 0761 30303).
Fine Italian cuisine in an Old German setting.

DONAUESCHINGEN
Baden-Württemberg
◇ **Ochsen** €
Käferstrasse 18
(tel: 0771 80990; www.hotel-ochsen-ds.de). Also ⑩ €.
45 rooms.

BAD SÄCKINGEN Baden-Württemberg
◇ **Goldener Knopf** €€
Rathausplatz 9
(tel: 07761 5650;
www.goldenerknopf.de).
Also ⑩ €€.
71 rooms.

BADENWEILER Baden-Württemberg
◇ **Ritter** €€€
Friedrichstrasse 2
(tel: 07632 8310;
www.hotelritter.de).
75 rooms.

◇ **Schwarzmatt** €€€
Schwarzmattstrasse 6A
(tel: 07632 82010;
www.schwarzmatt.de).
41 rooms.

⑩ **Romantik Hotel zur Sonne** €€€
Moltkestrasse 4
(tel: 07632 75080).
Italian and German food.

TOUR 20
BADEN-BADEN Baden-Württemberg
◇ **Merkur** €€
Merkurstrasse 8–10
(tel: 07221 3030; www.merkur-hotel.de). Also ⑩ €€.
36 rooms.

FREUDENSTADT Baden-Württemberg
◇ **Bären** €€
33 Lange Strasse
(tel: 07441 2729).
36 rooms.
⑩ **Jägerstüble** €€
Marktplatz 12
(tel: 07441 2387).
Hearty helpings of Swabian and German cooking.

⑩ **Warteck** €€
Stuttgarter Strasse 14
(tel: 07441 91920).
Formal Swabian and German cooking.

STUTTGART Baden-Württemberg
◇ **Mercure City-Center** €€
Heilbronner Strasse 88
(tel: 0711 255580;
www.mercure.com).
Also ⑩ €€.
174 rooms.

◇ **Ibis Stuttgart City** €
Presselstrasse 15
(tel: 0711 255510;
www.ibis.com).
132 rooms.

LICHTENSTEIN Baden-Württemberg
◇ **Adler** €
Heerstrasse 26
(tel: 07129 4041; www.adler-lichtenstein.de). Also ⑩ €/€€.
65 rooms.

ALPIRSBACH Baden-Württemberg
◇ **Rössle** €
Aischbachstrasse 5
(tel: 07444 2281; www.roessle-alpirsbach.de). Also ⑩ €.
26 rooms.

TOUR 21
SAARBRÜCKEN Saarland
◇ **Domicil-Leidinger** €€
Mainzer Strasse 10
(tel: 0681 93270;
www.domicil-leidinger.de.
Also ⑩ €€.
91 rooms.

KAISERSLAUTERN
Rheinland-Pfalz
◇ **Novotel Kaiserslautern** €€
St Quentin Ring 1
(tel: 0631 20150;
www.novotel.com).
Also ⑩ €€.
149 rooms.

MANNHEIM
◇ **Dorint Hotel Kongress** €€
Friedrichsring 6
(tel: 0621 12510).
287 rooms.

⑩ **Drehrestaurant Skyline** €€€
Hans-Reschke-Ufer 2
(tel: 0621 419290).
Regional cooking in revolving restaurant.

⑩ **Eichbaum Brauhaus** €
Käfertalerstrasse 168
(tel: 0621 35385).
Café/restaurant in a brewery.

BAD DÜRKHEIM
Rheinland-Pfalz
◇ **Gartenhotel Heusser** €€
Seebacher Strasse 50–52
(tel: 06322 9300; www.hotel-heusser.de). Also ⑩ €€.
84 rooms.

TOUR 22
TRIER Rheinland-Pfalz
◇ **Deutscher Hof** €€
Südallee 25
(tel: 0651 97780; www.hotel-deutscher-hof.de). Also ⑩ €€.
102 rooms.

COCHEM Rheinland-Pfalz
◇ **Burg** €€
Moselpromenade 23
(tel: 02671 7117).
46 rooms.

◇ **Lohspeicher** €€
Obergasse 1 (Am Marktplatz)
(tel: 02671 3976;
www.lohspeicher.de).
9 rooms.

🍽 **Weissmühle im Enderttal** €€€
Endertstrasse 1
(tel: 02671 8955).
German cooking, local trout specialities.

KOBLENZ Rheinland-Pfalz
◇ **Ibis** €
Rizzastrasse 42
(tel: 0261 30240;
www.ibishotel.com).
106 rooms.

◇ **Brenner** €
Rizzastrasse 20–22
(tel: 0261 915780;
www.hotel-brenner.de).
24 rooms.

BINGEN Rheinland-Pfalz
◇ **Rheinhotel Starkenburger Hof** €
Rheinkai 1–2
(tel: 06721 14341).
30 rooms.

TOUR 23
HEIDELBERG Hessen
◇ **Marriott** €€
Vangerowstrasse 16
(tel: 06221 9080; www.
marriott.com). Also 🍽 €€.
248 rooms.

BAD MERGENTHEIM
Baden-Württemberg
◇ **Alte Münze** €
Münzgasse 12
(tel: 07931 5560;
www.hotelaltemuenze.de).
30 rooms.

◇ **Haus Bundschu** €€
Cronbergstrasse 15
(tel: 07931 9330).
50 rooms.

◇ **Victoria** €€
Poststrasse 2–4
(tel: 07931 5930;
www.victoria-hotel.de).
78 rooms.

🍽 **Schurk** €/€€
Markelsheim, Hauptstrasse 57
(tel: 07931 2132).
Wide-ranging German menu and an extensive wine list.

HEILBRONN Baden-Württemberg
◇ **Insel-Hotel** €€
Willy-Mayer-Brücke
(tel: 07131 6300; www.insel-hotel.de). Also 🍽 €€.
125 rooms.

🍽 **Ratskeller** €€
Rathaus, Marktplatz 7
(tel: 07131 84628).
Reliable German/Swabian fare.

TOUR 24
FRANKFURT AM MAIN
Hessen
◇ **Astoria** €/€€
Rheinstrasse 25
(tel: 069 975600;
www.block.de/astoria).
60 rooms.

🍽 **Main Tower** €€/€€€
Neue Mainzer Strasse 52–58
(tel: 069 36504777).
Continental cuisine in a towering restaurant.

BAD HONNEF Nordrhein-Westfalen
◇ **Seminaris** €€
Alexander von Humboldt Strasse 20
(tel: 02224 7710; www.
seminaris.de/badhonnef).
Also 🍽 €€.
213 rooms.

RÜDESHEIM Hessen
◇ **Traube-Aumüller** €€
Rheinstrasse 6–9
(tel: 06722 9140, fax: 06722
1573). Also 🍽 €/€€.
119 rooms.

WIESBADEN Hessen
◇ **Nassauer Hof** €€€
Kaiser-Friedrich-Platz 3–4
(tel: 0611 1330).
169 rooms.

🍽 **Käfer's** €€€
Kurhausplatz 1
(tel: 0611 536200).
International, two restaurants in one.

🍽 **Zur Rose** €€€
Bremthaler Strasse 1
(tel: 06127 4006).
German and French, romance and nostalgia.

TOUR 25
KÖLN Nordrhein-Westfalen
◇ **Euro Garden Cologne Zentral** €€
Domstrasse 10–16
(tel: 0221 16490; www.euro garden-hotel-koeln.de).
85 rooms.

◇ **Ibis Köln Centrum** €
Neue Weyerstrasse 4
(tel: 0221 20960;
www.ibishotel.com.
208 rooms.

BONN Nordrhein-Westfalen
🍽 **Café Bistro Pendel** €€
Vivatsgasse 2a
(tel: 0228 9766064)
International cuisine.

🍽 **Roses Restaurant** €€€
Martinsplatz 2a
(tel: 0228 4330653).
Classy fare in elegant surroundings.

ANDERNACH Rheinland-Pfalz
◇ **Villa am Rhein** €
Konrad Adenauer Allee 3
(tel: 02632 92740; www.villa-am-rhein.de). Also 🍽 €€.
Closed Sat.
25 rooms.

AACHEN Nordrhein-Westfalen
◇ **Aquis-Grana Cityhotel** €€
Büchel 32,
Buchkremerstrasse
(tel: 0241 4430; www.hotel-aquisgrana.com.
97 rooms.

🍽 **Nobis Printen** €
Münsterplatz 3
(tel: 0241 968000).
Café, sandwiches, cakes.

PRACTICAL INFORMATION

TOUR INFORMATION
The addresses, telephone numbers and opening times of the attractions mentioned in the tours, including the telephone numbers of the Tourist Information Centres are listed below tour by tour.

TOUR 1

i Steinstrasse 7, Hamburg.
Tel: 040 30051300.

i Stadtverwaltung Manfred-Samusch-Strasse 5, Ahrensburg.
Tel: 04102 770.

i Schlosswiese 7, Ratzeburg.
Tel: 04541 858565.

i Markt 14, Schwerin. Tel: 0385 5925212.

i Markt 11, Wismar. Tel: 03841 19433.

i Holstentorplatz 1, Lübeck.
Tel: 01805 882233.

i Andreas Gayk Strasse 31, Kiel.
Tel: 0431 656700.

i Altstädter Markt, Rendsburg.
Tel: 04331 21120.

1 Ahrensburg
Schloss Ahrensburg
Lübecker Strasse 1.
Tel: 04102 42510.
Open Mar–Oct Tue–Thu, Sat–Sun 11–5; Nov–Feb Wed, Sat–Sun 11–5.

2 Ratzeburg
Kreismuseum
Domhof 12.
Tel: 04541 86070.
Open Tue–Sun 10–1, 2–5.

3 Schwerin
Schweriner Schloss
Lennéstrasse 1.
Tel: 0385 525 2920.
Open mid-Apr to mid-Oct, Tue–Sun 10–6; mid-Oct to mid-Apr, Tue–Sun 10–5.
Staatliches Museum
Alter Garten 3, Werder-strasse.
Tel: 0385 59580.
Open mid-Apr to mid-Oct daily 10–6; mid-Oct to mid-Apr, Tue–Sun 10–5.

5 Lübeck
Museum Holstentor
Holstentorplatz.
Tel: 0451 1224129.
Open Jan–Mar Tue–Sun 11–5; Apr–Dec daily 10–6.
Rathaus
Rathausplatz.
Tel: 0451 1221005.
Tours Mon–Fri 11, noon & 3.

For History Buffs
Buddenbrookhaus
Mengstrasse 4, Lübeck.
Tel: 0451 1224190.
Open Apr–Dec, daily 10–6; Jan–Mar, daily 11–5.

Back to Nature
Naturschutzgebiet Graswerder
Heiligenhafen.
Tel: 04362 90720.

For Children
Hansa-Park
Sierksdorf, north of Lübeck.
Tel: 04563 4740.
Open Apr–Oct, daily 9–6.

Special to...
Sommerspiele
Schlossgarten, Eutin.
Tel: 04521 80010.
Open Jul & Aug.

TOUR 2

i Am Bahnhofplatz 15, Bremen.
Tel: 01805 101030.

i Ernst-August-Platz 8, Hannover.
Tel: 0511 12345111.

i Vor der Burg 1, Braunschweig.
Tel: 0531 4702040.

i Willy-Brandt-Platz 3, Wolfsburg.
Tel: 05361 899930.

i Markt 14–16, Celle.
Tel: 05141 1212.

i Borsteler Strasse 6, Bispingen.
Tel: 05194 39850.

1 Hannover
Neues Rathaus
Trammplatz 2, Am Maschpark.
Tel: 0511 16845333.
Open Mar–Oct, Mon–Fri 9.30–6, Sat–Sun 10–6.30; Nov–Feb, daily 11–4.30.
Herrenhäuser Gärten
Herrenhäuser Strasse 4.
Tel: 0511 16844543.
Open daily 9am–sunset.
Kestner Museum
Trammplatz 3.
Tel: 0511 16842120.
Open Tue–Sun 11–6 (to 8pm on Wed).
Niedersächsisches Landesmuseum
Willy Brandt Allee 5–8.
Tel: 0511 9807686.
Open Tue–Sun 10–5, Thu 10–7.
Sprengel Museum
Kurt-Schwitters-Platz.
Tel: 0511 16843875.
Open Tue 10–8, Wed–Sun 10–6.

2 Braunschweig
Herzog-Anton-Ulrich Museum
Museumstrasse 1.
Tel: 0531 12250.
Open Tue & Thu–Sun 10–5, Wed 1–8.

3 Wolfsburg
Volkswagenwerk–Autostadt
Stadtbrücke.
Tel: 0800 288678238.
Open Apr–Oct, 10–8; Nov–Mar, 10–6.

Schloss Wolfsburg
Schlossstrasse 8.
Tel: 05361 828530.

4 Wienhausen
Kloster (Convent)
Tel: 05149 18660.
Open Apr to mid-Oct, guided tours Sun & church holidays noon–5, other days 10–11, 2–5.

Back to Nature
Serengeti-Park
Hodenhagen.
Tel: 05164 97990.
Open mid-Mar to Oct, 10–6.
Vogelpark Walsrode
Walsrode.
Tel: 05161 60440.
Open Mar–Oct, daily 9–6 or 7; Nov–Feb, daily 10–4.

For Children
Heide-Park
Soltau.
Tel: 01805 919101.
Open Apr–Oct, daily 9–6 (Sat to 8pm in summer).

TOUR 3

i Berlin Hauptbahnhof, Europaplatz 1, Berlin.
Tel: 030 250025.

i Brandenburger Strasse 3, Potsdam.
Tel: 0331 275580.

i Ehm-Welk Strasse 15, Lübbenau.
Tel: 03542 3668.

3 Museumsinsel
Pergamonmuseum
Tel: 030 20905577.
Open Tue–Sun 10–6 (Thu to 10pm). Check at all museums before visiting.
Bode-Museum
Tel: 030 20905577
Open Tue–Sun 10–6 (Thu to 10pm).
Alte Nationalgalerie
Tel: 030 20905577.
Open Tue–Sun 10–6, Thu to 10pm.

Altes Museum
Am Lustgarten.
Tel: 030 20905554.
*Open Tue–Sun 10–6
(Thu to 10pm).*

❹ Fernsehturm
Alexanderplatz.
Tel: 030 2423333.

**❼ Schloss
Charlottenburg**
Spandauer Damm 10–22.
Tel: 030 32091440.
*Open for tours Tue–Fri 9–5,
Sat–Sun 10–4.*

For Children
Zoologischer Garten
Hardenbergerplatz, Berlin.
Tel: 030 254010.
*Open daily 9–6 (to 5.30pm
Mar–Apr; to 6.30pm
May–Sep).*

Special to...
Checkpoint Charlie
Friedrichstrasse 44, Berlin.
Tel: 030 2537250.
Open daily 9am–10pm.

EXCURSION I

Potsdam
Schloss Sanssouci
Tel: 0331 9694190.
*Guided tours Tue–Sun 9–5
(to 4pm Nov–Mar).*
**Neue Kammern
(Orangerie)**
Tel: 0331 9694280.
*Guided tours mid-May to
mid-Oct, Tue–Sun 10–5.*
Schloss Cecilienhof
Tel: 0331 9694244
*Open Tue–Sun 9–5 (to 4pm
Nov–Mar).*

For History Buffs
Lutherstadt Wittenberg
Tourist Information Office,
Schlossplatz 2.
Tel: 03491 498610.
Lutherhalle
Collegienstrasse 54.
Tel: 03491 42030.
*Open Apr–Oct, 9–6;
Nov–Mar, Tue–Sun 10–5.*

EXCURSION 2

Lübbenau
Barge trip
Harbour.

Tel: 03542 2225.
*From 9am (weather
permitting).*

TOUR 4

i Richard Wagner
Strasse 1, Leipzig.
Tel: 0341 7104260.

i Markt 3, Meissen.
Tel: 03521 41940.

i Prager Strasse 2A,
Dresden.
Tel: 0351 49192100.

i Schlossallee 3b,
Moritzburg.
Tel: 035207 8540.

i Schreiberberg 2,
Königstein.
Tel: 035021 68261.

i Markt 12, Bad
Schandau.
Tel: 035022 90030.

i Markt 1, Colditz.
Tel: 034381 43579.

❶ Meissen
**Staatliche Porzellan
Manufaktur**
Talstrasse 9.
Tel: 03521 468700.
*Guided tours 9–6 daily.
Nov–Apr 9–5.*
Albrechtsburg
Domplatz 1.
Tel: 03521 47070.
*Open daily 10–6 (to 4pm
Nov–Feb).*

❷ Dresden
Zwinger Palace
Theaterplatz 1.
Tel: 0351 4914678.
Porzellansammlung
Zwinger, Sophienstrasse
2.
Tel: 0351 49142000.
Open Tue–Sun 10–6.

❸ Moritzburg
Schloss Moritzburg
Tel: 035207 8730.
*Open 10–5, Apr–Oct. Hourly
tours 10–4, rest of the year.*

❹ Königstein
Festung Königstein
Schreiberberg 2.

Tel: 035021 64607.
*Open Apr–Sep, 9–8; Oct,
9–6; Nov–Mar, 9–5.*

❻ Colditz
Colditz Castle
Tel: 034381 43777.
*Open Apr–Oct, Mon–Fri
8.30–5, Sat 9–5, Sun 10–5;
Nov–Mar, daily 10–5.*

Special To...
Weinstube Vincenz Richter
An der Frauenkirche 12,
Meissen.
Tel: 03521 453285.

For Children
Zoologischer Garten
Grosser Garten, Dresden.
Tel: 0351 478060.
*Open daily 8.30–6.30 (to
4.30pm Nov–Mar).*
Karl May Museum
Karl May Strasse 5,
Radebeul.
Tel: 0351 8373010.
*Open daily 9–6 (10–4
Nov–Feb).*

TOUR 5

i Markt 10, Weimar.
Tel: 03643 7450.

i Johannistrasse 23, Jena.
Tel: 03641 498050.

i Heinrichstrasse 35,
Gera.
Tel: 0365 8304480.

i Marktstrasse 13–15,
Friedrichroda.
Tel: 03623 33200.

i Markt 9, Eisenach.
Tel: 03691 79230.

i Ratsstrasse 20,
Mühlhausen.
Tel: 03601 404770.

i Hauptmarkt 33, Gotha.
Tel: 03621 50785712.

i Benediktsplatz 1, Erfurt.
Tel: 0361 66400.

❶ Jena
Zeiss Planetarium
Am Planetarium 5.
Tel: 03641 885488.
Shows Tue & Thu 11am &

*3pm, Wed & Fri 11am, Sat
& Sun 2 & 4pm.*

Optisches Museum
Carl Zeiss Platz 12.
Tel: 03641 443165.
*Open Tue–Fri 10–4.30, Sat
11–5.*

❸ Friedrichroda
Marienglashöhle
Friedrichroda.
Tel: 03623 304953.
*Open daily 9–5 (Nov–Mar
to 4pm).*

❹ Eisenach
Wartburg Castle
Tel: 03691 2500.
Open daily 8.30–5.
Thüringer Museum
Stadtschloss.
Tel: 03691 79230.
Open Tue–Sun 11–5.
Lutherhaus
Lutherplatz 8.
Tel: 03691 29830.
Open daily 10–5.
Bachhaus
Frauenplan 21.
Tel: 03691 79340.
Open 10–6.
Automobilbaumuseum
Friedrich Naumann Strasse.
Tel: 03691 77212.
Open Tue–Sun 10–5.

❺ Mühlhausen
Rabenturm
Frauentor.
Tel: 03601 816020.
Open Tue–Sun 10–5.

❻ Gotha
Schlossmuseum
Schloss Friedenstein,
Schlossberg.
Tel: 03621 823414.
*Open Tue–Fri 10–5
(Nov–Apr to 4pm).*

❼ Erfurt
Gartenbaumuseum
Cyriaksburg, Gothaer
Strasse 50.
Tel: 0361 2239700.
*Open Mar–Oct, Tue–Sun
10–6 (also Mon Jul–Aug).*
Dom (Cathedral)
Domstufen 1.
Tel: 0361 6461265.
*Open Mon–Fri 9–11.30,
12.30–5, Sat till 4.30, Sun
1–5.*

Angermuseum
Anger 18.
Tel: 0361 554560.
Open Tue–Sun 10–6.

For Children
Mon Plaisir Dolls'
Exhibition
Neues Palais, Arnstadt.
Tel: 0362 8602932.
Open Tue–Sun 9.30–4.30.

TOUR 6

i Markt 7, Goslar.
Tel: 05321 78060.

i Nordhäuser Strasse 4,
Bad Harzburg.
Tel: 05322 75330.

i Marktplatz 10,
Wernigerode.
Tel: 03943 5537835.

i Ritscherstrasse 4, Bad
Lauterberg.
Tel: 05524 92040.

i Marktplatz 32,
Herzberg.
Tel: 05521 852111.

i Dörgestrasse 40,
Osterode. Tel: 05522
318360.

i Bergstrasse 31,
Clausthal-Zellerfeld.
Tel: 05323 81024.

2 Wernigerode
Schlossmuseum
Schloss Adalbert.
Tel: 03943 553030.
*Open daily 10–6. Closed
Mon, Nov–Apr.*

6 Herzberg
Schloss
Tel: 05521 4799.
*Open Apr–Oct, Tue–Fri 10–1,
2–5 (6pm weekends);
Nov–Mar, Tue–Fri 11–1, 2–4
(5pm weekends).*

7 Clausthal-Zellerfeld
Oberharzer
Bergwerkmuseum
Bernhardtstrasse 16.
Tel 05323 98950.
Open daily 9–5.

Alte Silberminen
Wildemann. Tel tourist
office: 05323 6700.
Iberger Tropfsteinhöhle
Bad Grund.
Tel: 05323 81024,
*Open Apr–Oct, daily 9–4.30;
Nov–Mar, Tue–Sun 10–3.30.*

Back to Nature
Wild Deer Park
Haus der Natur, Bad
Harzburg.
Tel: 05322 559996.
Open daily dawn–dusk.

For Children
Märchenwald
Bad Harzburg.
Tel: 05322 23590.
Open daily 10–6.

Back to Nature
Wernigerode Wildlife
Park
Christianental.
Tel: 03943 25292.

TOUR 7

i Altes Rathaus, Markt 9,
Göttingen.
Tel: 0551 499800.

i Am Münster 6,
Northeim.
Tel: 05551 913066.

i Marktstrasse 13,
Einbeck.
Tel: 05561 3131910.

i Rathausstrasse 18–20,
Hildesheim.
Tel: 05121 17980.

i Deisterallee 1, Hameln.
Tel: 05151 957823.

i Marienplatz 2a,
Paderborn.
Tel: 05251 882980.

i Rathaus (Town Hall),
Lotzestrasse 2, Hann
Münden.
Tel: 05541 75313.

3 Hildesheim
Roemer-Pelizaeus Museum
Steine 1–2.
Tel: 05121 93690.
Open daily 10–6.

Schloss Marienburg
Pattensen.
Tel: 05069 407.
Open Apr–Oct, daily 10–6.

5 Paderborn
Dom (Cathedral) and
Diocesan Museum
Domplatz.
Tel: 05251 1251400.
Open Tue–Sun 10–6.

6 Hann Münden
Welfenschloss
Schlossplatz 5.
Tel: 05541 75202.
*Open Wed–Fri 10–noon,
2.30–5, Sat 10–noon,
2.30–4, Sun 10–12.30.*

For Children
Safaripark Stuckenbrock
Hollywood Park, Mittweg
16, Stuckenbrock.
Tel: 05207 952425.
*Open Apr–Oct, 9–6; Jun to
mid-Sep to 7.*

TOUR 8

i Rathaus, Obere
Königsstrasse 8, Kassel.
Tel: 0561 707707.

i Sachsenhäuser Strasse
10, Waldeck.
Tel: 05623 99980.

i Obermarkt 7–13,
Frankenberg.
Tel: 06451 505113.

i Pilgrimstein 26,
Marburg/Lahn.
Tel: 06421 99120.

i Markt 12, Alsfeld.
Tel: 06631 9110243.

i Markt 1, Bad Hersfeld.
Tel: 06621 201274.

1 Wilhelmsthal
Schloss Wilhelmsthal
Tel: 05674 6898.
*Open Mar–Oct, Tue–Sun
10–5; Nov–Feb, Tue–Sun
10–4. Guided tours.*

2 Waldeck
Hexenturm und
Burgmuseum
Schlosshotel.
Tel: 05623 5890.

*Open Mar–Oct, 9–6 Nov
Wed–Sun 10–4. Closed 16
Nov–Feb.*

4 Marburg/Lahn
Elisabethkirche
Tel: 06421 62245.
Open daily 9–6.
Schloss Marburg
Schlosspark.
Tel: 06421 2822355.
*Open Apr–Oct, Tue–Sun
10–6; Nov–Mar 11–5.*

Special to...
Glasshütte Süssmuth
Glasmuseum, Am Bahnhof
3, Immenhausen.
Tel: 05673 2060.
*Open Tue–Fri 10–5,
Sat 11–5, Sun 10–5.*

For History Buffs
Cistercian Abbey
Bahnhofstrasse 8–10,
Haina.
Tel: 06451 505113.
*Open Tue, Thu, Sat & Sun
10–noon.*

Special to…
Bad Hersfeld Stiftskirche
(ruins)
Tel: 06621 201274.
*Open Mar–early May &
Sep–Oct, Tue–Sun
10–12.30, 2–4.*

TOUR 9

i Rathausstrasse 13,
Hagen.
Tel: 02331 2075886.

i Theodor Heuss Ring
24, Iserlohn.
Tel: 02371 2171820.

i Neumarkt 6, Arnsberg.
Tel: 02931 4055.

i Dieplohstrasse 1,
Warstein.
Tel: 02902 2731.

i Von-Stephan-Strasse 2,
Meschede.
Tel: 0291 9022443.

i Derkere Strasse 10a,
Brilon.
Tel: 02961 96990.

[i] Rathaus (Town Hall),
Markt 2, Siegen.
Tel: 0271 4041316.

[i] Krottorfer Strasse 25,
Freudenberg.
Tel: 02734 43164.

[1] Iserlohn
Dechenhöhle
Iserlohn.
Tel: 023714 71421.
*Open Apr–Oct, daily
10–5; Mar–Nov, daily 10–4;
Dec–Feb, Sat–Sun 10–4.*

[2] Arnsberg
Sauerland Museum
Alter Markt 24–26,
Arnsberg.
Tel: 02931 4098.
*Open Tue–Fri 9–5, Sat–Sun
10–6.*

[3] Bilsteinhöhle
Städtisches Museum
Belecker Landstrasse 9,
Warstein.
Tel: 02902 1078.

[5] Ramsbeck
**Erzbergbaumuseum
(Mining Museum)**
Tel: 02905 250.
Guided tours.

[7] Siegen
Siegerland Museum
Oberen Schloss,
Burgstrasse.
Tel: 0271 230410.
Open Tue–Sun 10–5.

Back to Nature
Heinrichshöhle
Hemer.
Tel: 02372 61549.
*Open mid-Mar to Oct,
guided tours daily 10–6; Nov
to mid-Mar, Sat–Sun
noon–4.*

For Children
Fort Fun Abenteuerland
Bestwig, Wasserfall.
Tel: 02905 81123.
Open Apr–Oct, 10–5.

TOUR 10

[i] Congress-Centrum,
Würzburg.
Tel: 0931 372335.

[i] Herrngasse 4, Coburg.
Tel: 09561 74180.

[i] Marktplatz 5, Kronach.
Tel: 09261 97236.

[i] Luitpoldplatz 9,
Bayreuth.
Tel: 0921 88588.

[i] Geyerswörthstrasse 3,
Bamberg.
Tel: 0951 2976200.

[i] Rathausplatz 2, Ebrach.
Tel: 09553 92200.

[1] Coburg
Schloss Ehrenburg
Schlossplatz.
Tel: 09561 808832.
*Guided tours Apr–Sep,
Tue–Sun 9–5 every hour;
Oct–Mar, Tue–Sun 10–3
every hour.*
Veste Coburg
Festungstrasse.
Tel: 09561 8790.
*Open Apr–Oct, daily 9.30–5;
Nov–Mar, Tue–Sun 1–4.*

[2] Kronach
Schloss Rosenberg
Tel: 09261 60410.
*Open Mar–Oct, Tue–Sun
9.30–5.30; Nov–Feb,
Tue–Sun 11 & 2.*

[3] Bayreuth
Richard Wagner Museum
Tel: 0921 757280.
*Open Apr–Oct, 9–5 (to
8pm Tue & Thu); Nov–Mar,
daily 10–5.*
Festspielhaus
Tel: 0921 78780.
*Guided tours Tue–Sun 10, 2.
Closed Nov, during
rehearsals & afternoons
during festival.*
Opera House
Tel: 0921 7596922.
*Guided tours Apr–Sep, daily
9–4; Oct–Mar, daily
10–4. Closed days of perfor-
mance & rehearsals.*
Neues Schloss
Tel: 0921 7596921.
*Guided tours Apr–Sep, daily
9–6; Oct–Mar, daily 10–4.
Tours in English on request.*

[4] Bamberg
**Dom (Cathedral) and
Diocesan Museum**
Tel: 0951 502325.
Open Tue–Sun 10–5.

**Alte Hofhaltung and
Historisches Museum**
Tel: 0951 871142.
*Open Apr–Oct, Tue–Sun 9–5
(from mid-May daily 10–5).*
Neue Residenz
Tel: 0951 519390.
*Tours late Jul to mid-Oct,
daily 9–6.*

For History Buffs
Schloss Ermitage
Bayreuth.
Tel: 0921 7596937.
*Open Apr–Sep, daily 9–6,
Oct (first 2 weeks) 10–3.*

TOUR 11

[i] Königstrasse 93,
Nürnberg.
Tel: 0911 2336132.

[i] Oberer Markt 2,
Altdorf.
Tel: 09187 807100.

[i] Hallplatz 2, Amberg.
Tel: 09621 10239.

[i] Dr Pfleger Strasse 17,
Weiden.
Tel: 0961 4808250.

[i] Marktplatz 9,
Vohenstrauss.
Tel: 09651 922230.

[i] Marktplatz 1, Kallmünz.
Tel: 09473 94010.

[i] Marktplatz 2,
Kipfenberg.
Tel: 08465 941040.

[i] Domplatz 8. Eichstätt.
Tel: 08421 6001400.

[i] Martin Luther Platz 3,
Weissenburg.
Tel: 09141 907124.

[i] Weissenburger Strasse
1, Ellingen.
Tel: 09141 976543.

[i] Stillaplatz 1, Abenberg.
Tel: 09178 98800.

[i] Schloss Ratibor,
Hauptstrasse 1, Roth.
Tel: 09171 848513.

[5] Altdorf
**König Otto
Tropfsteinhöhle**
St Colomann, 3km (2
miles) north of Velburg.
Tel: 09182 93020.
Open Apr–Oct, daily 9–5.

[7] Eichstätt
**Dom and
Diözesanmuseum**
Tel: 08421 50742.
*Open Apr–Nov, Wed–Fri
10.30–5, Sat–Sun 10–5.*
**Fürstbischöfliche
Residenz**
Prince Bishops Palace.
Tel: 08421 98880.
*Guided tours Mon–Thu 11,
3, Fri 11, Sat 10.15, 3.30.*

[10] Abenberg
Burg Abenberg
Burgstrasse 16.
Tel: 09178 982990.

[11] Roth
Schloss Ratibor
Hauptstrasse 1.
Tel: 09171 848532.
*Open Apr–Sep, Tue–Sun
1–5. Also by arrangement.*

Special to...
Glass Road
Tourismusbüro Neustadt a
d Waldnaab.
Tel: 09602 79105:

TOUR 12

[i] Rathausplatz 3, Passau.
Tel: 0851 955980.

[i] Schulgasse 2, Regen.
Tel: 09921 60426.

[i] Propsteistrasse 46,
Cham.
Tel: 041 7803222.

[i] Altes Rathaus (Old
Town Hall), Rathausplatz 3,
Regensburg.
Tel: 0941 5074410.

[i] Donaupark 13,
Kelheim.
Tel: 09441 68340.

[i] Marktplatz 1,
Riedenburg.
Tel: 09442 905000.

[i] Rathausplatz 4,
Ingolstadt.
Tel: 0841 3053030.

[i] Rathaus, Altstadt 315,
Landshut.
Tel: 0871 922050.

3 Regensburg
Dom & Domschatz
Domplatz.
Tel: 0941 5865500.
*Open May–Oct, Mon–Sat
noon–6.30, Sun noon–6;
Nov–Apr, Mon–Sat 8–4, Sun
noon–6.*
Reichstagsmuseum
Rathausplatz 4.
Tel: 0941 5074410.
*Guided tours Mon–Sat 9.30,
10.30, 11.30, 2, 3, 4, Sun 10,
11, 12. English Mon–Sat 3.*
Schloss Thurn and Taxis
Emmeramsplatz.
Tel: 0941 5048133.
*Guided tours Apr–Oct,
Mon–Fri 11, 2, 3, 4, Sat–Sun
10, 11, 1, 2, 3, 4; Nov–Mar,
Sat–Sun 10, 11, 2, 3.*
Kepler Gedächtnishaus
Keplerstrasse 5.
Tel: 0941 5073442.
Open Sat–Sun 10.30–4

4 Donaustauf
Walhalla
Near Donaustauf.
Tel: 09403 961680.
*Open Apr–Sep, daily 9–5.45;
Oct, 9–4.45; Nov–Mar,
10–11.45, 1–3.45.*

5 Kelheim
**Befreiungshalle (Liberation
Hall)**
Kelheim.
Tel: 09441 682070.
*Open daily 9–6; mid-Mar to
Oct 9–4.*
Kloster Weltenburg
Tel: 09441 3682.
*Open mid-Mar to mid-Nov
8–7; closed Mon, Tue.*

6 Essing
**Grosse and Kleine
Schulerlochhöhle (caves)**
Infozentrum Naturpark
Altmühltal, Eichstätt.
Tel: 08421 98760.

7 Riedenburg
Rosenburg
Tel: 09442 2752.
Schloss Prunn
Tel: 09442 3323.
Schloss Eggersberg
Tel: 09442 91870.

8 Ingolstadt
**Bayerisches Armee-
museum**
Neues Schloss, Paradeplatz.
Tel: 0841 93770.
Open Tue–Sun 8.45–4.30.

9 Landshut
Burg Trausnitz
Alte Bergstrasse.
Tel: 0871 924110.
*Open Apr–Sep, daily 9–6;
Oct–Mar, 10–4.*
Stadtresidenz
Tel: 0871 41110.
*Tours Apr–Sep, Tue–Sun
9–6; Oct–Mar, Tue–Sun
10–4.*

TOUR 13

[i] Kufsteiner Strasse 4,
Rosenheim.
Tel: 08031 3659061.

[i] Alte Rathausstrasse 11
(Old Town Hall), Prien.
Tel: 08051 69050.

[i] Am Anger 1, Seebruck.
Tel: 0700 73327825.

[i] Kulturzentrum im
Stadtpark, Traunstein. Tel:
0861 9869523.

[i] Wittelsbacherstrasse
15, Bad Reichenhall.
Tel: 08651 60151.

[i] Maximilianstrasse 9,
Berchtesgaden.
Tel: 08652 9445300.

[i] Hauptstrasse 60, Ruh-
polding.
Tel: 08663 88060.

[i] Dorfstrasse 38, Reit im
Winkl.
Tel: 08640 80020.

2 Herrenchiemsee
Schloss Herrenchiemsee
Tel: 08051 68870.
Guided tours daily,

*Apr to mid-Oct, 9–6; mid-
Oct to Mar, 9.40–4.15.*
**Prien–Stock Landungssteg
Boat trips**
Tel: 0851 6090.

5 Bad Reichenhall
Alte Saline
Salinenstrasse.
Tel: 08651 702146.
*Tours May–Oct, daily
10–11.30, 2–4; Nov–Apr,
Tue–Thu 2–4.*

6 Berchtesgaden
Schloss
Schlossplatz.
Tel: 08652 947980.
*Guided tours mid-May to
mid-Oct, Sun–Fri 10–12,
2–4; mid-Oct to mid-May,
Mon–Fri 11, 2.*
Saltzbergwerk
Bergwerkstrasse 83.
Tel: 08652 600220.
*Guided tours May–Oct, daily
9–5; Nov–Apr, daily 1.30–3.*
Obersalzberg–Kehlstein
By bus from Berchtes-
gaden.
Tel: 08652 9670.
Open May–Oct.
**Rossfeld–Höhenring-
strasse**
Tel: 08652 9670.
Königsee boat trips
Tel: 08652 9670.
Open all year,

For Children
Freizeitpark
Vorderbrand 7, Ruhpolding.
Tel: 08663 1413.
*Open Apr–Oct, daily 9–6;
21 Dec–6 Jan, 10–7.*

TOUR 14

[i] Marienplatz, Neues
Rathaus, München.
Tel: 089 23396500.

[i] Bahnhofstrasse 11a,
Schliersee:
Tel: 08026 60650.

[i] Rathaus, Kirchenweg 6,
Gmund.
Tel: 08022 750527.

[i] Hauptstrasse 2,
Tegern-see.
Tel: 08022 927380.

[i] Rathaus Nördliche
Hauptstrasse 9, Rottach-
Egern.
Tel: 08022 671341.

[i] Adrian-Stoop-Strasse
20, Bad Wiessee.
Tel: 08022 86030.

[i] Kalmbachstrasse 11,
Kochel.
Tel: 08851 338.

[i] Prälatenstrasse 3,
Benediktbeuern.
Tel: 08857 248.

[i] Max Höfler Platz 1, Bad
Tölz.
Tel: 08041 78670.

3 Tegernsee
Schloss
Tel: 08022 4640.

8 Benediktbeuern
Benediktiner Kloster
Tel: 08857 880.
Guided tours all year round.

For Children
Alpamare Leisure Park
Bad Tölz.
Tel: 08041 509999.
Open daily 9–10.

TOUR 15

[i] Marienplatz, Neues
Rathaus, München.
Tel: 089 23396500.

[i] Wittelsbacherstrasse
2c, Starnberg.
Tel: 08151 90600.

[i] Ratsgasse 1, Berg.
Tel: 08151 5080.

[i] Weilheimer Strasse
1–3, Seeshaupt.
Tel: 08801 90710.

[i] Richard Strauss Platz
1a, Garmisch-
Partenkirchen.
Tel: 08821 180700.

[i] Elmau 10, Elmau.
Tel: 08823 180.

[i] Dammkarstrasse 3,
Mittenwald.
Tel: 08823 33981.

Practical • Information

ⓘ Ammergauer Strasse 8,
Ettal.
Tel: 08822 3534.

ⓘ Schloss Linderhof.
Tel: 08822 92030.

ⓘ Eugen-Papst-Strasse
9a, Oberammergau.
Tel: 08822 92310.

❶ Starnberg
Heimatmuseum
Tel: 08151 772132.
Open Tue–Sun 10–12, 1–5.

❷ Berg
Schlosshotel
Seestrasse 17.
Tel: 08151 9630.

❻ Mittenwald
**Geigenbau Museum and
Heimatmuseum**
Ballenhausgasse 3.
Tel: 08823 2511.
*Open Tue–Sun 10–5 (low
season 11–4).*

❼ Ettal
Kloster
Kaiser Ludwig Platz 1.
Tel: 08822 740.
*Open daily 8–6 (to 8pm in
summer).*

❽ Schloss Linderhof
Schloss
Tel: 08822 92030.
*Guided tours Apr–Sep, daily
9–6; Oct–Mar, daily 10–4.*

❾ Oberammergau
Passionsspielhaus
Tel: 08822 9458833.
*Tours May–Oct, 10–5;
Nov–Apr, 10–4.*

For History Buffs
Hotel Kaiserin Elisabeth
Feldafing.
Tel: 08157 93090.

Back to Nature
Osterseen
Landgasthof Osterseen,
Hofmark 9, Iffeldorf.
Tel: 08856 92860.

ⓘ Schiessgrabenstrasse
14, Augsburg.
Tel: 0821 502070.

ⓘ Rathausgasse 1,
Donauwörth.
Tel: 0906 789151.

ⓘ Rathaus, Königstrasse
37, Dillingen.
Tel: 09071 54108.

ⓘ Schlossplatz 1,
Günzburg.
Tel: 08221 200444.

ⓘ Münsterplatz 50, Ulm.
Tel: 0731 1612830.

ⓘ Marktplatz 3,
Memmingen.
Tel 08331 850172.

ⓘ Marktplatz 14,
Ottobeuren.
Tel: 08332 921950.

ⓘ Rathausplatz 24,
Kempten.
Tel: 0831 2525237.

ⓘ Rathaus, Kaiser-Max-
Strasse 1, Kaufbeuren.
Tel: 08341 40405.

ⓘ Rathaus, Hauptplatz
152, Landsberg.
Tel: 08191 128246.

❹ Ulm
Münster
Münsterplatz 1.
Tel: 0731 37994512.
*Open Nov–Feb, 9–5.45;
Mar, Apr, Sep, Oct, 9–6.45;
May–Aug, 8–6.45.*
Rathaus
Neue Strasse 1.
Tel: 0731 1610.
*Open Mon–Wed 7–4.30,
thu 7–6, Fri 7–12.*
Schwörhaus
Weinhof 12.
Tel: 0731 1614201.

❺ Memmingen
Stadtmuseum
Hermansbau, Zangmeister-
strasse 8.
Tel: 08331 850134.
*Open May–Oct, Tue–Sat
10–12, 2–4, Sun 10–4.*

❻ Ottobeuren
Klosterkirche
Tel: 08332 7980.
*Open daily Apr–Oct, 9–6;
Nov–Mar, 9–4.*

Kloster buildings
*Open Apr–Oct, daily 10–12,
2–5; Nov–Jan, 2–4;
Feb–Mar, Sat–Sun 2–4.*

❼ Kempten/Allgäu
Residenz
Residenzplatz, Kempten.
Tel: 0831 256251.
Basilika of St Lorenz
Stiftsplatz, Kempten.
Tel: 0831 5405600.

❽ Kaufbeuren
St Blasiuskirche
Blasiusberg 13.
Tel tourist office: 08341
40405.
**Stadtmuseum (Ganghofer
Museum)**
Tel: 08341 100232.

❾ Landsberg
Bayertor
Tel tourist office: 08191
128246.
*Open May–Oct, daily
10–noon, 2–5.*
Rathaus
Tel: 08191 128246.
*Open May–Oct, Mon–Fri
8–6, weekends 10–noon,
2–5; Nov–Apr, Mon–Wed
8–noon, 2–5, Thu 8–noon,
2–5.30, Fri 8–12.30.*

Special to...
Edwin Scharff Museum
Neu-Ulm.
Tel: 0731 9709526.

ⓘ Ludwigstrasse 68,
Lindau.
Tel: 08382 260030.

ⓘ Hugo-von-Königsegg
Strasse 8, Oberstaufen.
Tel: 08386 93000.

ⓘ Marienplatz 3,
Immenstadt.
Tel: 08323 914176.

ⓘ Rathausplatz 1,
Sonthofen.
Tel: 08321 615291.

ⓘ Marktplatz 7, Oberst-
dorf.
Tel: 08322 7000.

ⓘ Klein Walsertal, Austria,
Hirschegg im Walsertal.
Tel: 05517 51140.

ⓘ Kaiser-Maximilian-
Platz 1, Füssen.
Tel: 08362 93850.

ⓘ Unterer Grabenweg
18, Isny.
Tel: 07562 984110.

ⓘ Rathaus, Marktplatz 1,
Wangen. Tel: 07522 74211.

❻ Füssen
Rathaus
Former Benedictine Abbey,
Lechhalde.
Tel tourist office: 08362
93850.
*Open Apr–Oct, Tue–Sun
11–4; Nov–Mar, 2–4.*
Hohes Schloss
Ritterstrasse.
Tel: 08362 938512.
*Open Apr–Oct, Tue–Sun
11–4; Nov–Mar, 2–4.*
Schloss Hohenschwangau
Alpenseestrasse,
Schwangau.
Tel: 08362 930830.
*Open Apr–Sep, daily
8–5.30; Oct–Mar, daily
9–3.30.*
Schloss Neuschwanstein
Schwangau.
Tel: 08362 939880.
*Open Apr–Sep, daily 8–5;
Oct–Mar, daily 9–3.*

For History Buffs
Wieskirche
Near Steingaden.
Tel: 08862 932930.

ⓘ Bahnhofplatz 13,
Konstanz.
Tel: 07531 133030.

ⓘ Pirminstrasse 145, Insel
Reichenau.
Tel: 07534 92070.

ⓘ Landungsplatz 14,
Überlingen.
Tel: 07551 991122.

ⓘ Schulstrasse 12,
Unteruhldingen.
Tel: 07556 921620.

[i] Schloss Salem, Salem.
Tel: 07553 917515.

[i] Schulstrasse 5,
Heiligenberg.
Tel: 07554 998312.

[i] Saalplatz 7, Wilhelmsdorf.
Tel: 07503 9210.

[i] Münsterplatz 1,
Weingarten.
Tel: 0751 405125.

[i] Kirchstrasse 16,
Ravensburg.
Tel: 0751 82800.

[i] Bahnhofplatz 2,
Friedrichshafen.
Tel: 07541 30010.

[i] Kirchstrasse 4,
Meersburg.
Tel: 07532 440400.

❶ Insel Reichenau
Münster
Burgstrasse, Mittelzell.
Tel: 07534 246.
*Open 9–6, treasury May–
Oct, Mon–Sat 11–noon, 3–4.*

❷ Überlingen
Rathaus
Münsterplatz.
Tel: 07551 991011.
*Open Apr–Oct, Mon–Fri
9–noon, 2.30–5, Sat 9–noon;
Nov–Mar, closed Sat.*
Städtisches Museum
Reichlin von Meldegg Haus,
Krummebergstrasse 30.
Tel: 07531 991079.

❸ Unteruhldingen
Pfahlbaumuseum
Strandpromenade 6.
Tel: 07556 8543.
*Guided tours Apr–Sep, daily
9–7; Oct, 9–5; Nov–Feb,
weekends 9–5.*

❹ Salem
Münster and Schloss
Tel: 07553 81437.
*Guided tours Apr–1 Nov,
Mon–Sat 9.30–6, Sun
10.30–6.*

❻ Heiligenberg
Schloss
Tel: 07554 998312.

*Tours Apr–Oct, tue–Sun 9,
11, 2, 3.30.*

❼ Weingarten
Basilika
Martinsberg.
Tel: 0751 561270.
Open daily 8–6.

❽ Ravensburg
Mehlsack Turm
Mehlsackweg. Tel: 0751
82800.
Open Apr–Oct, Sun 10–2.

❾ Friedrichshafen
Zeppelin Museum
Seestrasse 22.
Tel: 07541 38010.
*Open Tue–Sun 10–7 (to
5pm Nov–Apr).*

❿ Meersburg
Altes Schloss Museum
Schlossplatz 10.
Tel: 07532 80000.
*Open Mar–Oct, 9–6.30;
Nov–Feb, 10–6.*
Neues Schloss
Schlossplatz.
Tel: 07532 440400.
*Guided tours in English by
arrangement.*
Weinbaumuseum
Vorburgstrasse 11.
Tel: 07532 82388.
*Open Apr–Oct, Tue, Fri, Sun
2–5.*

For History Buffs
Hohentwiel Ruins
Near Singen.
Tel: 07731 85264.

For History Buffs
Alemannenmuseum
Kornhaus, Karlstrasse 28,
Weingarten.
Tel: 0751 405125.
*Open Tue–Sun 3–5 (Thu to
6pm).*

Back to Nature
Mainau Island
Tel: 07531 3030.
Open daily.

TOUR 19

[i] Rathausplatz 2–4,
Freiburg im Breisgau.
Tel: 0761 3881880.

[i] Lindenstrasse 1,
Furtwangen.
Tel: 07723 92950.

[i] Wallfahrtstrasse 4,
Triberg.
Tel: 07722 866490.

[i] Rietgasse 2,
Villingen.
Tel: 07721 822340.

[i] Karlstrasse 58,
Donaueschingen.
Tel: 0771 857221.

[i] Strandbadstrasse 4,
Titisee-Neustadt.
Tel: 07651 98040.

[i] Meinrad Thoma Strasse
21, Todtnau.
Tel: 07671 969695.

[i] Kurgarten 1, St Blasien.
Tel: 07672 41430.

[i] Wallstrasse 26,
Waldshut-Tiengen.
Tel: 07751 833200.

[i] Waldshuter Strasse 20,
Bad Säckingen.
Tel: 07761 56830.

[i] Hauptstrasse 14, Wehr.
Tel: 07762 80601.

[i] Herrenstrasse 5,
Lörrach.
Tel: 07621 9408913.

[i] Hauptstrasse 18,
Kandern.
Tel: 07626 972356.

[i] Ernst-Eisenlohr-Strasse
4, Badenweiler.
Tel: 07632 799300.

[i] Am Marktplatz,
Sulzburg.
Tel: 07634 560040.

❶ Furtwangen
Deutsches Uhrenmuseum
Robert-Gerwig-Platz 1.
Tel: 07723 9202800.
*Open Apr–Oct, daily 9–6;
Nov–Mar, 10–5.*

❸ Villingen
Franziskanermuseum
Rietgasse 2.

Tel tourist office: 07721
822351.
*Open Tue–Sat 10–5; Sun &
holidays 11–5.*

❹ Donaueschingen
Schloss
Fürstenbergstrasse.
Tel: 0771 86563.
*Guided tours Easter–Sep,
Wed–Mon 9–noon, 2–5.*
Fürstenberg-Sammlungen
Karlsplatz 7.
Tel: 0771 86563.
*Open Apr–Nov, Tue–Sat
10–1, 2–5, Sun 10–5.*

❼ St Blasien
Dom
Fürstabt-Gerbert-Strasse.
Tel: 07672 678.
*Open May–Sep, 8–6.30;
Oct–Apr, 8–5.30.*

❾ Bad Säckingen
Hochrheinmuseum
Schloss Schönau,
Schönaugasse, Schlosspark.
Tel: 07761 2217.
Open Tue, Thu, Sun 2–5.

❿ Wehr
Haseler Tropfsteinhöhle
Tel tourist office: 07762
808601.
*Daily guided tours in
summer.*

⓫ Lörrach
Museum am Burghof
Baseler Strasse 143.
Tel: 07621 919370.
*Open Wed–Sat 2–5, Sun
11–1, 2–5.*

⓬ Kandern
Schlossmuseum
Schloss Bürgeln. Tel: 07626
237.
*Open for guided tours
Mar–Nov, Wed–Mon 11, 2,
3, 4, 5.*

⓮ Sulzburg
Bergbaumuseum (Mining
Museum)
Hauptstrasse 54.
Tel: 07634 560040.

TOUR 20

[i] Kaiserallee 3, Baden-
Baden.
Tel: 07221 275200.

i Marktplatz 64,
Freudenstadt.
Tel: 07441 8640.

i Marktplatz 5,
Herrenberg.
Tel: 07032 9240.

i Königstrasse 1a,
Stuttgart.
Tel: 0711 22280.

i An der Neckarbrücke
1, Tübingen.
Tel: 07071 91360.

i Listplatz 1, Reutlingen.
Tel: 07121 3032622.

i Rathausplatz 17,
Lichtenstein.
Tel: 07129 6960.

i Kirchplatz 12,
Hechingen.
Tel: 07471 940211.

i Färberstrasse 2,
Balingen.
Tel: 07433 170261.

i Hauptstrasse 20,
Alpirsbach.
Tel: 07444 9516281.

i Im Bahnhof Bleibach,
Gutach.
Tel 07685 19433.

i Winzerhof, Höllengasse
2, Gengenbach.
Tel: 07803 930143.

i Fischmarkt 2, Offenburg.
Tel: 0781 822000.

3 Stuttgart
Landesmuseum
Altes Schloss, Schillerplatz.
Tel: 0711 279 3498.
Open Tue–Sun 10–5.

4 Tübingen
Stiftskirche
Holzmarkt.
Tel: 07071 42046.
*Open Feb–Oct, 9–5;
Nov–Jan, 9–4.*

Hölderlinturm
Bursagasse 6.
Tel: 07071 22040.
*Open Tue–Fri 10–noon, 3–5,
weekends 2–5.*

6 Lichtenstein
Schloss
Hohenau.
Tel tourist office: 07129
6960.
*Open for guided tours
Feb–Mar, Nov, public holidays and weekends 9–noon,
1–5; Apr–Oct, Mon–Sat
9–noon, 1–5, Sun 9–5.30.*
Nebelhöhle
Unterhausen.
Tel tourist office: 07129
6960.
*Open Mar–Nov, daily
8.30–5.30.*

7 Hechingen
Burg Hohenzollern
Zeugenberg.
Tel: 07471 2428.
*Open daily 9–5.30 (to
4.30pm Nov to mid-Mar).*
Heimatmuseum
Altes Schloss, Schlossplatz.
Tel: 07471 6400.
Villa Rustica
*Open Tue–Sun 10–5 (daily
Jun–Oct).*

8 Balingen
Museum für Waage und
Gewicht
Zollernschloss.
Tel tourist office: 07433
170261.

9 Alpirsbach
Benediktiner Kloster
Ambrosius Blarer Platz.
Tel: 07444 51061.

Special to...
Mercedes-Benz Museum
Mercedesstrasse 100,
Stuttgart.
Tel: 0711 1730000.
Open Tue–Sun 9–6.
Porsche Museum
Porscheplatz 1, Stuttgart.
Tel: 0711 91125685.
Open Mon–Fri 9–4, weekends 9–5.

For Children
Europa-Park
Rust, Europa-Park Strasse
2. From Offenburg A5

south exit 576, west to
Rust.
Tel: 01805 776688.
*Open Apr–Oct, daily 9–6 (or
later); also some times in
winter.*

TOUR 21

i Reichsstrasse 1,
Saarbrücken.
Tel: 0681 938090.

i Poststrasse 12, Merzig.
Tel: 06861 72120.

i Freiherr-vom-Stein
Strasse 64, Mettlach.
Tel: 06864 8334.

i Graf-Siegfried-Strasse
32, Saarburg.
Tel: 06581 995980.

i Triererstrasse 5,
Nonnweiler.
Tel: 06873 6600.

i Hauptstrasse 419,
Oberstein.
Tel: 06781 56390.

i Fruchthallstrasse 14,
Kaiserslautern.
Tel: 0631 3652317.

i Neumarkt 14, Worms.
Tel: 06241 25045.

i Kurbrunnenstrasse 14,
Bad Dürkheim.
Tel: 06322 9566250.

i Hetzelplatz 1,
Neustadt.
Tel: 06321 926892.

i Exerzierplatzstrasse 3,
Pirmasens. Tel: 06331
842355.

2 Mettlach
Villeroy & Boch
Former Benedictine Abbey.
Tel: 06864 11020.
*Open 9–noon, 1–5,
Sun 10–1.*
Keramik Museum
Saaruferstrasse.
Tel: 06864 811294.
*Open Mon–Fri 9–6, Sat–Sun
9.30–4.*

5 Idar-Oberstein
Deutsches Edelsteinmuseum
Hauptstrasse 118.
Tel: 06781 900980.
*Open May–Oct, 9–6;
Nov–Apr, 10–5.30. Closed
Mon in Nov, Jan, Feb.*
Weiherschleife
Idar.
Tel: 06781 31513.
*Guided tours mid-Mar to
mid-Nov, daily 10–6; mid-Nov–mid-Dec, mid-Feb–
mid-Mar, Mon–Fri 10–4.*
Heimatmuseum
Hauptstrasse 436.
Tel: 06781 24619.
*Open Apr–Oct, daily
9–5.30; Nov–Feb, daily
11–4.30.*
Edelsteinminen
im Steinkaulenberg. Tel
tourist office: 06781 47400.
*Open mid-Mar to mid-Nov,
daily 9–5.*
Besucherbergwerk
Fischbach, 10km (6 miles)
northeast of Idar-Oberstein on road 41.
Tel: 06781 2304.
*Guided tours Mar to mid-Nov, daily 10–5; mid-Nov to
Feb, weekends and public
hols 10–noon, 1–3.*

7 Worms
Dom
Lutherring 9. Tel: 06241
6115.
*Open Apr–Oct, daily 9–6;
Nov–Mar, 9–5.*

9 Neustadt
Schloss Hambach
Hambach. Tel: 06321 30881.
Open daily 10–6.

For Children
Hassloch Holiday Park
Hassloch.
Tel: 06324 5993316.
*Open Apr–Sep, Mon–Fri
10–6; weekends, Oct and
public hols 9–6.*

**Recommended
Walks**
Burg Trifels
Annweiler, west on 10
from Pirmasens.
Tel: 06346 8470.
*Open daily 9–5 (Apr–Sep to
6pm).*

TOUR 22

[i] Porta Nigra, Trier.
Tel: 0651 978080.
[i] Gestade 6, Bernkastel-Kues.
Tel: 06531 4023.

[i] Am Bahnhof 5, Traben-Trarbach.
Tel: 06541 83980.

[i] Endertplatz 1, Cochem.
Tel: 02671 60040.

[i] Bahnhofplatz 17, Koblenz.
Tel: 0261 303880.

[i] Marktplatz, Altes Rathaus, Boppard.
Tel: 06742 3888.

[i] Heerstrasse 86, St Goar.
Tel: 06741 383.

[i] Rheinkai 21, Bingen.
Tel: 06721 184205.

[i] Kurhausstrasse 22–24, Bad Kreuznach.
Tel: 0671 8360050.

[1] Bernkastel-Kues
Mosel Weinmuseum
Cusanusstrasse 2, Kues.
Tel: 06531 4141.
Open daily 10–5 (from 2pm Nov to mid-Apr).

[3] Cochem
Reichsburg
Tel: 02671 255.
Guided tours mid-Mar to Nov, 9–5.

[4] Burg Eltz
Münsternaifeld.
Tel: 02672 950500.
Guided tours Apr–1 Nov, daily 9.30–5.30.

[5] Koblenz
Festung Ehrenbreitstein
Ehrenbreitstein.
Tel: 0261 66754000.
Open 10–5.
SchlossStolzenfels
Stolzenfels.
Tel: 0261 51656.
Open Apr–Sep, 9–6; Oct–Nov, 10–6; Jan–Mar, 10–5.

[6] Boppard
Alte Burg
Burgstrasse.
Tel tourist office: 06742 3888.
Open Apr–Oct, Tue–Sun 10–noon, 2–5.

[7] St Goar
Burg Rheinfels
Schlossberg 47.
Tel: 06741 7753.
Open Apr–Oct, daily 9–6; Nov–Mar, 9–5.

[8] Bingen
Heimatmuseum
Burg Klopp.
Tel tourist office: 06721 184205.
Open Apr–Oct, Tue–Sun 10–5.

[9] Bad Kreuznach
Römerhalle Museum
Hüffelsheimer Strasse 11.
Tel: 0671 800248.
Open Tue–Sun 10–5.

For Children
Spielzeugmuseum
Hauptmarkt 14, Trier.
Tel: 0651 75850.
Open daily 11–6.

For History Buffs
St Nikolaus-Hospital
Kues.
Tel: 06531 2260.
Open Sun–Fri 9–6, Sat 9–3.

TOUR 23

[i] Willy-Brandt-Platz 1, Heidelberg.
Tel: 06221 19433.

[i] Hauptstrasse 39, Bensheim.
Tel: 06251 5826314.

[i] Einhardspforte 3, Michelstadt.
Tel: 06061 706139.

[i] Rathaus, Engelplatz 69, Miltenberg.
Tel: 09371 404119.

[i] Am Spitzen Turm, Wertheim.
Tel: 09342 935090.

[i] Rathaus, Marktplatz 8, Tauberbischofsheim.
Tel: 09341 80313.

[i] Marktplatz 3, Bad Mergentheim.
Tel: 07931 574815.

[i] Rathaus, Marktplatz 2, Rothenburg ob der Tauber.
Tel: 09861 404800.

[i] Markt 9, Schwäbisch Hall.
Tel: 0791 751246.

[i] Kaiserstrasse 17, Heilbronn.
Tel: 07131 562270.

[i] Maximilianstrasse 13, Speyer.
Tel: 06232 142392.

[1] Bensheim
Schloss Auerbacher
5km (3 miles) north of Bensheim.
Tel: 06251 72923.

[2] Michelstadt
Einhardsbasilika
Tel: 06061 2447.
Open Mar–Oct, Tue–Sun 10–noon, 1–5; Nov–Feb, Tue–Sun 11–3.

[3] Miltenberg
Gasthaus zum Riesen
Hotel zum Riesen, Hauptstrasse 97.
Tel: 09371 989948.

[5] Tauberbischofsheim
Kurmainzisches Schloss
Tel: 09341 80333.
Open Easter–Oct, Tue–Sat 2.30–4.30, Sun 10–noon, 2.30–4.30.

[6] Bad Mergentheim
Deutschordensschloss Museum
Deutschordensplatz.
Tel: 07931 52212.
Open Apr–Oct, Tue–Sun 10.30–5; Nov–Mar, Tue–Sat 2–5, Sun 10.30–5.

[7] Rothenburg ob der Tauber
Ratsherrntrinkstube
Marktplatz 6.
Tel: 09861 404800.
Rathaus
Marktplatz.
Tel: 09861 4040.
Open Mon–Fri 8–6.
Wehrgang (rampart)
Rödertor.
Open Apr–Oct, daily 9–5.
Mittelalterliches Kriminalmuseum
Burggasse 3.
Tel: 09861 5359.
Open Apr–Oct, daily 9.30–6; Nov, Jan–Mar 2–4; Dec, 10–4.

[8] Schwäbisch Hall
Benediktinerkloster Comburg (Comburg Abbey)
Steinbach, 2km (1 mile) south of Schwäbisch Hall.
Tel: 0791 930200.
Now teachers' college.
Klosterkirche
Open daily 8–6.

[9] Heilbronn
St Kilian's Church
Kilianplatz.
Tel: 07131 381026.
Open daily 9–12, 2–6.

[10] Speyer
Kaiserdom Speyer
Maximilianstrasse 11, Speyer.
Tel: 06232 102118.
Open Apr–Oct, daily 9–7; Nov–Mar, daily 9–5.

For Children
Odenwald-und-Spielzeugmuseum
Michelstadt.
Tel: 06061 706193.
Open daily 10–5.

TOUR 24

[i] Am Römerberg 27, Frankfurt am Main.
Tel: 069 21238800.

[i] Markt 14–18, Hanau.
Tel: 06181 295950.

[i] Kurhaus, Louisenstrasse 58, Bad Homburg.
Tel: 06172 178110.

[i] Rathaus,
Katharinenstrasse 7,
Kronberg.
Tel: 06173 7030.

[i] Hospitalstrasse 2,
Limburg.
Tel: 06431 6166.

[i] Drachenfelsstrasse 11,
Königswinter.
Tel: 02223 917711.

[i] Bahnhofstrasse 3, Bad
Honnef.
Tel: 02224 882746.

[i] Kirchstrasse 1,
Lahnstein.
Tel: 02621 914171.

[i] Bahnhofstrasse 8,
St Goarshausen.
Tel: 06771 91020.

[i] Assmannshausen: see
Rüdesheim.

[i] Geisenheimer Strasse
22, Rüdesheim.
Tel: 06722 19433.

[i] Brückenturm am
Rathaus, Mainz.
Tel: 06131 286210.

[i] Marktstrasse 6,
Wiesbaden.
Tel: 0611 1729930.

[1] Hanau
Goldschmiedehaus
Altstädter Markt 6.
Tel: 06181 256556.
*Open Tue–Sun 10–noon,
2–5.*
Schloss Philippsruhe
Philippsruher Allee 45.
Tel: 06181 258010.
Open Tue–Sun 11–6.

[2] Bad Homburg
Römerkastell
Saalburg.
Tel: 06175 937408.
*Open Mar–Oct, daily 9–6;
Nov–Feb, Tue–Sun 9–4.*
Schloss
Schlossplatz.
Tel: 06172 9262147.
Open Tue–Sun 10–4 or 5.

[4] Limburg
Domschatz
Diözesanmuseum
Domstrasse 12. Tel: 06431
295327.
*Open mid-Mar to mid-Nov,
Tue–Sat 10–1, 2–5, Sun
11–5.*

[7] Lahnstein
Burg Lahneck
Tel: 02621 2244.
Tours Apr–Nov, daily 10–5.

[10] Rüdesheim
Schloss Brömserburg
Rheinstrasse 2.
Tel: 06722 2348.
*Open mid-Mar to Oct, daily
10–6.*

[11] Mainz
Dom, Treasury and
Museum
Domstrasse 3.
Tel: 06131 253412.
*Open Mon–Fri 9–6 (to 5pm
Oct–Apr), Sat 9–2, Sun
12.30–4 (not Sun Oct–Apr).*
Gutenberg Museum
Liebfrauenplatz 5.
Tel: 06131 122640.
*Open Tue–Sat 9–5,
Sun 11–3.*
Römisch-Germanisches
Zentralmuzeum im
Schloss
Ernst Ludwig Platz 2.
Tel: 06131 91240.
Open Tue–Sun 10–6.

For Children
Opel Zoo
Königsteiner Strasse 35,
Kronberg.
Tel: 06173 3259030.
*Open Jun–Aug, daily 9–7;
Apr–May, Sep–Oct, daily
9–6; Nov–Mar, daily 9–5.*

Back to Nature
Falconry
Grosser Feldberg,
Kronberg.
Tel: 06173 7030.

Special to...
Brömserburg
Oberstrasse 29,
Rüdesheim.
Tel: 06722 2348.
*Guided tours mid-Mar to
Oct, daily 10–6.*

TOUR 25

[i] Unter Fettenhennen
19, Köln.
Tel: 0221 22130400.

[i] Uhlstrasse 1, Brühl.
Tel: 02232 79345.

[i] Windeckstrasse 1 (at
Münsterplatz), Bonn.
Tel: 0228 775000.

[i] Bachstrasse 5,
Remagen.
Tel: 02642 20187.

[i] Läufstrasse 4,
Andernach.
Tel: 02632 298410.

[i] Klosterverwaltung,
Maria-Laach.
Tel: 02652 590.

[i] Nürburgring, Nürburg.
Tel: 02691 93020.

[i] Kölner Strasse 13, Bad
Münstereifel.
Tel: 02253 542244.

[i] Elisenbrunnen,
Friedrich-Wilhelm-Platz,
Aachen.
Tel: 0241 1802960.

[1] Brühl
Schloss Augustusburg
Tel: 02232 44000.
*Open for guided tours
Feb–Nov, Tue–Fri 9–noon,
1.30–4, Sat–Sun 10–5.*

[2] Bonn
Beethovenhaus
Bonngasse 18–26.
Tel: 0228 981750.
*Open Mon–Sat 10–6 (to
5pm Oct–Mar), Sun 11–6
(Oct–Mar to 5pm).*

Münster
Münsterplatz.
Tel: 0228 985880.
Open daily 7–7.
Rheinisches Landes-
museum
Colmantstrasse 14–18.
Tel: 0228 20700.
*Open Tue–Sun 10–6, Wed,
Fri 10–9.*

[3] Bad Godesberg
Schloss Godesburg
Auf dem Godesberg 5.
Tel: 0228 316071.
Open May–Oct, daily 9–6.

[5] Andernach
Runde Turm
Obtain key from tourist
office, Läufstrasse 4.
Tel: 02632 298410.

[7] Nürburgring
Erlebnis-Welt
Nürburgring
Tel: 02691 302602.
Open daily 10–6.

[8] Bad Münstereifel
Max Planck Institute
Effelsberg, 12km (7.5 miles)
southeast.
Tel: 02258 5250.
*Guided tours Tue–Sat 10,
11, 1, 2, 3, 4. Advance
bookings recommended.*

[9] Aachen
Dom und Schatzkammer
(Cathedral and treasury)
Münsterplatz.
Tel: 0241 477090.
*Open daily 7am–9pm
(Nov–May to 6pm).*

For History Buffs
Poppelsdorfer Schloss
Meckesheimer Allee 171.
Tel: 0228 732761.
*Open Apr–Sep, Mon–Fri
9–6, weekends 9–1;
Oct–Mar, Mon–Fri 9–4.*

For Children
Phantasialand
Berggeiststrasse 31–41,
Brühl.
Tel: 02232 36200.
*Open Apr–Oct, daily 9–6
(winter on application).*

INDEX

Index

Index & Acknowledgements

The Automobile Association

wishes to thank the following libraries and photographers for their assistance in the preparation of this book.

ALAMY 58/9, 155; WORLD PICTURES LTD 129, 130/1, 153.

The remaining photographs are held in the Association's own library (AA WORLD TRAVEL LIBRARY) with contributions from:
A BAKER 5, 21a, 40, 61, 63, 65, 66, 67, 68, 69, 72, 74, 75, 76/7, 78, 86/7, 91, 93, 94a, 95, 96, 97a, 97b, 98, 99, 104, 105, 106, 107a, 107b, 109, 111, 112, 112/13, 115, 116, 117, 118/19, 120, 121, 122, 123, 125, 126, 132, 133, 134, 135, 136, 136/7, 138, 139, 140, 141, 142, 143, 144, 145, 147, 149, 154, 156, 161, 163, 173; P BENNETT 13, 14, 15a, 27, 28, 28/9, 30, 30/1, 43; M JOURDAN 55, 60, 70, 70/1, 92, 108, 114; A KOUPRIANOFF 38, 39a, 47a, 127a, 127b, 150, 151, 152; S & O MATTHEWS 26; C SAWYER 2, 21b, 22, 24, 25, 84, 85, 88b, 90, 94b, 146; J SMITH 128; T SOUTER 23, 62, 73, 79, 80, 81, 83, 88a, 89, 100, 101, 102/3168; D TRAVERSO 6, 7, 8, 9, 10, 10/11, 12, 15b, 16, 18, 19, 32, 33, 34, 34/5, 35, 36, 37, 39b, 41, 43, 45, 46, 47b, 49, 50, 51a, 51b, 52/3, 54, 56/7; D TRAVERSO 44.

Contributors

Verifier: George McDonald **Original copy editors:** Emma Stanford, Dilys Jones **Indexer:** Marie Lorimer

Atlas

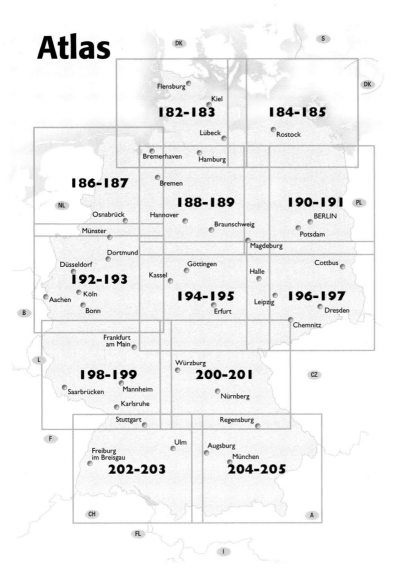

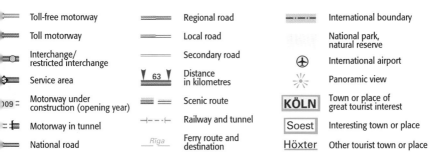

Toll-free motorway	Regional road	—·—·—	International boundary
Toll motorway	Local road		National park, natural reserve
Interchange/restricted interchange	Secondary road	⊕	International airport
Service area	▼ 63 ▼ Distance in kilometres	☀	Panoramic view
)09 = Motorway under construction (opening year)	Scenic route	**KÖLN**	Town or place of great tourist interest
= Motorway in tunnel	—+—+— Railway and tunnel	Soest	Interesting town or place
National road	*Rīga* Ferry route and destination	Höxter	Other tourist town or place

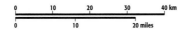

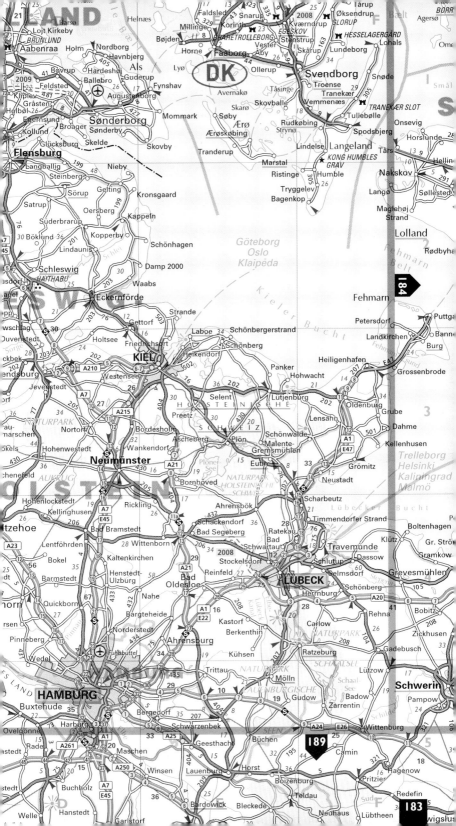

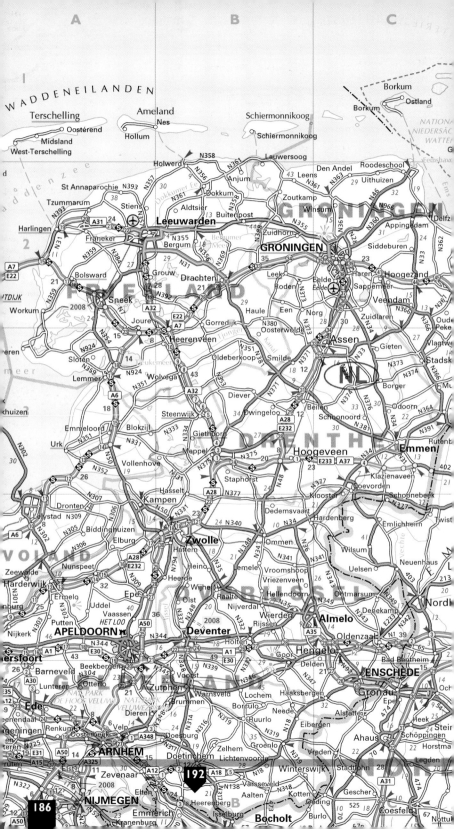

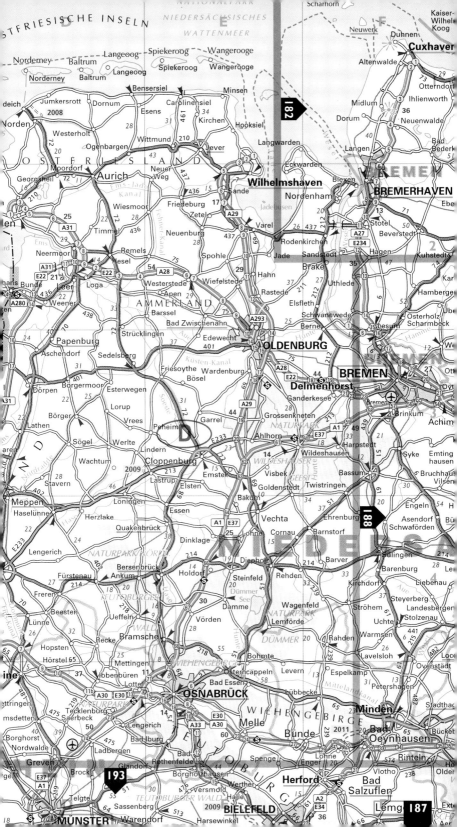

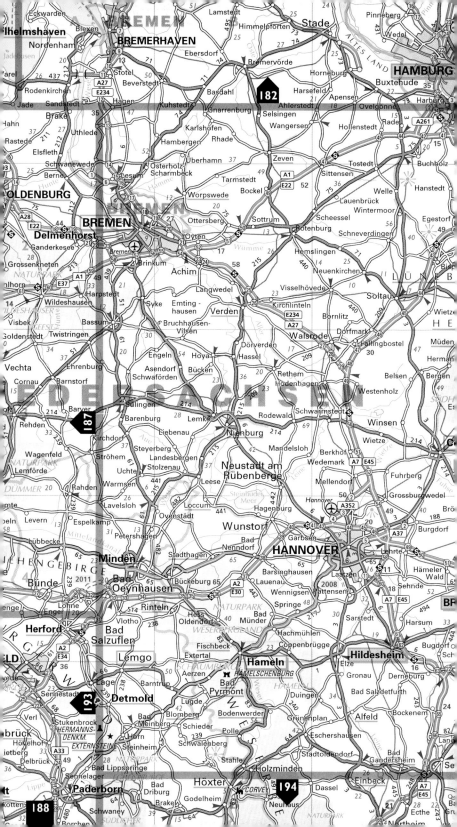

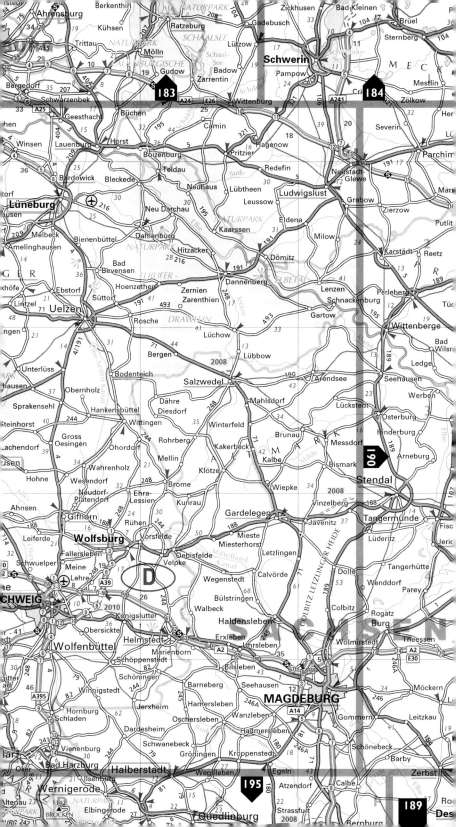

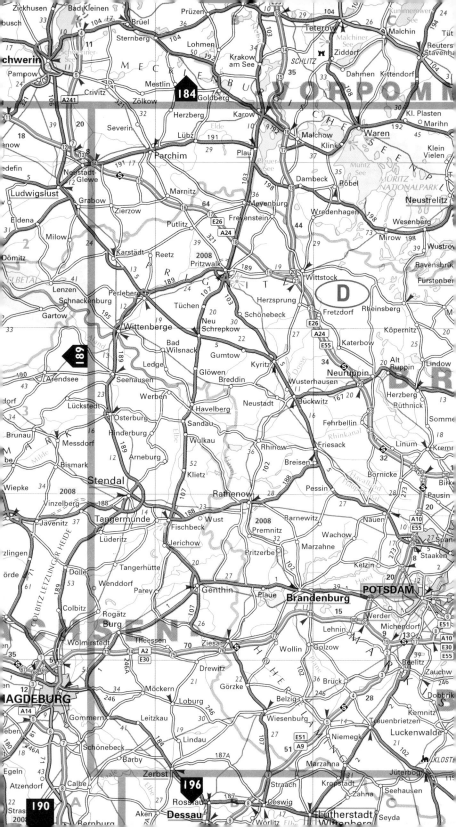

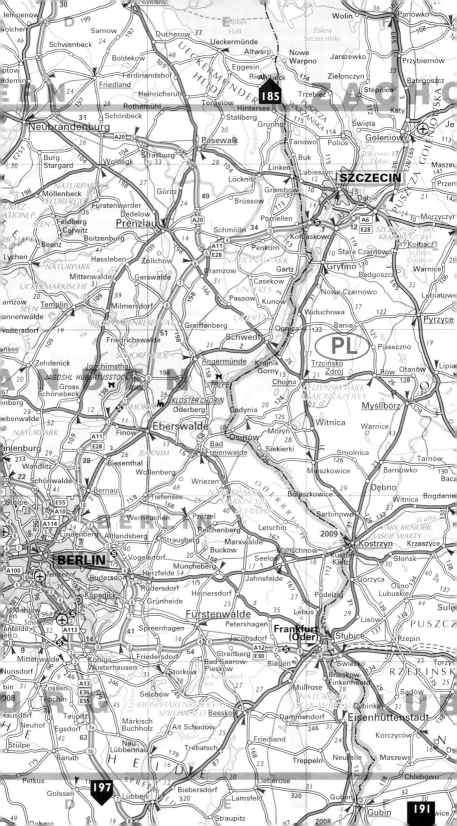

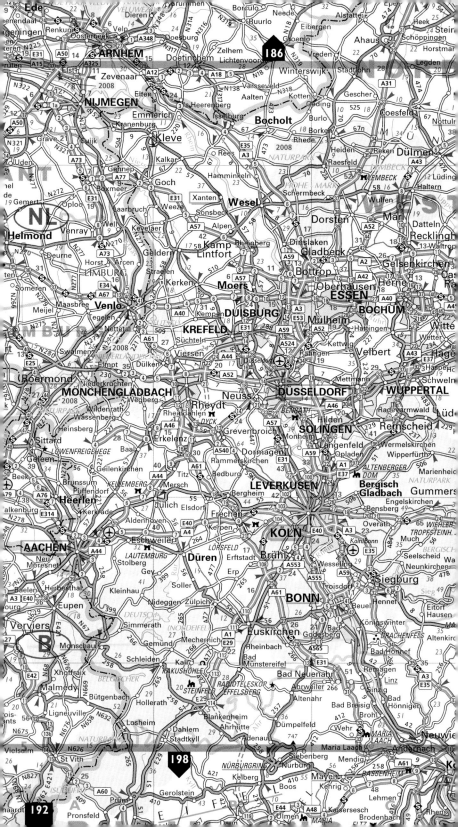

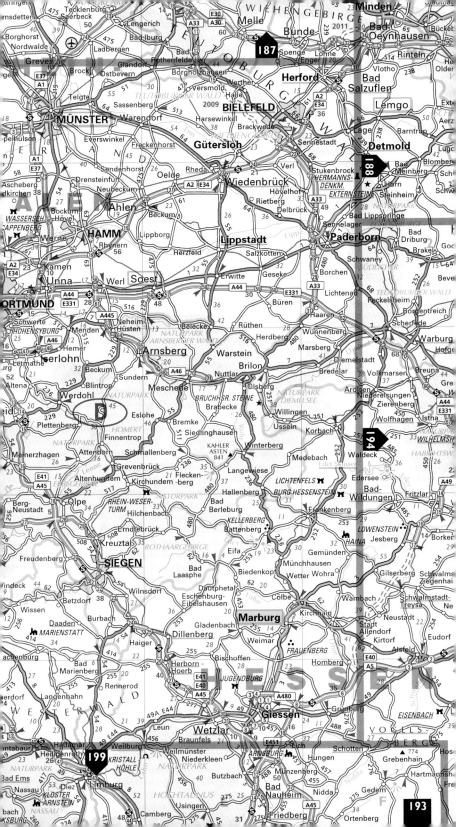

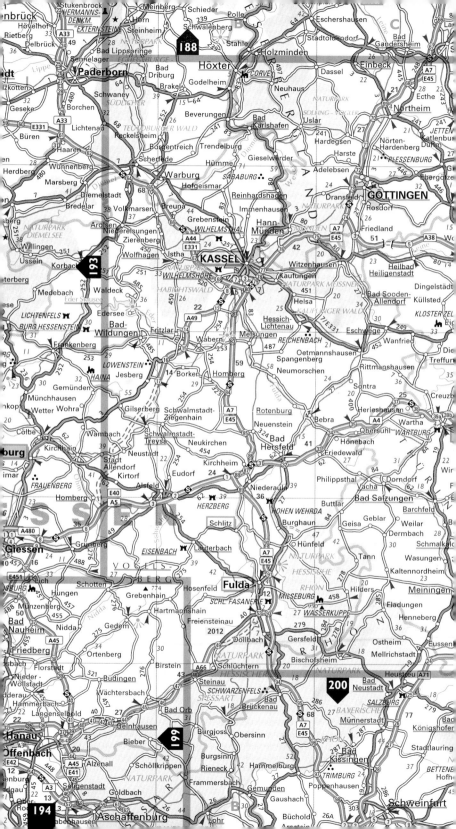

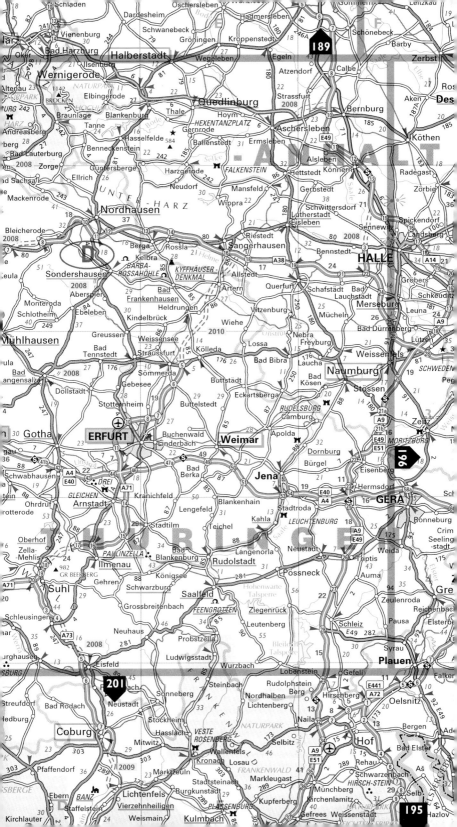

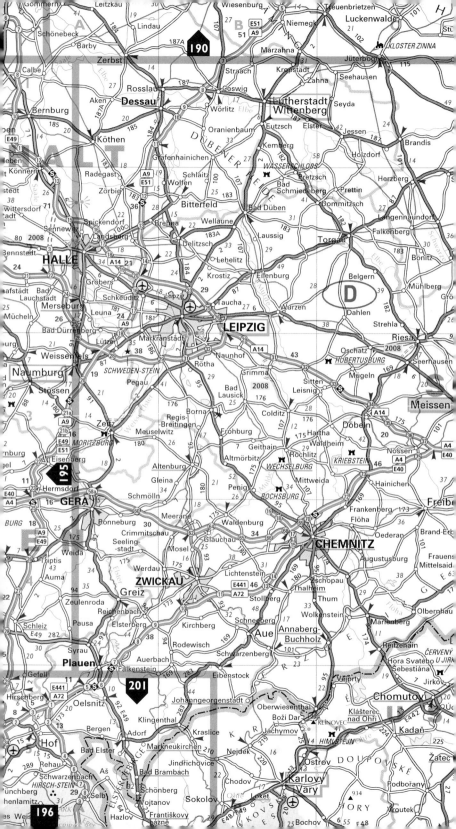

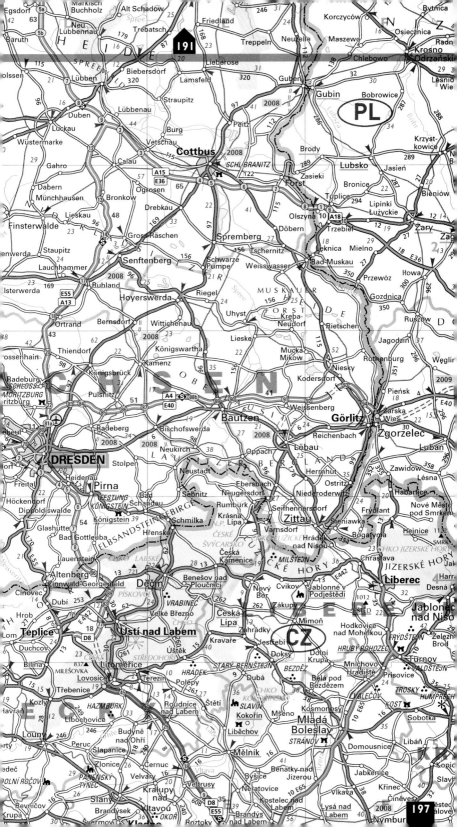

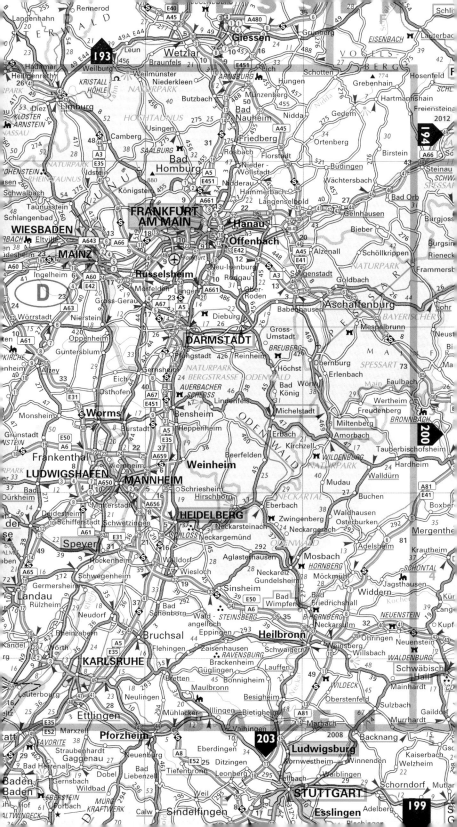

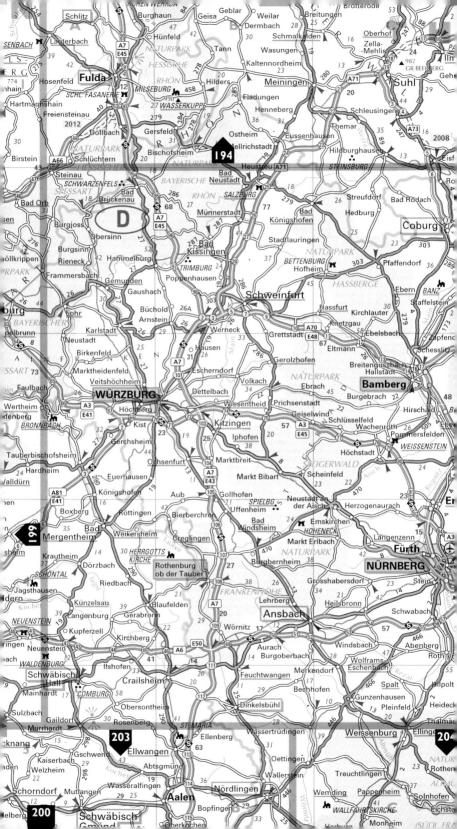

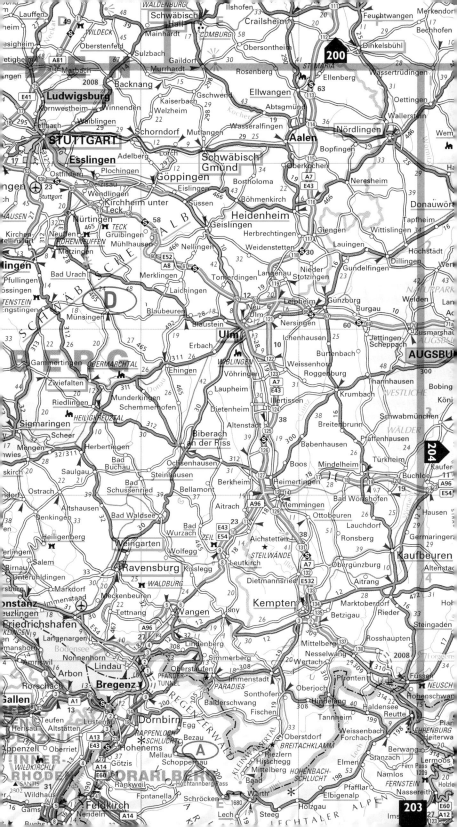

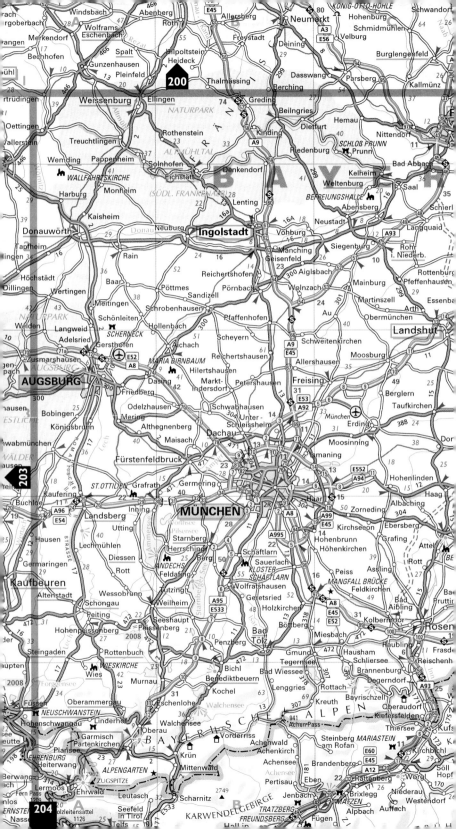

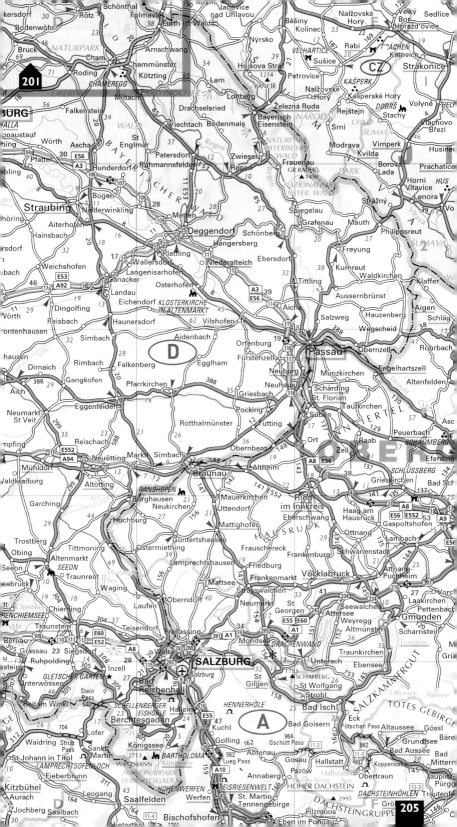

ATLAS INDEX

Atlas Index